Virtual Literacies

Routledge Research in Education

For a full list of titles in this series, please visit www.routledge.com

Virtual Literacies

Interactive Spaces for
Children and Young People

**Edited by Guy Merchant, Julia Gillen,
Jackie Marsh, and Julia Davies**

Routledge
Taylor & Francis Group
NEW YORK   LONDON

First published 2013
by Routledge
711 Third Avenue, New York, NY 10017

Simultaneously published in the UK
by Routledge
2 Park Square, Milton Park, Abingdon, Oxon OX14 4RN

*Routledge is an imprint of the Taylor & Francis Group,
an informa business*

Library of Congress Cataloging-in-Publication Data

Virtual literacies : interactive spaces for children and young people /
edited by Guy Merchant ... [et al.].
    p. cm. — (Routledge research in education ; 84)
1. Computers and literacy. 2. Virtual reality in education.
3. Education—Effect of technological innovations on. 4. Computers
and children. 5. Video games and children. I. Merchant, Guy.
    LC149.5.V57 2012
    371.33'468 2 23
    2012011895

ISBN: 978-0-415-89960-4 (hbk)
ISBN: 978-0-203-09646-8 (ebk)

Typeset in Sabon
by IBT Global.

Contents

PART I
Exploring Virtuality

PART II
Virtual Literacies in Everyday Life

Figures

Tables

Acknowledgements

The editors would like to thank all of those who contributed to this book for their excellent chapters and for keeping to some demanding deadlines. We would also like to thank the teachers, researchers, practitioners of various kinds, children and young people who have worked with us and contributed so much to current understandings of theory and practice in the exploration of virtual literacies. The chapters in this book are drawn from a UK Economic and Scientific Research Council (ESRC) Research Seminar Series, RES-451–26–0731, jointly organised by Lancaster University, the University of Sheffield and Sheffield Hallam University which ran from September 2009 to June 2010. We thank the ESRC, everyone who participated in those rich and diverse discussions, and in particular those who presented either in face-to-face sessions, via Skype or in Second Life. The ideas and work presented were often novel and inspirational, and they were always stimulating. We are very pleased to be able to share some of this work in the current publication.

Finally we would like to extend our sincere thanks to all those at Routledge who have worked on the project, especially Max Novick and Jennifer Morrow and to Ryan Kenney of IBT Global.

Introduction

Guy Merchant, Julia Gillen,
Jackie Marsh, and Julia Davies

The growth of interest and participation in virtual worlds and other online spaces raises important issues for literacy research and practice. Literacy is in a state of flux. New ways of producing and distributing texts, as well as new kinds of texts, co-exist with familiar genres and practices. Topics associated with the 'new' or 'digital' literacies are widely debated in both public and academic circles. And, as increasing numbers of children and young people are drawn into digital environments, both in their everyday lives and as part of their formal schooling, these new literacies have also become a key concern for educators, policy-makers, and practitioners. In this edited volume we draw together some influential current research in this area, and in so doing, provide an important resource for scholars, students, and teachers, as well as others with an interest in the role of digital literacies in the lives of young people.

The book is an outcome of a recent, and highly successful, ESRC-funded seminar series, 'Children's and young people's digital literacies in virtual online spaces'[1] (2009–10), which was directed by the editors of this volume. The aim of this seminar series was to investigate children's digital literacy practices in virtual worlds, online massive multiplayer games, and alternate or mixed-reality learning environments. We brought together scholars from a variety of fields in knowledge to explore, across five seminars and a one-day conference (half of which was conducted in the virtual world *Second Life*), the ways in which literacy is used and shaped in online virtual spaces. The chapters in this book are based upon contributions to the seminar series. They include some of the most engaging empirical research being undertaken on literacy in virtual worlds and online spaces both in and beyond educational institutions today. And, as befits the topic, it is international in scope, containing a variety of key studies from the UK, North America, and Australasia.

This is an important time for those researching virtual worlds, videogaming, and Web 2.0 technologies, since there is growing professional interest in their significance in the education and development of children and young people. Whether these technologies are associated with informal learning, and the extent to which they could or should be incorporated into classroom contexts, is hotly debated. This book adds to this debate by including a principled evaluation and appreciation of the learning and teaching that can occur in digital environments.

Mass media accounts of digital culture are often predicated on a technologically determinist vision, on the one hand promoting a utopian view of the future while on the other fuelling moral panic by emphasizing the potential risks of life online. In this book, children, young people, and those who work with them are revealed as active agents with possibilities to navigate new paths. The empirical research by contributors to this book provides evidence of the learning potential of virtual spaces in classrooms and elsewhere. It offers an opportunity for literacy researchers and educators to deepen their understanding of the range of multimodal literacy practices associated with virtual worlds, online games, social networking sites, and augmented reality games. Drawing on a sociocultural approach, with understandings brought from cognate disciplines such as literacy studies in applied linguistics and anthropology, distributed cognition in cultural psychology, and computer-mediated communication, it provides an account of new directions in research and practice.

We have organized the volume according to a four-part thematic structure. The first part is an exploration of what we mean when we talk about virtual and online spaces; the second part turns attention to research into children and young people's experiences 'in the wild' (Beavis, this volume) in their homes and out-of-school lives; the third provides some insight and reflection on innovatory school-based practices; and the final part examines the ways in which online communities can be formed in a variety of different contexts, offering diverse perspectives on issues relating to participation. As with any new field, terminology is problematic, tending to change with the evolving nature of our understanding. The authors contributing to this volume draw on different academic traditions and have their own intellectual history, and so we have decided to honor that by avoiding the temptation to offer definitions. However, in the first chapter, Julia Gillen and Guy Merchant do provide some groundwork by tracing the development of discourses about the 'virtual' in technology, and in doing so, problematize our understanding of what constitutes virtuality. The chapter examines the power of dichotomies in contemporary thinking—binaries such as offline/online, school/out-of-school, formal/informal—and shows how creative uses of new technologies may transcend these popular distinctions.

As we have seen, children and young people's participation in virtual worlds is currently attracting much interest, and the first part of this book offers two different perspectives on this. Firstly, Rebecca Black and Stephanie Reich look at how a sociocultural framework can be fruitful in exploring young children's engagement with online virtual worlds. The chapter describes how applying a sociocultural lens to the content and design of virtual worlds can help us to understand how such spaces might promote certain forms of literacy and learning while constraining others. The authors demonstrate how a sociocultural approach can illuminate how children make meaning and solve problems within virtual worlds, and how such activities carry across on- and offline spaces that extend beyond these virtual worlds. An alternative perspective is offered by Victoria Carrington, who examines a popular virtual world produced for young girls, Mattel's *BarbieGirls*, and a virtual world produced in India, Chimpoo.com. The chapter looks at issues of consumption and gender as a background context for a consideration of the textual practices modeled and made available in this particular virtual world.

In the second part of the book we turn our attention to the ways in which children and young people engage with videogaming and virtual worlds in their everyday lives, and to accounts of their meaning-making and popular textual practices 'in the wild.' Catherine Beavis focuses on interactions between players, games, and technology, and the active nature of play. Drawing on data from an Australian research project with teacher educators and secondary English teachers, she develops a model for games and literacy based upon data gathered from everyday gaming practices. The popular virtual world *Club Penguin* is the focus for Jackie Marsh's study, which examines the way in which children engage in a rich range of literacy practices when participating in virtual words. Drawing on data collected from 5–11-year-olds, she identifies how literacy practices are put to use in establishing and maintaining the social order in online gameplay. Children's use of virtual literacies to develop online social networks is considered in the light of wider media concerns about young children's online safety. This is followed by Alex Kendall and Julian McDougall's work with young male gamers, which provides an analysis of the localized practices of reading, telling, and meaning-making associated with *Grand Theft Auto 4*. They explore how boundaries between different kinds of textual practices might be constituted and insulated, and how participants play with, and against, these for different performance contexts and audiences.

While the studies that make up the second part of the book focus on practices that take place outside educational settings, the contributors all make reference to the relationships between these experiences and more formal learning. So it seems highly appropriate that in the third part we look at school-based projects that have created digital learning spaces that either cross or extend the physical boundaries of the classroom. In each of the four studies included, young people are seen as active agents engaged in digitally mediated meaning-making practices. This part of the book begins with Angela Colvert's case study of alternate reality gaming with 10- and 11-year-olds. Here we see children involved in designing and playing an alternate reality game (ARG). Angela Colvert shows how the children develop their understanding of the themes and structure of the narrative through using the communicative affordances of different modes and media as they involve younger children from the same school in their proj-ect. This is followed by Martin Waller's account of how teachers of young children can harness the hyperconnectivity of social networking to provide rich learning experiences. It provides a reasoned account of how *Twitter* can be used in a way that minimizes risk and supports the development of both traditional and digital writing. Howells and Robertson contrib-ute new understandings of the literacy opportunities offered by new media authoring environments through analyzing successful and less successful storytelling techniques used by 11–12-year-old learners in a 3D computer game-making project. They identify storytelling techniques enabled by the interactive and immersive nature of the medium, discuss some contrasts between this form of narrative and more traditional story writing tasks, and consider some of the implications for learners and educators.

In the last chapter Guy Merchant explores the issues associated with the wider adoption of digital literacies in the classroom. Based on a case study of a virtual world designed for educational purposes, the chapter focuses on the importance of investment and professional development in future work.

The fourth part of the book examines the ways in which digital literacies have been used in informal settings to develop meaningful engagement and learning that is unconstrained by time, place, and the institutional routines of schooling. We begin with Christine Greenhow's chapter on social net-working, in which she shows how social network sites function as power-ful sites for adolescent learning and for the development of novel forms of community. The chapter examines how these non-formal literacy practices inform our notions of knowledge, knowledge production, and community in the new media age, and how educators are currently putting these ideas to use in and out of schools. Julia Gillen, Rebecca Ferguson, Anna Peachey, and Peter Twining follow this with an exploration of the Schome project—an initiative that aimed to explore the potential of virtual worlds, and con-sider their capacity to act as spaces in which visions of future practices and pedagogies can be built and experienced. The project was centered on *Teen Second Life*, at the time probably the most advanced simulated 3D virtual world that could offer an 'enclosed' space, thus enabling children to take advantage of the rich affordances of the environment, while restricting access to credentialized project members. The authors explain how vital associated literacy domains were to the project, including a forum and wiki. Through interacting in these different environments, individuals and groups of teenagers, physically located in different countries and settings, including homes, after-school clubs, and classrooms, could negotiate tricky issues—for example, as regards access to limited resources. This chapter centers on one dispute after a teenager sought permission to construct a Gothic cathedral on the island, seemingly clashing with established cultural norms, despite the best of intentions. The analysis demonstrates the pos-sibilities of setting up conditions for rich, rational debates even on highly contentious issues, when great care is taken to establish and maintain a supportive community ethos.

The fourth part of the book concludes with investigations of the BBC's immersive virtual world, *Adventure Rock*, and massively multiplayer online games (MMOs). Lizzie Jackson's chapter studies the design and implementation of a virtual world for children, *Adventure Rock*, by the UK's public service broadcaster, the BBC. Her perspective is informed by her long experience in BBC production, and an understanding of its values, as well as her own appreciation of the importance of play in cognitive development. Through concern that unmoderated interactions between children (or perhaps others) in-world might be harmful, the BBC designed the world so that interactions would be between children's avatars and the environment, including bots. Social interaction opportunities were catered for on associated websites. Lizzie Jackson's work, including a concluding "13 Tips for Producers of Virtual Worlds for Children," recognizes the difficulties and opportunities associated with this key design constraint. She also demonstrates some imaginative participatory research methods when working with children. Crystle Martin, Caroline C. Williams, Amanda Ochsner, Shannon Harris, Elizabeth King, Gabriella Anton, Jonathon Elmergreen, and Constance Steinkuehler draw on their ethnographic data of young people's gameplay to reconceptualize MMOs as a literacy space, and the act of gaming as traversal through that space. Using *World of Warcraft*, the authors detail the topology of the literacy space in terms of its constitutive texts and other semiotic resources. With this conceptualization in place, they then describe gameplay as traversal of that space with the game itself acting as a springboard.

The editors conclude the volume by drawing together the threads that run through the chapters and revisiting some of the key questions that emerge. We present some encouragement, and also some cautions, regarding the implementation of virtual worlds and other interactive online spaces into school curricula. More specifically we identify five themes that could shape further research and practice. These are: the new ways of meaning-making associated with virtual literacies; the playful, imaginative, and creative aspects associated with these practices; the theme of changing sociability; the importance of critiquing the explicit and hidden pedagogies of virtual environments; and, finally, the methodological issues and challenges that have been raised by the studies reported in the book.

What the chapters in this book offer, collectively, is an overview of some of the key issues that are embedded in children, young people, and adults' literacy practices in online, virtual spaces. Inevitably, as with any collection, there are areas that we did not have sufficient space to address, such as regulatory issues and debates, or analyses of brain-computer interfaces (BCI) and games. We decided not to include discussion of university students' online literacies since we are aware of other ongoing research specializing in that area. In addition, there are aspects of literacy that are not the focus of study in these chapters, including multilingual literacy practices in online spaces. These areas offer rich potential for future research and we suggest that the studies outlined in these pages provide an important and critical basis for this work.

NOTES

1. http://www.lancs.ac.uk/fass/events/digital-literacies/

Part I
Exploring Virtuality

1 From Virtual Histories to Virtual Literacies

Julia Gillen and Guy Merchant

INTRODUCTION

In calling this book *Virtual Literacies*, we intend to signal our shared interest in the ways in which a diversity of literacy practices are involved in the social construction of online spaces. These practices could be seen as being *virtual* from a number of points of view; however, the literacies that initially attracted our attention were those used to mediate social interaction in virtual worlds and video games. But while virtual worlds have been an important context for our own work (Gillen, 2009; Merchant, 2010), in developing the seminar series on which this book is based, we were also keen to look at the similarities and differences between these worlds and a variety of other online spaces and their related practices—particularly those that are beginning to attract the attention of children and young people in their homes, in schools, and elsewhere. Our collaboration with teachers and classroom researchers has helped us in the exploration of these new forms of literacy, which, while diverse and often intricately interwoven with print literacy, were united by the fact that they were being used to create online spaces—spaces that in turn encouraged new kinds of communicative interaction. Current usage of the word *virtual* seems to us to be a useful way of trying to capture and describe these developments, and although we have no ambition to add to the burgeoning list of kinds of literacies (see Barton, 2007), it does seem important here to explore the concept of virtuality[1] and why it is a central theme in this work. Therefore in this chapter we focus our efforts on some important groundwork, firstly by exploring contemporary understandings of the virtual, and secondly by tracing some of its historical antecedents.

HOW THE VIRTUAL BECOMES REAL

Popular ways of talking about the role of digital technologies in contemporary life often include the word virtual as a way of referring to an alternative or parallel social space—a space that it is believed that *we* or *they* inhabit for some, or most of the time. This space is variously conceived of as an extension of the 'real world' or an unhelpful, distracting, or even perilous escape from it. Interestingly, it is less common to apply the same label and evaluations to more established technologies of communication. Even though phone conversations or radio broadcasts share some of the same features, in that the participants are not normally physically co-located, it is unusual to use the term virtual in these contexts. Similarly, forms of entertainment such as literature, film, or even drama, which often draw us into a kind of shared and imaginal reality, tend to be described in different ways. Yet video games and other sustained computer-based interactions are regularly bracketed together with virtual worlds, and experimental work with head-mounted displays and datagloves, to constitute a popular perception of the virtual. In these discourses, prolonged immersion in niche digital environments and the capacity to act upon or within them are perhaps the most salient unifying features. This prolonged immersion repeatedly becomes the focus of moral panic in which the risks of addiction and alienation, or exposure to violence or corporate marketing are regularly cited. Fears that stem from the interactive and communicative affordances of the virtual—particularly those associated with inappropriate language and behavior, or sexual predation—add to the catalogue of perceived risks. The existence of this moral panic as well as the non-application of 'virtual' as a modifier to well-established media technologies, such as cinema and radio, are perhaps both clues to the novel and innovatory qualities of the new technologies—qualities that would appear to give rise to social uncertainties.

While the perceived risks are certainly worthy of serious attention, the unfortunate result of their repeated identification with online activity reinforces the idea that the virtual is somehow separate from other aspects of everyday life. Concerns that young people will withdraw from the world and will be deprived of the sorts of interaction that promote the development of social skills have regularly been associated with video games, virtual worlds, and other digital environments (Palmer, 2006; Wolfe & Flewitt, 2010). Although there is little research evidence to support these claims, and in fact there are some strong counterclaims, these fears are a persistent theme in popular opinion. And furthermore they give strength to a particular view that dichotomizes the *real* and the *virtual*, and this, we will argue, is an unhelpful distinction to make.

In everyday conversation we routinely use the expression *virtually* to describe how an action was almost, but not quite, accomplished. Similarly, if people reported that they felt as if they were 'virtually in the same room' as someone else, they communicate the same feeling of proximate if not total presence or reality. As Hine (1998: 4) has suggested, not only is there the suggestion that the virtual is "not strictly the real thing," but also the association with "the uncertainty of relation to time, location and presence" that is produced by the technology. From this sort of account it is easy to imagine the virtual as a sort of spectral reality: one that is almost, but not quite, real. Against this we argue that the environments written about in this volume—*Club Penguin, Second Life,* and *Active Worlds* to name but a few—are real enough in the sense that they are more or less easy to access, they are recognizable, persistent, and you can 'go' to them and even do things 'in' them. Although they may be distinguishable from some facets of what we might provisionally call everyday life (if that is seen in terms of the immediate material and physical world), for many of us, encounters with distanced representations are increasingly common.

As with books, films, and other media, the new virtual environments are actually experienced as an integral part of many people's everyday lives, and they constitute a very real experiential phenomenon for users and players. This becomes a particularly important point when authors, such as those writing in this volume, refer to the seamless blending of online and offline activity, the to-and-fro that characterizes ARGs (alternate reality games), virtual world gameplay, or the various uses of social media in maintaining and developing relationships. The online environments involved may have distinguishing characteristics that set them apart from other contexts, but that does not mean they should be dismissed as not being real. In developing an alternative perspective, then, we take the view that virtuality bridges the material world and the world of information and data. It as if one realm of materiality is separated from another, by the screen. Sakr (2008: 8) argues that "Virtuality is a negotiation between materiality and information," although with Hayles (1990), we would include the screen itself, the servers, and all the rest as constituent parts of that materiality. Information and data can never evade material existence. The key negotiation is one that takes place through interactions between people and technology—at least in the sorts of virtual environments that we are concerned with here.

Virtual worlds provide a vivid example of this negotiation between people and technologies in that they provide users with a real-time animated view of an online space that simulates aspects of their familiar physical world. Although the environment itself is actually constructed from bits of data, or 'information,' the material affordances of the computer and screen allow these users to see, to inhabit, and often to modify that world—and in doing so they become material. At the same time the keystrokes, mouse-clicks, and other operations provide a physical interface for users to navigate their way around online space, to interact with others, and to act on the environment. Although the user may feel immersed in the virtual world, and there are plenty of accounts of how this happens (e.g., Schroeder, 2002; Childs, 2010), she is bodily situated in space and time, and participates in the virtual through physical interactions with material objects. The phenomenon of immersion, perhaps something akin to Coleridge's idea of 'the willing suspension of disbelief,' gives experiential depth to virtuality. But just as in the consumption of literature or film, this experience is created, at least in part, through the process of mediation.

The cultural historian Williams (1982: 84) argues that nineteenth-century technologies "made possible the material realization of fantasies which had hitherto existed only in the realm of imagination"—for instance, as electricity was employed in urban environments in spectacular lightshows, fairs, and expositions and to illuminate department stores showcasing luxury goods.

> Electricity created a fairytale environment, the sense of being, not in a distant place, but in a make-believe place where obedient genies leap to their master's command, where miracles of speed and motion are wrought by the slightest gesture, where a landscape of glowing pleasure domes and twinkling lights stretches into infinity. (Williams, 1982: 84–85)

In a similar vein, technologies of representation trace a similar arc of development towards material realization. In their seminal work on new media, Bolter and Grusin (2000) describe the long history of visual realism as one that unites the techniques of linear perspective used in drawing and painting with the development of photography and moving image. Through recounting this history they are able to trace a desire to "put the viewer in the same space as the objects viewed" (p. 11). This effect is enhanced in situations and technologies in which the virtual objects are foregrounded and the medium, as well as the process of mediation, recedes from our awareness. Bolter and Grusin use the word 'immediacy' to describe this phenomenon, suggesting that new technology is propelling us towards these heightened experiences of visual realism and in doing so opening up new possibilities. Children and young people who are growing up in technologized and densely mediated environments may well be more at home with the resulting interplay between the material and the virtual. Not only do we have much to learn from them, but also there are pressing issues to explore, particularly if we are to prepare the young adequately for the digital future. If Hayles' (1990: 48) prediction is accurate, "We will increasingly live, work, and play in environments that construct us as embodied virtualities." A more nuanced account of the virtual may be necessary if we are to take this forward.

So far, then, we have explored popular perceptions of the virtual and identified some of the problems associated with opposing the real with the virtual. We have suggested that virtual environments are created when technology provides a bridge between the person and a newly conceived world of information—one that is perceived by that person as simultaneously both remote and immediate. From this view, virtual environments are constructed, mediated spaces that offer new ways of interacting with others. In some versions of the virtual, the desire to create an experience of 'being there' through visual and audio realism is a defining feature and it is this phenomenon that we explore in the following section.

MATERIALITY, MEDIATION, AND
THE VIRTUAL IN THE CLASSROOM

Here we tease out some of the issues at stake in contextualizing the virtual, by focusing specifically on the relationship between mediation, imagination, and belief. We begin with an example—an exploration of how video, a technology not normally associated with virtuality, can become part of a school classroom. This will help us in addressing the business of mediation, referred to earlier, and will enable us to identify some important points of similarity and difference. We begin by looking at the materiality of the classroom space.

Classrooms, like many institutional settings, are full of stuff. Visit an empty classroom and there is the furniture, the instructional equipment, the stack of textbooks, and the traces of those who have inhabited that place—the abandoned writing tools, the forgotten schoolbag, and so on. Although we are by now accustomed to talking about classrooms as social spaces, they are constituted as much by the arrangement of things as they are by the social beings that inhabit them. And in some ways the contemporary classroom, with its educational apparatus, its purpose-built teaching resources, and its technological infrastructure, reminds us of the Marxian notion of 'frozen labor'—the labor that is embodied in objects with a global circulation that enter the increasingly commodified spaces of schooling.

Classrooms have always been places in which learners and teachers interact with material objects. Following Socrates, most teachers need the equivalent of a stick and sand to illustrate the fundamentals of geometry, or whatever else is on the curriculum. So we think of classrooms as a space in which social interaction "takes place in an artefact-saturated medium that includes language" (Cole & Wertsch, 1996). In this sense the twenty-first-century classroom does not seem too different—maybe the level of saturation has increased, and maybe the young are exposed to more sophisticated tools, but the basic formula is in many ways unchanged. Classrooms are social spaces, arranged and resourced for learning. But it does seem that new technology introduces a new dimension. Consider the following observation made in the course of a study conducted by Merchant:

> *I am watching a class of 5 year-olds in a classroom in Rotherham. Most of them are looking at the whiteboard which is showing a short extract from an educational television programme. The screen shows the presenter Rod who is wearing a blue t-shirt with a large white letter 'S' on the back. The only trouble is, he doesn't know which t-shirt he's wearing—or so the story goes—and he needs help from the children. And since this is the era of 'interactivity', the classroom teacher chooses Tamsin, a ready volunteer, who picks her way through the children. Their fidgety legs and unpredictable movements make it a bit like an obstacle course. Rod, the presenter, turns so the letter 'S' on the*

back of his t-shirt all but fills the screen. 'Trace the letter on my back!'
he says, encouragingly. By now Tamsin is next to the whiteboard,
looking up and ready to comply. Ready, but for one small obstacle . . .
the whiteboard, the letter 'S' and the figure of Rod are out of reach.
The obliging teacher hastily and resourcefully produces a milk crate
from behind her chair. Tamsin, confidently if rather unsteadily, clam-
bers up on to the upturned milk crate to trace the letter 'S' on Rod's
back. With a smile on her face the forefinger of her right hand follows
the curves on Rod's t-shirt on the surface of the whiteboard. 'Oh now
I know, it's S!' says Rod.

Watching this enactment of teaching, we might say that the video image
and the whiteboard can easily take their place alongside all the other stuff
that fills up classroom spaces. They are objects that you can use, or refuse
to use. Of course, educational technologists might claim you can use them
'effectively' or 'ineffectively,' but that is another discussion. Yet somehow,
Tamsin's progress from sedentary audience to active participant is not simply a matter of teaching approach, nor is her use of an invented solution to a
real-world problem as she clambers on the upturned milk crate. This is just
the preamble to a rather strange interaction between Tamsin and an ethe-
real presence from elsewhere. The interaction is carefully choreographed
by the wily programmers. Rod can't actually feel Tamsin tracing the letter
'S,' he wouldn't know if she got it wrong, and the segment would roll on
even in the absence of an audience; but we can safely assume that she is not
fooled by the artifice, and that she willingly suspends her disbelief in order
to trace the letter shape. Tamsin performs this little drama in front of her
classmates and under the watchful eye of her teacher. The idea of 'people on
screens' is most likely to be very familiar to her, through the accumulation
of many hours of television watching. Likewise, we can suppose that stepping up on to the milk crate is also very familiar, through the accumulation
of many hours of practice in stepping and climbing.

It is clear to us, though, that we need a better account of the sort of mediated interaction that has been described. Here is a start: the whiteboard in
this particular example is essentially a medium, or surface, for displaying
the virtual. So the focus could simply remain with that surface—but yet the
very 'thingness' of the board seems to recede from our gaze (Ihde, 2005), as
the teachers and children operate at the interface. From this perspective, the
technological sophistication begins to approach the 'ideal' state described
by Bolter and Grusin (2000) as the "logic of transparent immediacy." It
is as if the material world is screened from a virtual world with its lifelike
representation of a person called Rod, just by the thinnest of windows. In
this way technologies may seem to extend classroom spaces or to overlay
them with the virtual (Burnett, 2011). And, of course, the idea of the virtual has already entered into educational discourse through the widespread
adoption of learning platforms (managed learning environments). Here the

idea of working in *virtual* learning environments (VLEs) is regularly used to talk about the various practices associated with the intranet systems provided and often bounded by school boards and local authorities. The virtual is characteristically seen as a way of extending learning beyond what was previously possible. The online environment becomes "an extension of the classroom" (Stone, 2011).

It is the emergence of this kind of virtuality that constitutes a break with more traditional classroom environments. Media realism has become normalized—children, and young people, are actually quite at home with this virtuality, as our vignette clearly illustrates. After all, their day-to-day lives are already densely mediated. In this context we are reminded of Miller and Slater, who argue that:

> . . . virtuality—as the capacity of communicative technologies to constitute rather than mediate realities and to constitute relatively bounded spheres of interaction—is neither new nor specific to the Internet. Indeed it is probably intrinsic to the process of mediation itself. (Miller & Slater 2000: 6)

According to this view of virtuality, the intersection between mediation and imagination—what we referred to earlier as 'the willing suspension of disbelief'—is central. Following the work of Hayles, we could then take the virtual to describe what happens at the interface between data, as an impossibly idealized abstraction, and its material instantiation.

> Virtuality is the cultural perception that material objects are interpenetrated by information patterns. (Hayles, 1990: 13)

This suggests that in embracing a broader conception of virtuality than that which is normally evoked in the discussion, say, of virtual worlds, we may approach a more fruitful understanding of the virtual. Our re-reading of the video episode pays closer attention to issues of mediation, representation, and perception, all embedded in the particular historical and geographical context of the classroom. To examine these ideas more closely and to test the arguments we are advancing, it may help to examine the historical antecedents of virtual technology, imbued as they are with the idea that technical knowledge might somehow alter, augment, or fracture taken-for-granted reality.

VIRTUAL TECHNOLOGY: THE HISTORICAL ANTECEDENTS

Histories of virtual world technologies need to be located in a broader discourse of technological, social, and cultural development. We will demonstrate how tracing this broader discourse is helpful, while recognizing that since every recently marketed virtual world boasts technical innovation, it is common for users to feel assured that "Virtual worlds are a 21st century phenomenon" (Sheehy & Seamans, 2010: 17). As we have already indicated, we draw upon a number of significant academic works that have attempted to take stock of technological and cultural changes and that have propelled the crafting of new connections in theoretical ideas around virtuality. Among these, we have already referred to Bolter and Grusin's (2000) account of remediation, and Hayles' (1990) exploration of the concept of virtuality in science and literary fiction. In addition to these we draw on a more philosophical exploration of virtual reality in Heim (1993), and the ethnographic account of *Second Life* provided by Boellstorff (2008). In this section, we construct a history of the virtual by interweaving perspectives from historical and contemporary media sources, and this is followed by a brief acknowledgment of how popular narrative has also played a part in shaping our views of virtual space.

Initially, our approach is based on the work of Soler and Gillen (2009), who used the Nexis newspaper database to search for key terms in national English-language newspapers worldwide. First, they established that 1990–2009 was the period in which the term 'virtual worlds' emerged as a focal term in the press. After pilot work with a number of possibilities, they identified these search terms: 'virtual worlds,' 'literacy,' 'teenagers,' and/or 'children.' Using these, they assembled a corpus (Baker, 2006) of newspaper articles. Analyzing these, Soler and Gillen (2009) were then able to identify three distinct strands in media coverage. These related to: 1) virtual reality prosthesis; 2) the emergence of videogaming; and 3) the early development of virtual communities. They were then able to assemble a collection of ten articles that exemplify these strands, a collection we will refer to as our mini-corpus, and which is in outlined Table 1.1. We build on that work

Table 1.1 Exemplar Articles from the Newspaper Search (from Soler & Gillen, 2009)

Year	Newspaper	Shortened title
1992	The Independent (UK)	Almost anything is possible—virtually
1995	Dallas Observer (USA)	Caught in the web
1999	The Guardian (UK)	Think Piece: Victorian classroom values
2000	The Guardian (UK)	Wicked world: Grapevine where schools share good ideas
2008	The Times (UK)	When hatred comes to your home page
2009	The Times Educational Supplement (UK)	Virtual learning- Untangled Web

here by extending the descriptions of these strands interweaving references to and quotations from the featured articles. These illustrate social views as reflected in or shaped by the press, and can therefore be seen as one way of narrating the development of virtual environments in the period between the end of the twentieth century and the early twenty-first century.

1. VIRTUAL REALITY PROSTHETIC DEVICES

As we mentioned earlier, part of the discourse about the virtual devices from scientific developments in which wearable technology has been used to immerse subjects in a data-driven experience. This has involved the use of head-mounted displays (HMDs), datagloves, and other prosthetic devices to simulate reality. A newspaper report describes this kind of immersive experience:

> The helmet, rather like a personal flight simulator, contains a tiny display screen on to which the software projects its version of reality. If you turn your head, the virtual world turns with you. (Watts, 1992)

The helmet—by definition an HMD—cuts off the sensory experience of the everyday world and replaces this with computer-generated sensations. Some early prototypes of this technology were used and developed by the U.S. Air Force for training pilots. As Heim (1993: 112) points out, the history of these innovations easily pre-dates the use of the term 'virtual reality.' In fact, the first HMD system, rather ominously named 'The Sword of Damocles,' was developed by the computer scientist Ivan Sutherland in the mid-1960s. But it was not until the work of Jaron Lanier that the idea of this kind of virtual reality was sufficiently developed to capture the popular imagination. It is widely held that Lanier himself coined the phrase "virtual reality" (Lanier, 1992).

Clearly this kind of virtual reality is a specialist domain, but it has a parallel in contemporary and popular uses of technology. We might, for example, consider the motion-sensitive interfaces developed for *Nintendo Wii* and *Xbox Kinnect* gaming, in which real-time bodily movements influence what is heard and seen on screen. On the other hand, it could be argued that these developments fall considerably short of the concept of total immersion written into Lanier's idea of virtual reality. For an example of how prediction is always a gamble, Lanier's idea, put forward in 1991, has never really taken hold:

> Approximately two years from now there will be head-mounted home entertainment systems [. . .] By approximately the end of the century, my working assumption is that there will be what I consider to be a high enough quality machine to deserve to be called the virtual reality machine available for home use. (Lanier, 1992: 153)

As it turned out, technical development, consumer demand, and the influence of both lone innovators and large corporations have taken the idea of virtual technology in other directions.

This brief history of virtual prosthetic devices helps to illustrate one way in which the concept of virtuality has been framed. In this version, the technology enables a representation of another world that is sufficiently sophisticated to create a sense of total immersion. Here we have gone several steps further than video, surround-sound, or even 3D film, because the user is 'in' the virtual environment and can, albeit with some limitation, direct her own gaze and movement within this environment.

2. VIDEO GAMES

One of the most commercially successful spin-offs of recent technological innovation has been the video game. The UK's National Media Museum in Bradford chronicles this commercial development in a Games Lounge, which traces the development of digital gaming since 1952. It houses arcade, console, and table games, allowing people who remember their mass emergence to replay *PingPong, Tetris, Space Invaders, Pacman, Street Fighter II*, and the rest. The display demonstrates how visual qualities were always important, moving from very basic graphics, such as paddles and sets of colored blocks, through to elaborate simulations. We can also see how the history of such games has been punctuated by landmarks in which the so-called 'realism' of the environment has increased, as graphics technology improves and becomes more affordable and more accessible (Bolter & Grusin, 2000). The year 1997, for example, saw the launch of *Grand Theft Auto*—a game that achieved some notoriety for its depiction of crime, violence, and sexuality (see Kendall & McDougall, this volume)—but that was also a landmark in achieving a level of visual realism in its representation of the contemporary urban environment.

Our mini-corpus indicates the development of an understanding of virtual worlds as simulations—and this emerges in the early 1990s. For example, the 1992 piece, referred to earlier, explains the use of an "animation" of a shooting incident produced by a "ballistics expert and computer programmer" in a legal case, and places this alongside more mundane applications of virtual technologies:

> Architects and designers are using virtual worlds to convince supermarkets they need new warehouses—by showing how efficient these would be. ("Almost anything is possible—virtually")

Strategic simulation games with multifarious goals, such as *Sim City*, first released in 1989, and later versions such as the *The Sims*, significantly increased the range of decisions that players could take, and began to offer something like a 'world' in which players could act. Widespread availability of broadband then led to the rapid development of video games, which allowed gamers to interact online while not necessarily being physically co-present. In the mini-corpus we find articles that greet the development of multiplayer online games with some enthusiasm, suggesting that they herald new kinds of engagement and agency:

> TV is passive; on the Internet you're using your imagination, and you're actually with other people. It's not like a drug. It's more comparable to reading—your brain's engaged, it's a broadening experience . . . a Discovery Zone for bright adolescents. ("Caught in the Web," 1995)

One of the most commercially successful spin-offs of recent technological innovation has been the video game, designed for specific platforms, such as video game consoles and personal computers. From an early stage games had two controller inputs, allowing competition; as local area network technologies developed, more gamers could compete against one another. Achieving worldwide popularity, massively multiplayer online games like *World of Warcraft*, which by June 2010 boasted 11.1 million user accounts and over 60% of the market share of the games market (Cifaldi, 2011), are run by high-revenue media companies. A massively multiplayer online game has been defined in terms of the way in which it "provides roles, goals and an underlying narrative" (White & Le Cornu, 2010: 184). It usually involves players representing themselves as avatars who interact with others who are online, and present in the same 'region,' to explore, fulfill tasks, engage in combat, or simply hang out in a shared virtual space.

Although the history of video games traces a rather different path to that of virtual prosthetic devices, and has clearly garnered more commercial success, we note, in passing, some similarities. As game technology has developed, so have the complexity and visual realism of the environments represented. This has led to a more immersive experience—in fact gamers frequently report that they are 'in' the game, or so immersed ('in the zone') that they lose track of time. (See the discussion of temporality in playing *World of Warcraft* by Martin and colleagues, this volume.) While this experience has obvious parallels with other media such as cinema, these game experiences may be distinguished by the simple fact that gamers can act and *inter*-act within their game worlds.

3. MUDS AND MUVES

The early development of virtual communities emerged from the small-scale use of MUDs (Rheingold, 1993). MUD is a generic term used to describe a computer-generated multi-user domain (although sometimes the 'd' is used to stand for 'dungeon' or 'dimension'). MUDs developed from text-based adventure games and were originally played in small networked communities before the advent of the Web. They involved real-time interactions with limited semiotic possibilities, being essentially limited to exchanges of written text (see Rheingold, 1993; Markham, 1998; and Sunden, 2003, for examples). Players had to use their imaginations to construct a vivid world behind these short lines of dialogue that often represented the journeys of fantasy characters—monsters, magicians, and mythological creatures—as they moved from one fictional room or space to another. The creator of the first Multi-User Dungeon at Essex University, in the UK, was prescient in envisaging the possibilities:

> What I would like to see—and it's a long, long way off—is some local or national network with good graphics, sound effects and a well designed set of worlds of varying degrees of difficulty. In this true meritocracy, you will forever be encountering new situations, new difficulties, new solutions, and above all new people. Everyone starts off on an equal footing in this artificial world. (Bartle, 1983:130)

We can see in this the prefiguring of popular online games, such as *World of Warcraft*, as well as virtual worlds, such as *Second Life*. But the original MUDs and even their later developments were never as mainstream and commercial as the video console games referred to earlier. They were, however, the forebears of what have come to be known as MUVEs (multi-user virtual environments) as well as video games.

The most popular MUVEs are usually described as virtual worlds (e.g., *Second Life* and *Active Worlds*), and they are distinguished from video games by the simple fact that they "have no prescribed structuring of activity and allow varying degrees of creative freedom" (White & Le Cornu, 2010: 184). Games may sometimes be developed by those participating in virtual worlds, but they are not part of their basic architecture. Virtual worlds encourage a greater emphasis on sociality, the building of community, and the co-construction of the environment itself. Although these activities can also be found in other virtual spaces, they remain as key characteristics of virtual worlds. Morningstar and Farmer were part of the team that designed one of the first virtual worlds, Lucasfilm's *Habitat*, a commercially viable system that could support a population of thousands. Their account, which uses the terms 'cyberspace' and 'virtual world' throughout, is a fascinating piece, partly because of the insights it gives into virtual citizenship, governance, and, of course, design itself. They describe the growth of a virtual world community in which:

> users can communicate, play games, go on adventures, fall in love, get married, get divorced, start businesses, found religions, wage wars, protest against them, and experiment with self-government. (Morningstar & Farmer, [1991] 2008: 1)

Although visual representation in *Habitat* was rather limited, we can clearly see the beginnings of the idea of a virtual space constructed by the interaction of an online community of participants.

In *Habitat*, users were represented on-screen as a simple figure or 'avatar.' This idea of an avatar that represents, or in some accounts 'is' the user, is strongly associated with MUVEs. Although the term has a long history, the idea of an avatar as the representation, projection, or extension of a player first appears in the *Oxford English Dictionary* in 1986. It undoubtedly became common currency through the growing popularity of Neal Stephenson's (1992) novel *Snow Crash*, the MUVE *Second Life* launched in 2003, and more recently the (3D) science fiction film *Avatar* (2009). Our mini-corpus provides evidence of use in respect to children's use of virtual worlds:

> Almost immediately they were finding ways to interact with their friends' avatars . . . The children began communicating with the Orkney pupils through the avatars they met in the virtual world . . . Time for them to create landscapes of their own. ("Wicked world: Grapevine where schools share good ideas," 2000)

Once again the idea of building a virtual community and developing new collaborative skills comes to the fore, as in innovative classroom work that describes how children engage with new technologies in the construction of a virtual world:

> Through programming, children would be able to actually do things, create things, make things happen. ("Think piece: Victorian classroom values," 1999)
> They're developing teamwork skills and communication, as well as literacy and numeracy skills. ("Virtual learning—Untangled Web," 2009)

Overall, the picture that begins to emerge through the development of MUVEs is in line with Bolter and Grusin's (2000) concept of 'transparent immediacy'—a state in which the subject feels sufficiently connected to what is represented on-screen that it begins to take on some of the characteristics of a place. Furthermore, in such an environment, or world, encounters with representations of others begin to construct it as a social space, one in which one can meet others and do things. And it is at this point that the three strands (virtual reality prosthesis; the emergence of videogaming; and the early development of virtual communities) converge into a single discourse about virtual spaces. Clearly a significant theme is that of immersion, for there is no doubt that some users' experiences of virtual worlds, like those of avid gamers, lead to a sense of immersion. This is sometimes described in terms of being 'in a place'—a place that is shared with a distributed online community (Taylor, 2002).

The phenomenon of immersion has provoked a range of reactions. For some it associates with escapism, and even addiction—fears that are reminiscent of early reactions to novel-reading (Vogrinčič, 2008) and just about every media development since. Yet for others, the same experience is seen as a way of increasing levels of interaction. The mini-corpus manifests the moral panic that is so often associated with identification of immersion in a context thought to be inappropriate:

> . . . she believed her daughter was wasting real emotions on something which was 'unreal' since it took place online. ("When hatred comes to your home page," 2008)

VIRTUAL WORLDS: TOWARDS MORE SUBTLE UNDERSTANDINGS?

Soler and Gillen (2009) identified in their original corpus tendencies in newspaper coverage for both hyperbole and moral panic in treatment of virtual worlds. Yet the mini-corpus, investigated in more detail here, fleshed out with other historical accounts, also reveals a development of more subtle understandings, giving some grounds for optimism for those interested in virtual literacies that a richer understanding of the possibilities for virtual literacies is indeed possible. Yet before we leave this particular story of development of virtual worlds as seen through the lens of 'non-fiction' print media, we feel we it is useful to mention one significant landmark. It is a step towards academic respectability and an indication that a field of scholarship has arrived when a research article is printed in *Science*. In 2007 Bainbridge published "The scientific research potential of virtual worlds," an attempt to briefly explain virtual worlds (specifically *World of Warcraft* and *Second Life*) while simultaneously discussing appropriate research methodologies.

This article can be read as a culmination of the point of view that virtual worlds are so new—"a major historical transition" (Bainbridge, 2007: 472)—that they contain different kinds of activities from those found in the real world and that therefore new approaches to research are warranted. To be more precise, it seems to us that in likening, for example, *World of Warcraft* to the Cold War, Bainbridge paints a somewhat apocalyptic vision: "There is some evidence that they [virtual worlds] serve as hatcheries for new cultural movements; for example, facilitating the consolidation of post-Christian religious ideologies and are substituting for disintegrating social institutions in the real world" (Bainbridge, 2007: 474). Asking sensible questions as to the feasibility of obtaining informed consent in online environments, and the difficulty of separating realms of public from private interactions, he also harks back with nostalgia to days when social scientists could join small social movements and study them covertly, suggesting: "Thus, a team of agents provocateurs who are researchers in disguise would positively contribute to everybody's dramatic experience, if they promoted a movement that simultaneously supported the mythos and permitted scientifically relevant observations of human behavior."

The chapters that follow demonstrate how ethical principles need not be thrown overboard in the face of challenging virtual worlds. We hope that in this chapter we have dug some foundations that enable the study of literacies in virtual worlds to be conceptualized, not as opposed to the study of literacies in all other environments, for such would be a false dichotomy. Yet such a dichotomy is still a real perception, as expressed by Bainbridge's final conclusion—comparing a world in which the virtual exists against an actually unknowable comparison:

> Probably for better, but conceivably for worse, virtual worlds are creating a very new context in which young people are socialized to group norms, learn intellectual skills, and express their individuality. (Bainbridge, 2007: 475)

OTHER STORIES: CONSTRUCTING THE VIRTUAL IN THE POPULAR IMAGINATION

A number of commentators have drawn attention to the symbiotic relationship between popular narrative and technological innovation. The ways in which such stories are told relates strongly to the cultural legacies appropriated by the teller; it is possible to tell stories of the construction of virtuality that derive from Scandinavian fairy tales, from early Soviet science fiction, and from a variety of cinematic genres. While writing this chapter, one of us was startled to see a reproduction of Leonora Carrington's (1963) painting "El Mundo Mágico de Los Mayas/The Magic World of the Mayans" (Museo Nacional de Antropología, 1964). Colorful, seemingly unrelated tiny figures against a surreal landscape evoked atmospheres and motifs of games such as *EverQuest* and *World of Warcraft* as well as the *Lord of the Rings* films. In societies that draw heavily on North American culture and scholarship, such as our own, Hayles' (1990) work is resonant. She interweaves an analysis of new media theory and research with critical commentaries on authors like Gibson and Stephenson.

Gibson's work is often cited in the literature in virtual worlds, and it has been influential on how we view what is often referred to as 'cyberspace.' Reflecting on the way in which he originally conceived of the idea of cyberspace when writing his 1984 classic *Neuromancer*, Gibson says:

> Somehow I knew that the notional space behind all of the computer screens would be one single universe. (Gibson, 2011: n.p.)

Case, the central character of *Neuromancer*, uses 'dermatrodes' to physically plug into cyberspace and, in so doing, sees a "transparent 3D chessboard extending to infinity," which is "a graphic representation of data abstracted from the banks of every computer in the human system"—a sort of parallel universe that he can act within. Here, Gibson constructs an idea of the virtual that draws on ideas of prosthesis and immersion as Case enters the 'single universe' of cyberspace.

The fictional construct of a parallel universe is a regular trope in oral and written narratives in many cultures, both ancient and modern. Its enduring appeal is exemplified by the commercial success of the film *Avatar*, in which Sully, the central character, has to adopt the body of an avatar in order to become part of the culture of the inhabitants of the distant planet, Pandora. What is interesting here is the way in which this narrative has combined with new technology to renew popular enthusiasm for 3D cinema. In other words, the theme of immersion through 'transparent immediacy,' which we explored earlier, crosses once again into the experience of an alien or virtual world.

CONCLUSIONS

There is no space here for a full exploration of the ways in which the virtual is represented in fiction, but we do feel that it is important to underscore how radical innovations such as 'virtual worlds' have been shaped through interaction with the wider cultural narratives. If narratives of hidden kingdoms, parallel universes, and alternate realities capture our imagination, then it is entirely predictable that virtual worlds (or online gameworlds) might do the same. The impulse to imagine these realms as distinct spaces—or even places—is perhaps most strongly stated in Boellstorff's ethnography of *Second Life* (Boellstorff, 2008). In a useful review of this and other recent contributions to Internet studies, Postill (2010) teases out the tension between accounts of the virtual as a separate domain, and those that see online worlds as part of everyday lives—a supplement rather than a distinct alternative. We appreciate that for some users on some occasions, virtual spaces may constitute a distinct domain, and Boellstorff argues this with some lucidity. This separation is in fact shown in some of the chapters in this collection, but in the final analysis, we would argue that interactions in virtual worlds are always related to the agency of human beings in material circumstances. We find understandings that tether virtual environments to everyday experiences to be more helpful in describing the back-and-forth nature of the practices we wish to study. The key negotiations in virtual literacies take place through interactions between people and technology. In this sense keystrokes, mouse-clicks, and other operations provide a physical interface for users to navigate their way around virtual space, to interact with others, and to act on the environment itself.

To conclude, we hope to have demonstrated that historical study can contribute to an understanding of how technologies have developed; this is both interesting and relevant. But still more important for our purposes, as we hope to have shown, is the attempt to demonstrate how our re/telling of these developments can display our understandings of our past, present, and future virtual literacies to ourselves. This, we feel, can help us to reimagine our futures.

NOTES

1. It is worth noting that our use of the terms virtual and virtuality applies to literature and debate around new technologies. The terms have a rather different connotation in the work of Deleuze and other philosophers (see Massumi, 2002).

REFERENCES

Bainbridge, W.S. (2007). The scientific research potential of virtual worlds. *Science,* 317: 472–476.

Baker, P. (2006). *Using Corpora in Discourse Analysis.* London: Continuum.

Bartle, R. (1983). A voice from the dungeon. *Practical Computing* December: 126–130. Retrieved October 17, 2011 from http://mud.co.uk/richard/.

Barton, D. (2007). *Literacy: An Introduction to the Ecology of Written Language* (2nd ed.). Oxford: Blackwell.

Boellstorff, T. (2008). *Coming of Age in Second Life: An Anthropologist Explores the Virtually Human.* Princeton: Princeton University Press.

Bolter, J. D. & Grusin, R. (2000). *Remediation: Understanding New Media.* London: MIT Press.

Burnett, C. (2011). The (im)materiality of educational space: Interactions between material, connected and textual dimensions of networked technology use in schools. *E-Learning and Digital Media* 8(3): 214–227.

Childs, M. (2010). *Learners' Experience of Presence in Virtual Worlds.* (Unpublished doctoral dissertation). Coventry: University of Warwick.

Cifaldi, F. (2011). World of Warcraft subscriptions continue to decline. *Gamasutra.* August 3. Retrieved October 28, 2011 from http://www.gamasutra.com/view/news/36351/World_of_Warcraft_Subscriptions_Continue_To_Decline_Though_More_Slowly.php.

Cole, M. & Wertsch, J. (1996). Beyond the individual-social antimony in discussion of Piaget and Vygotsky. *Human Development* 39: 250–256.

Davies, J. & Merchant, G. (2009). *Web 2.0 for Schools: Learning and Social Participation.* New York: Peter Lang.

Gibson, W. (2011). Interview: The art of fiction no. 211. Interviewed by David Wallace-Wells. *The Paris Review* 197 (Summer 2011). Retrieved October 17, 2011 from http://www.theparisreview.org/interviews/6089/the-art-of-fiction-no-211-william-gibson.

Gillen, J. (2009). Literacy practices in Schome Park: A virtual literacy ethnography. *Journal of Research in Reading* 32(1): 57–74.

Hayles, N. K. (1990). *How We Became Posthuman: Virtual Bodies in Cybernetics, Literature and Informatics.* London: University of Chicago Press.

Heim, M. (1993). *The Metaphysics of Virtual Reality.* New York: Oxford University Press.

Herring, S. (1992). Interactional coherence in CMC. *Journal of Computer-Mediated Communication* 4(4). Retrieved October 17, 2011 from http://jcmc.indiana.edu/vol4/issue4/herring.html.

Hine, C. (1998). *Virtual Ethnography.* London: Sage.

Ihde, D. (1990). *Technology and the Lifeworld: From Garden to Earth*. Bloomington: Indiana University Press.

Lanier, J. (1992). An insider's view of the future of virtual reality. Interview with Frank Biocca. *Journal of Communication* 42(4): 150–172.

Lankshear, C. & Knobel, M. (2011). *New Literacies 3/e: Everyday Practices and Social Learning*. Maidenhead: Open University Press.

Markham, A. (1998). *Life Online: Researching Real Experience in Virtual Space*. London: AltaMira.

Massumi, B. (2002). *Parables for the Virtual: Movement, Affect, Sensation*. London: Duke University Press.

Merchant, G. (2010). 3D virtual worlds as environments for literacy teaching. *Education Research* 52(2): 135–150.

Miller, D. & Slater, D. (2000). *The Internet: An Ethnographic Approach*. Oxford: Berg.

Morningstar, C. & Farmer F. R. (2008 [1991]). The lessons of Lucasfilm's *Habitat*. *Journal of Virtual Worlds Research* 1(1): 1–20.

Palmer, S. (2006). *Toxic Childhood: How Modern Life Is Damaging Our Children… and What We Can Do about It*. London: Orion.

Postill, J. (2010). Researching the Internet. *Journal of the Royal Anthropological Institute* 16(3): 646–650.

Rheingold, H. (1993). *The Virtual Community: Homesteading on the Electric Frontier*. Reading, MA: Addison-Wesley.

Sakr, L. S. (2008, March18). Virtual embodiment. Paper presented at the Embodiment Conference, University of California, Santa Cruz. Retrieved October 17, 2011 from http://vjumamel.com/files/embodiment.pdf.

Schroeder, R. (Ed.). (2002). *The Social Life of Avatars: Presence and Interaction in Shared Virtual Environments*. London: Springer-Verlag.

Sheehy, K. & Seamans, D. (2010). Virtual worlds: The states of play. In K. Sheehy, R. Ferguson, & G. Clough (eds.), *Virtual Worlds: Controversies at the Frontier of Education*. Hauppauge, NY: Nova Science Publishers.

Soler, J. & Gillen, J. (2009, July 11). A threshold moment for virtual worlds: Literacy issues relating to children and teenagers portrayed in the newspaper media. Paper presented at the 45th UK Literacy Association International Conference, University of Greenwich, London.

Stone, G. (2011). Virtual Learning Environments as an extension to the classroom reading environment. *English 4–11* 43: 14–16.

Sunden, J. (2003). *Material Virtualities: Approaching Online Textual Embodiment*. New York: Peter Lang.

Taylor, T. L. (2002). Living digitally: Embodiment in virtual worlds. In R. Schroeder (ed.), *The Social Life of Avatars: Presence and Interaction in Shared Virtual Environments*. London: Springer-Verlag.

Vogrinčič, A. (2008). The novel-reading panic in 18th-century in England: An outline of an early moral media panic. *Media Research* 14(2): 103–124.

White, D. & Le Cornu, A. (2010). Eventedness and disjuncture in virtual worlds. *Educational Research* 52(2): 183–196.

Williams, R. (1982). *Dream Worlds: Mass Consumption in Late Nineteenth-Century France*. Berkeley, CA: University of California Press.

Wolfe, S. & Flewitt, R. (2010). New technologies, new multimodal literacy practices and young children's metacognitive development. *Cambridge Journal of Education* 40(4): 387–399.

2 A Sociocultural Approach to Exploring Virtual Worlds

Rebecca W. Black and Stephanie M. Reich

INTRODUCTION

Lacey, a 10-year-old girl, and her 14-year-old brother, Ben, sit on the floor of his room preparing to explore a virtual world on his laptop. The process begins with some confusion, as they discuss which avatar to use and complain about the design of the world's opening user interface. While playing, these siblings hand off control of the mouse frequently, with Ben completing one activity while Lacey directs his attention to objects on the screen. Then they switch, with Lacey controlling the avatar while Ben advises her on where to go next. At one point, they visit a section of the world where avatars are able to interact with each other; however, they quickly lose interest in this activity, citing the restrictive nature of the chat system as a reason. Moving on to a different part of the world, Lacey and Ben share responsibility for reading the in-world text, sometimes taking turns and other times reading the same sentence collaboratively, working together to figure out the cryptic in-game clues. Lacey, who has struggled with reading due to dyslexia, takes the initiative on seeking out these in-game texts, searching for information about how to complete various puzzle-like challenges. At one point, she suggests searching the Web for a text-based 'walk-through' to help them complete a particularly difficult quest; however, Ben persuades her to work though the activity with him using a process of trial and error. At one point they both jump for the keyboard at the same time, rushing to turn off an ad embedded in the world before the pop-up images have a chance to appear on the screen.

This vignette, culled from observation data, can be used as an illustration of how a sociocultural framework can help researchers to capture the many facets and social intricacies of children's play and learning in virtual worlds. In particular, it highlights three fundamental elements of a sociocultural approach that will serve as foci throughout the analyses and discussion in this chapter. The first element, *the role of mediation in learning*, is evident in the computer itself, as it provides a cultural tool with text, icons, and images that shape and influence Ben and Lacey's interactions with each other and their meaning-making practices within the game. The second element, *the interplay of social and individual processes in development*, can be seen as Lacey and Ben explore the world together, with Ben supporting Lacey's reading and Lacey in turn helping Ben to strategize and navigate spatial aspects of the world. The potential influence of the social on individual gameplay is also present in the fan-created walk-throughs that Lacey frequently uses to improve her strategies for play. The third element of a sociocultural perspective, which is closely related to the second, involves *the influence of cultural and historical contexts on learning* and, for the purposes of this chapter, on children's digitally mediated activities. This influence emerges in the popular cultural content of the virtual world, the safeguards that restrict Lacey and Ben's communication with other players within the world, and in the advertising that they rush to turn off. In this chapter, we will expand on the ways in which these three intertwined elements of a sociocultural framework can be used to understand the complex interplay of social, cultural, and meditational factors that afford and constrain children's learning, development, and play in virtual worlds. In particular, our discussion will focus on how these elements of a sociocultural perspective enhance our knowledge about: 1) scaffolded learning; 2) mediated communication; and 3) culture and community in a virtual space called *Webkinz World*.

STUDY CONTEXT

While this chapter focuses primarily on the Ganz Corporation's *Webkinz World* site, the data and examples discussed in this chapter stem from a larger project involving comparative case studies of several virtual worlds for children between the ages of 6 and 13 years (see Black, 2010; Black & Reich, 2011; Black & Reich, in press.) These cases are based on participant observation and qualitative content analysis of the learning, literacy, and developmental features of these sites. Data include maps of site contents, records of games and activities within each world, screenshots, observations of users in public spaces, and literacy artifacts. Content analysis was conducted using open-ended qualitative protocols focused on technical and aesthetic design features, literacy-related texts and activities, educational and problem-solving-based activities, and community-building features of each site. Data were analyzed using discourse (Gee, 1999) and inductive thematic analyses (Coffey & Atkinson, 1996). Texts were also analyzed using grade level and readability measures.

Webkinz (Ganz, 2005) are stuffed animals that come with a special code that allows access to an avatar version of that animal within the online world of Webkinz. After visiting the Adoption Center to register, name, choose a gender for, and obtain information about their newly adopted Webkinz avatar, players receive a room for their pet and 2000 Kinzcash, a monetary unit that allows them to participate in the *Webkinz World* economy. Popular activities in the world of Webkinz include visiting the Webkinz Shop to purchase items for pets such as clothing or furniture, playing Arcade games, and visiting the Kinzville Park or Clubhouse to socialize with other players.

The virtual world is colorful and has an abundance of both text and images. The dock at the bottom of the screen provides information about such things as the avatar's possessions, amount of Kinzcash, and levels of health, happiness, and hunger. Tabs above the dock provide quick links to popular pages, such as My Room (the avatar's home) and Today's Activities (time-sensitive activities that provide Kinzcash or items). There is also a map of the different spaces in *Webkinz World*. Interestingly, while there is a map depicting the geographic layout of the world of Webkinz, the interface does not allow avatars to physically navigate from one space or activity to another. Rather, clicking on the desired destination triggers a page to load while the avatar remains in a static position. For most areas of *Webkinz World*, printed instructions are available, and for more frequently visited spaces, short tutorial videos are also provided.

SCAFFOLDED LEARNING IN VIRTUAL WORLDS

Applying a sociocultural lens to learning in virtual worlds draws our attention to the ways in which a child's mental functioning emerges through the development of psychological tools and the manipulation of cultural material (Karpov & Bransford, 1995). This includes play that is mediated by symbolic systems such as language, as well as by tools and artifacts such as toys and books. From this perspective, a virtual environment such as *Webkinz World* can mediate children's learning in multiple ways. For example, the world of Webkinz serves as the sociocultural context for interaction and activity and provides many of the tools and cultural artifacts that are relevant to in-game activities. While some artifacts are unique to the virtual environment, most activities and interactions mirror activities that children may see in their daily lives, ranging from gardening and decorating a backyard to working at the Employment Agency and socializing with others over coffee. Such activities provide young children with an opportunity to engage in sociodramatic play and experiment with the adult social roles, vocabulary, and language forms associated with these real-world events.

The design of virtual worlds can play a significant role in shaping children's in-game learning. In a space such as *Webkinz World*, the digital environment often serves as the expert or more capable other that supports young players' learning experiences within online spaces. For example, in *Webkinz World* support features include video tutorials, text- and image-based instructions, as well as subtle visual and audio cues that guide players' participation. The following paragraphs will illustrate how a sociocultural perspective can illuminate how such site features both afford and constrain children's opportunities for learning in *Webkinz World*.

According to sociocultural theorists, much of children's learning stems from the "appropriation of modes of speaking, acting, and thinking that are first encountered in collaboration with adults or more capable peers" (Minick, Stone, & Forman, 1993). This process is often discussed in terms of scaffolding or supporting learning within the zone of proximal development (ZPD) (Vygotsky, 1978). According to Vygotsky, the ZPD "is the distance between the actual developmental level" of a child "as determined by independent problem solving and the level of potential development as determined through problem solving under adult guidance, or in collaboration with more capable peers" (Vygotsky, 1978: 86). In this process, the expert or more capable other supports a novice or child in reaching his/her problem-solving potential using a variety of strategies, such as recruiting the novice's interest, reducing degrees of freedom within the activity, sustaining goal orientation, focusing attention on critical task features, and demonstrating possible solutions (Wood and associates, cited in Stone, 1993). In essence, the adult or more capable other designs the learning experience to support the learner's success.

While we see this sort of face-to-face scaffolding between siblings in the introductory vignette for the chapter, this metaphor of scaffolded learning also can be applied to our understandings of how a virtual world may be designed to act as a more capable other and provide supports for players' learning in *Webkinz World* using similar strategies. This perspective also can inform our understandings of how such a design may result in incomplete scaffolding that may limit the ZPD and constrain children's opportunities for deeper learning and subsequent cognitive development.

To illustrate, the world of Webkinz uses a range of meditational means to support young children's learning and participation and to make the site accessible even to novice technology users and early readers. The main user interface, known as the dock, uses a mixture of text and icons to help players with important tasks, such as keeping track of their in-game inventory, monitoring their pet's condition, and moving around the world. For example, a pet's levels of happiness and hunger are represented by a smiley face and fork respectively, while the inventory and action tabs are represented by colored building blocks and bouncing balls coupled with text. This combination of icons and text can help pre-readers to navigate the game more easily, and also allow early readers to develop print awareness and begin making the connections between the concepts represented by the icons and the words for these concepts. In addition, by placing the pet's happiness, hunger, and health level indicators, as well as action buttons for the pet's inventory and for certain popular areas of the site in prominent positions on the dock, the site design is supporting players' successful navigation of the site by drawing new players' attention to and continuously highlighting features that are integral to the overall *Webkinz World* narrative (adopting, caring for, and purchasing items for a pet).

Webkinz World also uses numerous video tutorials and animated non-player characters (NPCs) (characters that are fixtures within the game rather than player-controlled avatars) to support children's learning and participation in the site. These features leverage the affordances of the virtual environment by using a synthesis of sound, color, and movement to draw children's attention to important aspects of and demonstrate possible strategies for excelling at games and activities. These features also support players' comprehension of site materials. For example, NPCs offer instructions both aurally and textually via text bubbles that appear above the NPC's head while it is speaking. In addition, as the NPC introduces aspects of the user interface, it will often point, tilt its head, and/or direct its eyes towards the object or portion of the screen being discussed as a way of emphasizing important game items and vocabulary.

Some of these NPCs also have interactive components that provide customized feedback depending on what action a player has taken. For example, in the Employment Agency, the feline office worker T. Von Meow will tell players who have already visited the agency during an eight-hour period (players are able to complete only one job every eight hours) that they are a bit early and will direct their attention to a digital clock on the wall that counts down the time remaining until they are eligible for another job. As another example, Arte, the canine proprietor of the Curio Shop, changes his greeting for players depending on how much they purchase and tip in his shop. At the highest level of purchasing and tipping, Arte holds up a sign to indicate when players can purchase rare items (virtual clothing and furniture items that serve as status symbols) in the shop. This information is valuable because without the exact time, players must use a system of trial and error, visiting the Curio Shop repeatedly at random times in order to find rare items. Moreover, Arte prevents players from "gaming" this system by refusing to accept more than one tip per day from each player. In this way, the site can guide players away from prohibited activities and towards desired actions.

While the actions of the NPCs, video tutorials, and multimodal instructions for *Webkinz World* activities provide strong support for learning to navigate site features, the site does not provide the sort of higher-level feedback that would allow for deeper and richer understanding of the concepts introduced through games and activities (see Black & Reich, 2011 for a detailed discussion of the zone of proximal development in *Webkinz World*). In fact, incomplete or inadequate scaffolding may limit children's opportunities for development and independent problem solving. For instance, the Jellybean Challenge is an activity on *Webkinz World* in which users are shown a glass jar filled with jellybeans and are given three opportunities to guess how many jellybeans are inside. While providing multiple opportunities to complete the challenge is laudable, the structure of the activity provides no information that would improve a user's performance over time. No information is provided about the size of the jar or how many jellybeans it could hold when full. Further, after each incorrect guess, the user will encounter one of four responses: "Wow, that was way off!", "You'll need to be closer!", "Not a bad guess!", or "Oooo, that was close!" No feedback is provided about whether the guess is too high or too low or if subsequent guesses are closer, or at least heading in the correct direction. Interestingly, an Internet search of Webkinz fan sites found that these four responses are clues (e.g., "Wow, that was way off!" = guess is off by 1,000 or more jellybeans, "Oooo, that was close!" = guess is off by fewer than 200 jellybeans). There is no way, however, for users on the site to know that these answers are associated with information on how to complete the challenge. Thus, while users get multiple chances to successfully complete the task, there is no scaffolding to support users' reasoning and performance on the task.

These examples demonstrate how sociocultural theory can help researchers to better understand the efficacy and fallibility of the *Webkinz World* site design for supporting children's learning. In addition, we are able to see the important role that human interaction can play in scaffolded learning, as players' contributions to external fan sites provide more detailed feedback for successful navigation of Arte's Curio Shop and for successful completion of the Jellybean Challenge than the game itself provides. In the next section, we use a sociocultural framework to further examine the affordances and constraints of the *Webkinz World* site for human interaction and player learning.

MEDIATED COMMUNICATION IN VIRTUAL WORLDS

A sociocultural perspective on learning emphasizes the relationship between human mental processes and social contexts (Wertsch, 1991). Through this lens, children's interactions with people and objects in their immediate social environments play a crucial role in their cognitive development. When looking at children's learning and participation in virtual worlds, such a perspective draws attention to the sorts of interactions taking place between players and the ways in which the site design mediates these interactions. In the following paragraphs, we discuss how the design of communication features within *Webkinz World* both affords and constrains children's opportunities to teach and learn from each other.

Within many virtual worlds for young children, pre-structured and dictionary chat systems are the primary mediators of in-game social interaction. With pre-structured systems, players are able to choose from a set of pre-constructed words, phrases, and sentences, while with dictionary systems, players are able to type in their own messages provided their words are included in the site's list or "dictionary" of permissible words. To illustrate,

KinzChat is a pre-structured messaging system that is available to all players in *Webkinz World*. KinzChat allows players to choose from a set of topically organized, pre-constructed phrases that focus almost exclusively on Webkinz-related topics. On the one hand, because most of the phrases are simple and contextually situated within the game context, this form of messaging may make it easier for early readers and writers to discern word meanings and construct and interpret messages, thus affording them opportunities to interact and coordinate activities with other players.

On the other hand, while KinzChat does afford opportunities for interaction, concerns about online safety have shaped the design of such systems. As a result, KinzChat is limited in its potential for fostering authentic communication between players and promoting young children's language and literacy development. The most obvious problem with pre-structured messaging systems, such as KinzChat, is that they do not allow children to practice putting their thoughts into words or expressing themselves. In fact, the *Webkinz World* Frequently Asked Questions for parents clearly states that "There is no way for users to type what they want, exchange any personal information, ask or say anything inappropriate. We control everything the users are able to say" (Ganz, 2009, para. 1). Another problem with the pre-structured system is that users must scroll through numerous topical categories to find the one option that best approximates the information that they are trying to convey. This not only is time-consuming but also may result in a stilted and somewhat unoriginal communicative context. Moreover, as discussed by Black and Reich (2011), the process of choosing an option that is embedded in topical categories may be developmentally untenable for younger players (or even some adults, for that matter) who lack sophisticated class inclusion abilities. As such, the designers of these types of pre-structured messaging systems miss many opportunities for constructing chat in ways that would scaffold children's linguistic development and awareness.

KinzChatPlus, which requires parental approval, is the other in-game messaging system in *Webkinz World*. Similar to a dictionary messaging system, KinzChatPlus allows users to type in their own messages "as long as they are not on the excluded list of words and phrases developed for this form of chat" (Ganz, 2009). According to Ganz, excluded words include those such as proper names and numbers in an attempt to discourage users from sharing personal information about themselves. Other types of exclusions include words and phrases that might be considered profane, insulting (e.g., ugly, stupid), sexually suggestive (e.g., on you, coming, baby), or words that are culturally specific (e.g., piano is allowed but not sitar). This less restrictive type of chat system allows children much greater freedom for conveying their own thoughts and making meaningful social connections with other players than the pre-structured system. However, because the system prohibits misspellings, certain words, and turns of phrase as a means of preventing players from circumventing the rules for exclusion, it seriously curtails opportunities for early writers to use invented spelling, simple misspellings, and many of their preferred syntactic choices to convey meaning. In addition, because the dictionary messaging system is composed of a selection of words and phrases that is generated by adults who are operating from a particular sociocultural context (i.e., the sorts of adults who design and create content at a large North American corporation), children are restricted to utterances from within that worldview.

While there is concern from parents and policy-makers about Internet safety and children's communication with unknown others online (U.S. Department of Justice Federal Bureau of Investigation, n.d.), how decisions are made about what is included or excluded in pre-structured chat systems is unclear. As Grimes (2008) astutely pointed out, the term 'safety' remains vague and undefined with little, if any, "nuanced discussion of how the pre-approved words and sentences become approved in the first place: How are they selected, who selects them, and on what basis" (Grimes, 2008: 2). While an in-depth discussion of how decisions about word selections in KinzChatPlus are made is beyond the scope of this chapter, the issue is particularly relevant to understanding how the sociocultural context of *Webkinz World* can significantly impact the shared meanings and experiences that children are able to develop through their play.

In addition to the restrictions of the KinzChat and KinzChatPlus systems, the ways in which users can access and communicate with one another in *Webkinz World* are additionally restrictive. Users in the world of Webkinz are able to connect to other users in two ways. They can, when their avatars are in close proximity or through an asynchronous message (if the username is known), request a user to be their friend (which will need to be reciprocated for access to be granted), or they can opt to 'speak' while in public spaces and wait for another avatar to also publicly announce something. In the latter case, communication is not directed to any specific person and will not necessarily elicit a response from others in the space.

When users are 'friends' (i.e., a friend request was sent and accepted by the other), they can then communicate via their cell phone (located on the dock). This phone also enables users to invite others over to their homes (My Room). For a successful phone call, both users must be on the same color channel. Unfortunately, there are varying numbers of colors depending on the type of account each user has purchased (i.e., standard or deluxe) and there is no option in the KinzChat system that identifies phone color choices. Thus, users must, through trial and error, change colors until they arrive at the same color as their friend. So while there is a messaging system, it is somewhat prohibitive in allowing planned communication with known (or at least online-befriended) others.

In the subsequent section, we discuss how a sociocultural framework draws our attention to the ways in which participation in a virtual world, as a cultural activity, can influence children's social and cognitive development, not only through exchanges with the game and with other users, but also through 'interactions' (Rogoff, 1995: 174) with other social and historical 'players,' such as profit-driven corporations, advertisers, and game designers, to name just a few. Moreover, many of these interactions are mediated through the multimodal texts and literacy-related artifacts of the site; thus, this section will pay particular attention to the role of linguistic, semiotic, and technical mediation in creating culture in virtual worlds.

COMMUNITY AND CULTURE IN VIRTUAL WORLDS

Another primary focus of sociocultural theory is the connection between individuals embedded in a social and historical context (Vygotsky, 1978; Wertsch, 1991). As such, learning is first an intermental process (between people) prior to becoming an intramental one (John-Steiner & Mahn, 1996). From this perspective, children's learning and development are part of a process of socialization into shared cultures and "systems of meaning" (Göncü & Katsarou, 2000: 223) of a given sociohistorical context. In order to use a sociocultural lens in studying *Webkinz World*, attention must be paid to the cultural underpinnings of the site and, to a larger extent, how community is or is not manifested in this virtual space.

In many ways, the world of Webkinz is modeled after consumerist, Western society, in which wealth and attractiveness are believed to be important components of health and happiness. These values are conveyed through the artifacts on the site (e.g., the dock prominently displays possessions; almost all games in the Arcade terminate with the image of a piggybank being filled with coins), as well as through contact with NPCs and even the site-generated speech bubbles from one's own avatar. Thus, these cultural norms are conveyed through the majority of the texts, activities, and areas of *Webkinz World*. To illustrate, when playing Quizzy's Question Corner, one's own avatar will comment with "wow, we're making money now," and when visiting the KinzStyle Outlet, PJ Collie (the trendy-dressed dog NPC) will welcome you with "This is where you will find all the hip, funky, and fashionable threads that will keep your pet lookin' stylish!" Even when logging on, the initial page (the Kinzville Times newspaper) will highlight things to buy, play, or shop for, such as "if you're a shopaholic, you've got to check out Spree, a fabulous game in the Arcade!" Throughout the virtual world, children then enact (and perhaps internalize) these values through gameplay; earning Kinzcash, shopping and dressing their avatar, and expanding and decorating their avatar's home. These consumer values are also reinforced through banner advertisements around the gameplay screen and periodic in-game commercial campaigns for such things as movies and books.

Webkinz World also expresses values such as responsibility and caring for others. For example, users are instructed to care for their Webkinz pets, the messaging system is structured to restrict negative interactions, users must regularly water and maintain fruits and vegetables in their yard, and additional pay features, such as the Caring Valley (enable users to plant virtual trees), contribute money towards children's charities. It is worth noting, however, that these messages about responsibility and caring are not integral to successful play in the site. For instance, while one's garden will die if not tended to within a seven-day period, there are few consequences for not caring for one's avatar. When the Webkinz pet's health, happiness, or hunger meter becomes low, a thermometer will appear in its mouth and a heating pad will rest on its head. However, having health and hunger at zero (out of 100) will not affect gameplay. The avatar will not be slower, lethargic, or unable to access any area of *Webkinz World*.

While a self-proclaimed "educational" environment, the culture of *Webkinz World* does not appear to value education, the process of learning, or being smart. Instead, users can compete to be the prettiest or best dressed, but no such competitions exist for knowing more than others or excelling in intellectual pursuits. Further, many of the comments made in the virtual world about school are quite disparaging and few activities focus on learning specifically. For instance, one's own avatar, while playing in the Arcade or in Quizzy's Question Corner, will make such comments as "If only this counted as homework, huh?" or "Maybe we won't have to go to school now." Such statements seem to belittle the importance of school and perhaps even learning in general. While some comments are made about intelligence—"oh, I'm getting smarter by the moment" or "I'm going to be the smartest Webkinz around"—few activities focus on learning new material. Rather, the games are based on the demonstration of already known facts (trivia), spelling, or addition. On the whole, most activities are focused on earning Kinzcash, rather than educational benefit or the simple acquisition of knowledge. Even the Kinzville Academy, where pets can take courses, is in no way associated with academic subject learning. Instead, lessons focus on strength, agility, speed, creativity, style, cooking, and grooming. There is one intelligence course that involves solving word puzzles. While there is no traditional academic focus in these activities, there is a financial incentive, as completing these courses then enables users to take higher-paying jobs at the Employment Agency.

While there are clearly cultural norms on *Webkinz World*, whether the virtual world is a community is unclear. As Rogoff (2003) noted, "People develop as participants in cultural communities. Their development can be understood only in light of the cultural practices and circumstances of their communities" (p. 3–4). It is this awareness that leads to an additional question of whether the world of Webkinz is indeed an online community or simply a virtual space, mirroring dominant cultural norms. While many have theorized about what makes a community, some key tenets seem to be a sense of interdependence, communication, and emotional connection (Dalton, Elias, & Wandersman, 2001; Sarason, 1974). In looking specifically at online communities, the ability for personal expression, sharing information, and establishing social connections also seem to be important (Nip, 2004; Reich, 2010).

In some respects, *Webkinz World* provides many opportunities for personal expression. Users can select what type of Webkinz pet to purchase, pick clothing for their avatar, arrange the layout of the avatar's home (My Room), and decorate the space with purchased and won items. In addition, there are some means for establishing personal connections with others through the KinzChat, KinzChatPlus, and KinzPost systems. However, as discussed earlier, these clothing and furniture items, as well as the messages in the pre-structured and dictionary communication systems, are created by adult game designers and restrict young players' freedom of expression. In exploring how interdependence—a level of reciprocal influence—might be established in *Webkinz World*, we see few opportunities for users to contribute meaningfully to the world or to other users. As Robbins (2005) points out, from a sociocultural perspective, the ability of the individual to influence and be shaped by his or her community is of utmost importance.

> Individuals and their social partners and the activities in which they engage are continually transforming and developing in mutually integrated ways. Likewise, communities or contexts are constantly changing and being changed, which in turn results in changed opportunities for learning and development. (p. 143)

In looking at the structure of *Webkinz World* and users' abilities to shape their environment, or at least communicate with others, contribute ideas, or create new games or activities, there is little available. Users can email the site administrators and suggest changes be made, but there is nothing more direct. Instead, it appears that users may be using the fan sites around *Webkinz World* to promote communication, collaboration, expression, and interdependence.

Fan sites such as the *Webkinz Insider* assist newcomers and more novice users in navigating the world of Webkinz through a forum and Twitter updates. The communication features are not very restrictive and tips, explanations, and cheats are readily available. Similarly, *Everything Webkinz*, a site created by three mothers of Webkinz users, hosts many virtual events that may also engender a sense of connection. These events include room decorating contests, holiday parties, raffles, and scavenger hunts that encourage interaction between users and facilitate more cooperative interactions, if not more scaffolded learning opportunities. Further, the site administrators continually solicit member input, providing another mechanism for users to meaningfully participate.

While *Webkinz World* may not demonstrate the key components of an online community, it does promote distinct cultural values. Further, the fan sites associated with *Webkinz World* appear to provide more community-like opportunities and interactions for users. As such, our understandings of the affordances and constraints that *Webkinz World* offers for children's learning are improved by the widening of research boundaries to include the additional fan spaces around *Webkinz World*.

CONCLUSIONS

To date, the bulk of socioculturally oriented theory and research has explored the cultural influences of offline spaces. However, in modern societies, the artifacts, signs, social norms, and communicative practices of online spaces increasingly make up the cultures or shared "system of meaning" (Göncü & Katsarou, 2000: 223) into which children are socialized. Therefore, it is appropriate to extend this perspective to the study of online and technology-mediated spaces as well. Recent research on children's engagement with new technologies has provided insight into many specific elements of a sociocultural framework. This includes explorations of how expert others scaffold children's development of "technoliteracies" (Marsh, 2004) and contextually appropriate gaming literacy practices (Steinkuehler, 2007), examinations of the role of technological (Gillen, Gamannossi, & Cameron, 2005) and popular cultural media (Wohlwend, 2009) artifacts in mediating children's literate play, as well as investigations of the impact of culture and community both online (Black & Reich, in press) and in classroom contexts (Merchant, 2009) for children's learning in virtual worlds. These studies have all contributed greatly to our understandings of the varied roles of new technologies and media in children's development. However, building on insights gained from these studies, as well as from the observations and content analysis discussed in this chapter, we suggest that the focused and systematic use of a sociocultural framework can assist researchers in identifying design features that facilitate or limit children's technology-mediated play and learning in virtual worlds. More specifically, the sociocultural lens can provide insights into the intertwined elements of scaffolded learning, mediated communication, and culture and community that shape the explicit and implicit lessons that children are learning in these online spaces.

As the opening vignette demonstrates, digital environments often provide rich opportunities for meaningful interactions between children. However, virtual worlds can be viewed as the social and cognitive partners in children's development as well. The designed space, activities, feedback, and implicit values of these worlds can impact users—from serving as the more competent other in scaffolded interactions to conveying social and cultural meaning in gameplay. While decades of research have applied a sociocultural perspective to children's daily lives, we argue that this lens should be expanded to include children's play in virtual worlds as these sites attract millions of unique users each month (Compete, Inc., 2011). Virtual worlds, like *Webkinz World*, can serve as both a social partner and a space rich with cultural norms and values. Further, fan sites around these virtual worlds may provide online communities where users are able to continually transform and develop the space in integrated ways.

ACKNOWLEDGMENTS

The first author would like to thank the National Academy of Education and the Spencer Foundation for their generous support of this research.

REFERENCES

Black, R. W. (2010). The language of Webkinz: Early childhood literacy in an online virtual world. *Journal of Digital Culture and Education* 2(1): 7–24.

Black, R. W. & Reich, S. M. (in press). Culture and community in a virtual world for young children. In C. A. Steinkuehler, K. D. Squire, & S. A. Barab (eds.), *Games, Learning, and Society: Learning and Meaning in the Digital Age*. New York: Cambridge University Press.

Black, R. W. & Reich, S. M. (2011). Affordances and constraints of scaffolded learning in a virtual world for young children. *International Journal of Game-Based Learning* 1(2): 52–64.

Coffey, A. & Atkinson, P. (1996). *Making Sense of Qualitative Data: Complementary Research Strategies*. Thousand Oaks, CA: Sage.

Compete, Inc. (2011). Site comparison of webkinz.com (rank #542), clubpenguin. com (#647), poptropica.com (#518). *Compete*. Retrieved June 6, 2011 from http:// siteanalytics.compete.com/webkinz.com+clubpenguin.com+poptropica.com/.

Dalton, J., Elias, M., & Wandersman, A. (2001). *Community Psychology: Linking Individuals and Communities*. Stamford: Wadsworth.

Ganz (2009). For parents. Retrieved July 17, 2009 from http://www.webkinz.com/ us_en/faq_parents.html.

Gee, J. P. (1999). *An Introduction to Discourse Analysis: Theory and Method*. New York: Routledge.

Gillen, J., Gamannossi, B. A., & Cameron, C. A. (2005). "'Pronto, chi parla? (Hello,who is it?)': Telephones as artefacts and communication media in children's discourses. In J. Marsh (ed.), *Popular Culture, New Media and Digital Literacy in Early Childhood*. New York: RoutledgeFalmer.

Göncü, A. & Katsarou, E. (2000). Commentary: Constructing sociocultural approaches to literacy education. In K. A. Roskos & J. F. Christie (eds.), *Play and Literacy in Early Childhood: Research from Multiple Perspectives*. Mahwah, NJ: Lawrence Erlbaum Associates.

Grimes, S. (2008). I'm a Barbie Girl, in a BarbieGirls world. *The Escapist*. September 2. Retrieved July 9, 2009 from http://www.escapistmagazine.com/articles/ view/issues/issue_165/5187-Im-a-Barbie-Girl-in-a-BarbieGirls-World.3.

John-Steiner, V. & Mahn, H. (1996). Sociocultural approaches to learning and development: A Vygotskian framework. *Educational Psychologist* 31(3/4): 191–206.

Karpov, Y. & Bransford, D. (1995). L. S. Vygotsky and the doctrine of empirical and theoretical learning. *Educational Psychologist* 30: 61–66.

Marsh, J. (2004). The techno-literacy practices of young children. *Journal of Early Childhood Research* 2(1): 51–66.

Merchant, G. (2009). Literacy in virtual worlds. *Journal of Research in Reading* 32(1): 38–56.

Minick, N., Stone, C. A., & Forman, E. A. (1993). Integration of individual, social, and institutional processes in accounts of children's learning and development. In E. A. Forman, N. Minick, & C. A. Stone (eds.), *Contexts for Learning: Sociocultural Dynamics in Children's Development*. New York: Oxford University Press.

Nip, J. (2004). The relationship between online and offline communities: The case of the Queer Sisters. *Media, Culture, and Society* 26: 209–229.

Reich, S. M. (2010). Adolescents' sense of community on MySpace and Facebook: A mixed methods approach. *Journal of Community Psychology* 38(6): 688–705.

Robbins, J. (2005). Contexts, collaboration, and cultural tools: A sociocultural perspective on researching children's thinking. *Contemporary Issues in Early Childhood* 6(2): 140–149.

Rogoff, B. (2003). *The Cultural Nature of Human Development*. Oxford: Oxford University Press.

Rogoff, B. (1995). Observing sociocultural activity on three planes: Participatory appropriation, guided participation, and apprenticeship. In J. V. Wertsch, P. Del Rio, & A. Alvarez (eds.), *Sociocultural Studies of Mind*. New York: Cambridge University Press.

Sarason, S. B. (1974). *The Psychological Sense of Community: Perspectives for Community Psychology*. San Francisco: Jossey-Bass.

Steinkuehler, C. A. (2007). Massively multiplayer online gaming as a constellation of literacy practices. *E-Learning* 4(3): 297–318.

Stone, C. A. (1993). What is missing in the metaphor of scaffolding? In E. A. Forman, N. Minick, & C. A. Stone (eds.), *Contexts for Learning: Sociocultural Dynamics in Children's Development*. New York: Oxford University Press.

U.S. Department of Justice Federal Bureau of Investigation (n.d.). A parent's guide to Internet safety. *The FBI Federal Bureau of Investigation*. Retrieved June 6, 2011 from http://www.fbi.gov/stats-services/publications/parent-guide/.

Vygotsky, L. S. (1978). *Mind in Society: The Development of Psychological Processes*. Cambridge, MA: Harvard University Press.

Wertsch, James V. (1991). *Voices of the Mind: A Sociocultural Approach to Mediated Action*. Cambridge, MA: Harvard University Press.

Wohlwend, K. (2009). Damsels in discourse: Girls consuming and producing identity through Disney princess play. *Reading Research Quarterly* 44(1): 57–83.

3 Barbies and Chimps
Text and Childhoods in Virtual Worlds

Victoria Carrington

INTRODUCTION

Virtual worlds, computer-based online communities that create and sustain online spaces inhabited by users in the form of avatars, are becoming a major site of social interaction and entertainment for growing millions of young people. In 2010 virtual world registrations passed the 1 billion mark. 46% of this figure comes from registrants identifying as between 10 and 15 years of age (Kzero Worldswide, 2011). In all, users between the ages of 10 and 15 currently account for 468 million virtual world registrations. These figures suggest that *a lot* of children and young people are hanging out in the social and gaming spaces provided by virtual worlds. They are therefore sites of interest for those of us concerned with the ways in which texts are encountered and engaged with in online contexts.

Acknowledging this growing prominence, this chapter sets out to examine two contemporary virtual worlds designed for children. One of the worlds, *barbiegirls.com*, is based in the U.S. and run by one of the world's most successful toy companies; the other, *chimpoo.com*, is based in India and is the latest offering of one of the world's most successful online game companies. Both sites target children between the ages of 5 and 12 years of age. Both sites offer tiered access to activities and goods within the world and both claim to create safe and engaging environments for children. My particular interest in examining these worlds relates to the kinds of textual practices and models of childhood on display.

CHIMPOO.COM

The India-based online gaming company Games2Win[1] launched its first virtual world, *Chimpoo.com* (hereafter *Chimpoo*), in March 2010. By the end of the third quarter of 2010 the site was closing in on 4 million registrations. According to Kzero.com (2011), a large proportion of these registrations are drawn from India although the site presents in English and attracts a growing global online audience. The site is aimed at children aged 5–12 years (the average age of users is 10 years) and provides free basic registration that includes access to the world, gameplay, and a 'home' sandcastle. There is, in addition, a subscription model that releases access to a broader range of clothing and furnishings.

The economy of the site runs on a combination of subscriptions and currency earned by gameplay. Local, in-world currency, or 'coins' is earned by playing games, which may be either solo or with another player, and used to purchase costumes and decorator items. It is also possible, and encouraged, to buy additional access to *Chimpoo* goods. Players can purchase a month-by-month subscription, or 'Golden Bananas,' which allows the purchase of "exclusive stuff" without the necessary accumulated currency: "Buying exclusive stuff as you go along . . . Buying exclusive stuff when you don't have enough coins." Such a purchase requires payment via credit card or PayPal account, which, in turn, requires the consent and participation of an adult/caregiver with a current credit card. As evidenced by the very notion of 'exclusive stuff' and 'Golden Bananas,' there is tiered access to the higher order consumption available on the site. This range of exclusive goods, which includes themed chimp sandcastle interiors and catalogue items, is visible to but not available for purchase by players who do not buy either a subscription or Golden Bananas. The accumulation and display of goods are constructed to be both fun and creative; however, it is linked to the economic model of the game and the demonstration of success at playing games and accumulating currency. The 'home' sandcastle sits within a township of other sandcastles and predominantly provides a space for the display of furnishings and decorative pieces purchased with currency earned in the games or provided by credit card.

As a virtual world one of the key functions of *Chimpoo* is to provide a space and capacity for social interaction. Accordingly, the *Chimpoo* virtual world is made up of a set of destinations, each linked to a range of online games. Public zones enable *Chimpoo* users, via their chimp avatar, to share space in the city, at the beach, at school, and in a theme park. The structure of registration means that both 'guest' chimps (users who have created a chimp in order to visit the world and play a range of games, but who are unable to earn currency and create and furnish a home) and registered chimpoos can play and interact. Registered players have the further option of chatting and emailing each other and forming new, or reinforcing existing, 'buddy' relationships, and registration is repeatedly recommended to guest players as they move through the world and games. Sharing space means that the avatars are in the same virtual place and have the opportunity to interact in real time. *Chimpoo* does this through its email and live-chat function as well as by providing shared social spaces and the opportunity for shared gameplay. Email, or 'Secret Mail,' as it is called, can be used to leave messages for players' 'buddies' who are not currently online. Buddies who are online together can 'Chit-Chat' in real time using the chat program internal to the world. All email and live messages are monitored by both live censors and keyword check programs. The information in the sign-up for email, provided via a character called 'Lifeguard Chimpoo,' tells players, "We want to make sure no one sends you bad stuff. So, I will be keeping an eye on all the mails and make sure no one is being naughty." The site is clear but informal in relation to online safety. The messages to parents are brief, reassuring, and friendly and reference the site's compliance with the Children's Online Privacy Protection Act (COPPA), the industry U.S. standard for safety:

> . . . Chimpoo.com complies with the highest standards for protecting your child's personal information and your child can play in an absolutely safe environment. Further, we ensure your child's safety through pre-defined chat messages and filtering of messages that other children can post on your child's game play areas. (Chimpoo.com, 2011)

The range of text inside the site is varied. The instructional texts combine images and text for ease of understanding and gameplay, combining screenshots with blow-up bubbles with pictures to assist with some words (e.g., a picture of a cupboard instead of the word 'cupboard'). Likewise, game instructions mix images with print. Combinations of icon/image and limited text make game instructions accessible and attractive. This last feature is not necessarily linked to easing the vocabulary burden of instructions: the text includes words such as 'catalog,' 'collection,' 'rotate,' and 'decorating' without the assistance of an image icon. The site makes use of large amounts of high-quality and very colorful imagery to construct a chaotic and yet visually complete virtual world. Color is used to add depth and intensity to the 2D representation of the city and provides one way of differentiating individual chimp avatars. The games provided on the site reflect its parent company's experience and expertise around casual online gaming, providing a diverse range of fun and well-designed games that are easy to play and entertaining. The visual images embedded in the game instructions and elsewhere continue this theme and provide opportunities for young children to navigate the site and play the games without adult supervision and mediation.

While there is a lot of color and 2D activity, there is limited print text embedded in the landscapes of *Chimpoo*. Navigation around the site is limited to clicking on various images while game instructions are composed of a mix of icons and brief spurts of text. The site itself is limited in terms of opportunities for engagement with a range of environmental and other forms of text. Where an offline cityscape would provide many and ongoing opportunities to see multiple forms of text in action, the carefully sculpted virtual worlds are relatively text-free and the texts that are on display are predominantly functional. The home sandcastles that are filled with increasing numbers of goods from the catalogue display little if any text and it seems that accumulation of stuff is more important than style or arrangement. In fact, the decorator items available for purchase are entirely out of proportion relative to the space available in sandcastles to display them. The result is a jumble of giant objects inside each sandcastle as players continue to accumulate more and more, effectively using the home sandcastle as a storage facility.

While playing games provides the opportunity to purchase outfits and decorator items, the shopping options are, in fact, quite limited. All in-world shopping in *Chimpoo* is done via catalogues: one for clothing and another for décor items. The décor catalogue, as an example, is presented in the form of a book with turning pages (bottom right-hand page corner is turned in, with the word 'NEXT' visible; bottom left-hand page has the word 'PREVIOUS' on the folded corner). In this it reflects the use of e-books in offline contexts and, quite possibly, the growth of online catalogue shopping. The goods for sale are shown via a set of large, colorful images with simple, humorous labels—for example, 'Peapod Hammock,' 'Ice Cream Clown 5000,' 'Ye Ole Boot House.' The colorful and detailed visual image of each catalogue item renders the text superfluous. As noted earlier, the text embedded in gameplay is limited but effective in providing scaffolding for young children to play independently. While *Chimpoo* is free of in-world advertising, sponsored advertising pops up as players navigate between in-world areas. The advertising material fills the screen while the chosen game loads. Advertising space is seemingly sold to external organizations and displayed in these transitional moments.

Chimpoo, then, is a games-focused virtual world built around colorful graphics, a variety of games, limited text, and the accumulation of currency to allow the purchase of a contained range of goods from either a décor or clothing catalogue. However, there is an aspect of this virtual world that adds an interesting dimension. *Chimpoo* links explicitly to a companion blog site—chimpoo.com/blog (see also iluvchimpoo.com)—that encourages a wider engagement with and production of text. It does this in a range of ways. It mixes adult content, including job descriptions, and updates about the development of the virtual world aimed at parents and potential advertisers, with entries directed specifically towards children. There are activities around coloring, writing, drawing, and designing along with photography, including invitations and opportunities for children to write and post stories about the chimpoo characters they have created, design clothing and accessories for a chimpoo, or design and decorate a new chimpoo house. These activities come with instructions to print the base picture, sketch the outfit or design onto it, scan and then email it to the blog. Each design then has the potential to be displayed in the Chimpoo Art Gallery located inside the virtual world.

The blog brings with it a tacit acknowledgment that young people move in and out and across a range of online and offline sites: the blog links to the virtual world but there is an assumption that undertaking the writing and photographic 'challenges' is an offline activity that is then uploaded to the blog and virtual world. The blog thus serves to create a space of intersection between the offline and online. It also demonstrates quite clearly the assumed technical expertise and access that *Chimpoo* users have: in order to complete the design activity a player would need to have, in addition to a networked computer, a printer and scanner alongside access to email. It is additionally assumed that children either possess the necessary skills themselves or can access assistance when required. Remembering that this is a site designed to be used relatively independently by children from five years of age—evidenced by the high levels of imagery, simplistic design, and heavy use of icons to support instructions—this is interesting. These skills and technologies, not all that long ago the preserve of IT professionals and early adopters, are so deeply embedded in the everyday of children and families around the world that they are now naturalized in the game instructions of a global site for children.

BARBIEGIRLS.COM

BarbieGirls™ (hereafter *BarbieGirls*) launched in beta in April 2007 and within 28 days had attracted 1 million registrations. By the end of 2008 it had 13 million registrations, 86% of which identified as girls eight years of age and over (Gigaom.com , 2008) and by 2009 the site was passing 14 million registrations. One of the first virtual worlds for children, it is well known and until recently, well established.[2]

While basic registration—which allows access to a 'home' bedroom, games, and the accumulation of in-world currency—is free, a VIP subscription enables access to a range of exclusive products, including hairstyles, facial features, clothing, accessories, and furniture. The world is composed of a series of destinations, including a theme park, home bedroom complex, cinema, and shopping mall. *BarbieGirls* offers players, in the form of their Barbie-esque avatars, opportunities to play games and watch promotional videos in order to earn currency. The currency is then used to purchase clothing, furniture, accessories, and new character features, within the world. The semi-private space of a loft-style bedroom and public spaces such as the various shops and theme park provide spaces for socializing. The bedroom space is particularly important in *BarbieGirls*. Reflecting the central role of the bedroom for middle-class youth (Hodkinson & Lincoln, 2008), the bedroom is the 'home' site for each player, providing a space for the display of purchased and carefully arranged consumer goods and in-world socializing (Carrington & Hodgetts, 2010).

Inside *BarbieGirls* the majority of activities are directly linked to the accumulation of in-world currency. The activity of shopping in malls and shops is encouraged explicitly through the public valuation of styled bedrooms and avatars, and implicitly through the available activities. Both explicitly and implicitly, shopping is constructed as a pleasurable leisure activity. Rappaport (2001) outlined the close connection between the construction of gendered bourgeois identities centered on the pleasure of shopping and consumption and the emergence of a public role for women who were constructed as natural consumers. *BarbieGirls*, in this view, provides a public space, a "commodity-filled urban marketplace" (Rappaport, 2001: 130), in which young girls develop gendered identities as consumers. The link between identity, pleasure, and consumption is reinforced by the life-size fit of clothing and accessories.

There is a lot of text at work in *BarbieGirls*. The public spaces provide opportunities to read and interpret a range of texts at various levels across billboards, street signage, pop-up menus, and announcements. The central shopping area, for instance, displays a series of shop fronts, street signs, and relatively uncomplicated billboards. Each game is accompanied by instructions and often by hosts, who give advice via conversation bubbles. The game instructions and conversational texts make limited demands on decoding and comprehension skills; however, the in-world texts are not insignificant. Text is always created and deployed with purpose. *Barbie-Girls* actively uses text to build an informal familiarity with players and to support gameplay and shopping activities. It does this through the use of familiar and casual language such as 'hey, girl,' 'we're,' 'fast n' fun.' *BarbieGirls* is an artificial world constructed by a U.S.-based global toy company and the language used within the site is artfully designed to create the illusion of familiarity. In *BarbieGirls*, text is also used to explicitly recognize and reward the purchase and display of consumer items and the creation of gendered consumer identities. Speech bubbles allow shop assistants to greet and assist shoppers, billboards publicly display a picture and the name of players voted as the most stylish and creative in terms of dressing up their avatar and designing a pleasing and unique bedroom space, and game instructions show how to win the currency needed to purchase consumer items. Much of the text in *BarbieGirls* is deployed to support practices of gendered consumption and identity work.

As a virtual world, a key feature is the provision of space for interaction. The use of in-world chat and email facilitates this social interaction within the world. Participants can make use of pre-set conversational items in the chat function and pre-set email subjects to communicate directly via the Barbie chat program or via email. While this menu-click conversation style allows young players to build limited interaction with other players, these and other interactions are monitored. Longer-term players are also able to create original messages to send via Barbie Chat or email (see also Grimes, 2010 for an important discussion of the ways in which players circumvent and subvert the monitoring and pre-programming). All texts created by the players in *BarbieGirls* and *Chimpoo* are monitored both electronically and by human moderators. These pre-selected or moderated chat texts are the only player-produced texts created in *BarbieGirls*.

BARBIES AND CHIMPS: TEXTS AND CHILDHOODS

In terms of the uses of text and the ways in which identities and childhood are articulated, there is, I believe, some significance in the ways these two virtual worlds position themselves. In both virtual worlds, the in-world textual landscapes are used to create a particular relationship with players/users. *Chimpoo* is landscaped around simple and colorful graphics and fun elements, buildings with faces, giant pink mushrooms: all inhabited by chimps. It is explicitly about fast fun, playing games and purchasing often humorous and over-sized items for display in home sites. Text is functional and simple; the world is cartoonish and bears only a passing resemblance to the offline world. The textual landscape built around *BarbieGirls* is dominated by texts that work to build familiarity and encourage consumption.

While on the surface mimicking the types of texts found in the urban sites it recreates, the texts found within the site are contained and limited in scope. While this control ensures that the site is a safe play destination it also works to create a closed and limited social space. Within this controlled space, texts are gendered and pedagogic as they work to encourage and reward particular types of behavior and consumer activities. Elsewhere, this has been termed 'literacy lite' (Carrington & Hodgkins, 2010): "a literacy that is static and controlled; a literacy that takes place online but does not reflect any of the powerful identity and community practices with text made possible via web 2.0" (p. 681). In comparison to the flowing in and out of texts made possible on *Chimpoo*, *BarbieGirls* attempts to control the movement of text in, out, and within the world. This 'fortress' *BarbieGirls* approach is linked both to issues of safety and to the particular gendered model of childhood that underpins the virtual world.

The array of texts made available to children, either as models of adult activity or resources to use in their own literacy practices, sheds light on the ways in which childhood is perceived in various contexts. It is in this sense that the texts associated with these two quite different virtual worlds for children become interesting in a broader sense and, I would suggest, point to quite different positionings of children. There is a limited set of models of childhood designed to reflect increasingly digital lives. Prensky (2001) coined the term 'digital native' to capture the embedding of young children in digital cultures, making assumptions about their innate technological capacities. This modeling of a new childhood lived online is reflected in terms such as the 'net generation' (Tapscott, 1997), 'generation m(edia)' (Cvetkovic & Lackie, 2009; Roberts, Foehr, & Rideout, 2005), and the 'gamer generation' (Beck & Wade, 2006). This model of childhood is arguably technologically determinist as it works to overlay generational identity with technological competence. Inherent to this view is an assumption that digital practices displace others, making the presumed affinity of young people with these practices all the more important. Those of us born too early to be 'natives' must become immigrants, struggling to master the skills, practices, and spaces to which natives are naturally attuned. The either/or categorization of native versus immigrant or the inherent assumption of technological affinity is not helpful in understanding the complexity and challenges of the activities and identities developed by young people in contemporary digital cultures.

The 'digital natives' model does, however, provide a useful counter for models that position early adolescence and childhood as both risky and a risk as they engage with the new digital technologies and in the social spaces emerging around them. Contemporary models of early adolescence are often used to suggest that children moving into this age category are at risk of making poor choices, becoming alienated, disengaging from schooling, and engaging in risk-taking behavior of various forms (Carrington, 2006). There is another dimension to the 'at risk' argument. In an information economy, skills in relation to digital technologies have come to be associated with lifelong learning, preparedness for the new work econoscapes, and, as a result, job security. Following this argument, children growing up in a digitally oriented, post-industrial economic context are at risk—of unemployment, underemployment, social and economic marginalization, and associated social, psychological, and physiological implications—if they do not develop adequate facility with new technologies and the practices associated with them. This view of risk and the digital natives arguments both suggest mastery of digital technologies and the development of digital literacies as a form of human capital. However, the model of risk also attaches negative value to this exact venture: children are often constructed to be at risk of experiencing harm or, alternatively, causing harm when online. According to this modeling, children who move into the online social spaces made available by digital technologies are at heightened risk of being the victim or perpetrator of sexual predation or bullying, of social isolation, and of access to too much information and too little privacy. They may become children who are simultaneously at risk and a risk.

Reflecting this interest in risk, *BarbieGirls* expends considerable energy on safety and surveillance and parental engagement in their daughters' safety. The site in fact likens play inside *BarbieGirls* to outdoor play in the offline world, making assumptions about the ways in which young girls are surveilled for their own safety. The site observes: "We believe that you should be aware and approve of your child's online activities at all times. Just as you might observe your daughter through a window while she plays outside, we want to give you a virtual window—to our digital playground—as she plays online." Games2Win does not ignore its legislative responsibilities for protecting the safety of the young people who visit *Chimpoo*; however, where *BarbieGirls* effectively linked its surveillance and site security to gender, *Chimpoo* implemented the legislative requirements and posted information stating that this was the case.

BarbieGirls turns young girls (and other players) into petite, pretty avatar Barbie dolls who inhabit affluent urban zones. *Chimpoo* reshapes children as chimps, responsive to bright primary colors, and opportunities for fun. It does not go to the trouble of creating an alternate urban complex in which to create and trial gendered identities around the activities of consumption and design of the self. Instead it builds a two-dimensional cartoon city peopled by chimps that may or may not display a gender preference. This is a childhood of play, humor, and adventuring that includes, I would argue, an assumption of competence alongside childhood imagination and willingness to suspend 'reality.' While *BarbieGirls* makes use of technological terminologies in word search games and assumes access to the Internet, the framing of childhood is, by comparison to *Chimpoo*, dated. The in-world texts provided by *Chimpoo* are arguably limited; however, they scaffold all players into independent activity within the site, and, crucially, the virtual world has direct links to a text-rich blog that assumes technological competence and encourages multimodal textual participation that cuts across off-world, blog, and virtual world. This compensates for the limited text in-world, particularly as the linking of blog and virtual world acknowledges the complex and interconnected social, textual, and technological worlds of contemporary children.

Black and Steinkuehler (2008: 271) noted the existence of a "constellation of literacy practices" revolving around online sites. Reflecting this pattern of connected texts and practices, both worlds are associated with a range of paratexts (Burk, 2010). In the case of *BarbieGirls* these take the form of videos of the site and descriptions of cheats and codes, chat conversations about using codes in-world to gain additional currency or access to clothing, as well as fan sites, industry information, and reviews. These paratexts provide opportunities to connect with other fans, to offer critiques, and to create and circulate other media such as videos. These ancillary texts provide important engagements in linked social and textual engagements. However, while the users may move back and forth between the virtual world and the various outer rim sites, the texts themselves do not travel. *Chimpoo* has a similar layer of paratexts surrounding it. The difference, however, is the existence of the intersecting companion blog. The blog works to facilitate communication and explicitly recognize the production and sharing of various texts, including artworks, photos, and pieces of writing. This provides the opportunity to recognize and reward text created by players outside the virtual world and uploaded to the linked and co-branded blog. Artworks created offline are, for example, uploaded to the blog and then displayed inside the artist gallery located in the *Chimpoo* virtual world; competitions encourage children to participate in a range of text production. Thus recognition for the creation of poetry and stories along with the creation of innovative designs and drawings is provided within the virtual world as well as the blog. As in the world outside, *Chimpoo* texts travel between social and technological fields, allowing their creators to participate in a range of social contexts. Rather than a series of layers of rotating paratexts in orbit around the virtual world, an overlapping space is created between the blog and the virtual world.

As an intersecting text, the blog (chimpoo.com/blog; see also iluvchimpoo.com) in effect augments the textual depth and range of the virtual world. While Internet access is an entry requirement for accessing both worlds, *Chimpoo* presumes that young children and their families have access to and expertise with an additional range of technologies that include scanners, printers, digital cameras, and the software to upload scanned images and documents. The use of these technologies to create and upload texts to the blog provides the opportunity for *Chimpoo* players—predominantly young children—to use their skills with a range of texts to participate in this particular online space. Participating players are honing a range of powerful practices with technology and with text at the same time that they are engaging in the hypersociality and public social spaces provided by virtual worlds.

The more contemporary aesthetic reflected in assumptions about technology access and competence can be seen in other areas of *Chimpoo*. Via the costumes, clothing, and games provided on the site, players are provided with opportunities to identify as male, female, or as ungendered chimpoos. The economic model embedded in the site requires the accumulation of currency in order to purchase costumes and décor items; however, these goods are generally so fanciful that they are unlikely to exist in the offline world. *Chimpoo* provides us with a window to another model of contemporary childhood. This model of childhood would show us a child who is using informal networks and peer-to-peer learning opportunities to build the skill sets necessary to create multimodal, multiplatform texts that perform in on- and offline fields, who is learning to competently navigate the online world, and who is appropriately aware of the risks and potentials alongside the responsibilities of participating in online communities.

CONCLUSIONS

The reality is that children and young people are spending increasing amounts of time online and in virtual worlds, building and interacting across and within a number of social networks. *Chimpoo* and *Barbie-Girls* are virtual playgrounds but, just like their offline counterparts, they are important social and pedagogic sites. They are where children learn the rules of online engagement and ethical participation; where they learn what kinds of children they are; where they learn which literate practices are required and valued and which are not. They are sites where children experience and learn about surveillance, and they are sites where they are exposed to a particular economic model. Consequently, the skills and attitudes around sociality, public engagement, and the uses of text that are developed in these worlds are not insignificant. If virtual worlds and other sites of hypersociality such as *Facebook* have indeed become key sites for social interaction and identity display, and the registration and traffic statistics suggest they are, the ways in which text is entwined with these themes are key. The range of texts available, the ways in which the use of text is modeled, and the representations of appropriate textual practices all contribute to the range of literate practices and identities available to players. This is where *Chimpoo* and its intersecting paratext become particularly interesting.

This is not to argue that *Chimpoo* is an ideal textual destination. It is not. It is a site designed for online entertainment and gaming for a global youth audience rather than for thoughtful engagement with a range of carefully chosen texts and practices. The difference, I would argue, lies in two key aspects: the type of childhood model that underwrites each site and the bridges established (or not) between each virtual world and external texts and textual practices. While launched only three years earlier, *BarbieGirls* is premised upon an older, strongly gendered model of childhood. In this model, children and particularly girls are constructed as proto-consumers rewarded for displays of style, fashion, and cheeriness. *BarbieGirls* is another social site where clearly articulated gender characteristics are foregrounded. By comparison, *Chimpoo* appears to make available a space where gender is not, by default, foregrounded and where intersections between online and offline textual practices and competencies are constructed.

Somewhat unexpectedly, *Chimpoo* embeds many of the principles associated with Jenkins et al.'s (2006) notions of participatory culture. While Jenkins' view of participation via digital technologies may be critiqued for being overly optimistic in terms of access to technology and the presence of guilds of willing mentors and collaborators, it nonetheless provides a useful model of best practice in online and other communities. In a participatory culture it is increasingly valuable to be able to create and engage with multimodal texts that operate across a range of platforms, to rapidly critique information from a range of sources, to move back and forth between basic skill in print literacies and skill in multiliteracies, to work in peer learning contexts and informal settings (Carrington, 2009). Many of these skills and attitudes parallel those identified as core to engaging meaningfully in the contemporary civic; many may be performed communally and collaboratively. In turn, the skills and attitudes associated with these participatory practices assume a competence that is developed via the peer networks, opportunities for engagement, and access to information. As children engage with *Chimpoo* and the associated blog they are encouraged to read, create, and display multimodal texts in a range of genres. They are also encouraged to make use of a number of digital technologies, including computers, scanners, and cameras, as they create and share these texts. These digital practices take place in concert with print-based practices around writing narrative, labeling, and drawing. In this, *Chimpoo* reflects the ways in which new and older forms of text and technology co-exist across multiple social fields and practices and it embeds an assumed competence with a range of technologies. Rather than a surveilled childhood that attempts to ameliorate risk or assumptions of innate technological ability, a model that views children as competent allows them the opportunity to engage, play, learn, share, and develop skills with a range of multimodal texts for a variety of reasons.

As the virtual world market matures, it is increasingly clear that not all virtual worlds are the same. They are increasingly differentiated, both in terms of the audience to which they appeal and in relation to the types of textual identities and practices encouraged within them. As the discussion here points out, each world reflects particular constructions of gender, childhood, and identities, and delivers different opportunities to engage with texts and digital technologies. For those of us who track shifts in online spaces, and the social and civic engagements and textual practices that are facilitated and/or discouraged within them, these differentiations are important to note and to examine.

NOTES

1. Founded by Alok Kejriwal and Mahesh Chambadkonw, Games2Win was launched in 2007 and now attracts more than 20 million consumers each month across its various properties. The Mumbai-based company runs server farms in the U.S. and on Amazon Cloud. It owns and operates www.games2win.com, www.gangofgamers.com, www.chimpoo.com, and www.inviziads.com.
2. Mattel officially closed *BarbieGirls*™ on June 1, 2011, after this chapter was written. No official reason has been provided for the closure; however, online speculation by fans includes the failure of the VIP subscription model, lack of servers, and the growing incidence of inappropriate behavior and language by 'boys' and others. The majority of games have been moved to Barbie.com; however, players lost access to their home apartments, avatars, and purchased online goods.

REFERENCES

Beck, J. & Wade, M. (2006). *The Kids Are Alright: How the Gamer Generation Is Changing the Workplace*. Cambridge, MA: Harvard Business School Press.

Beck, J. & Wade, M. (2004). *Got Game: How the Gamer Generation Is Reshaping Business Forever*. New York: Harvard Business Press.

Black, R. & Steinkuehler, C. (2008). Literacy in virtual worlds. In L. Christenbury, R. Bomer, P. Smagorinsky (eds.), *Handbook of Adolescent Literacy Research*. New York: Guilford Press.

Burk, D. (2010). Copyright and paratext in computer gaming. In C. Wankel & S. Malleck (eds.), *Emerging Ethical Issues of Life in Virtual Worlds*. Charlotte, NC: Information Age Publishing.

Carrington, V. (2009). From blog to bebo and beyond: Text, risk, participation. *International Journal of Reading Research* 32(1): 6–21.

Carrington, V. (2006). *Rethinking Middle Years: Early Adolescents, Schooling and Digital Culture.* Sydney: Allen & Unwin.

Carrington, V. & Hodgetts, K. (2010). Literacy-lite in BarbieGirls. *British Journal of Sociology of Education* 31(6): 671–682.

Chimpoo.com (2011). Parents: Welcome to Chimpoo.com. Retrieved May 23, 2012 from http://www.chimpoo.com/chimpooworld/parents.

Cvetkovic, V. & Lackie, R. (2009). *Teaching Generation M: A Handbook for Librarians and Educators.* New York: Neal-Schuman Publishers.

Gigaom.com (2008). Virtual Worlds' Real Money Deals at VW 2008. Retrieved May 23, 2012 from http://gigaom.com/2008/04/07/virtual-worlds-real-money-deals-at-vw-2008/

Grimes, S. (2010). *The Digital Child at Play: How Technological, Political and Commercial Rule Systems Shape Children's Play in Virtual Worlds.* (Unpublished doctoral dissertation). Simon Fraser University, Burnaby.

Hodkinson, P. & Lincoln, S. (2008). Online journals as virtual bedrooms? *Young* 16(1): 27–46.

Jenkins, H., Clinton, K., Purushotma, R., Robison, A., & Weigel, M. (2006). *Confronting the Challenges of Participatory Culture: Media Education for the 21st Century.* The John D. & Catherine T. MacArthur Foundation Reports on Digital Media and Learning. Cambridge, MA: MIT Press.

Kzero Worldswide (2011). Age profiles: All worlds. *Kzero Worldswide.* August 18. Retrieved August 30, 2011 from www.kzero.co.uk/blog/?cat=101.

Prensky, M. (2001). Digital Natives, Digital Immigrants. *On the Horizon.* 9 N(5): 1–6.

Rappaport, E. (2001). *Shopping for Pleasure: Women in the Making of London's West End.* Princeton, NJ: Princeton University Press.

Roberts, D., Foehr, U., & Rideout, V. (2005). *Generation M: Media in the Lives of 8–18-Year-Olds.* A Kaiser Foundation Study. Menlo Park, CA: Henry J. Kaiser Family Foundation.

Tapscott, D. (1997). *Growing Up Digital: The Rise of the Net Generation.* New York: McGraw-Hill.

Virtual Worlds News (2008). Mattel Keynote: Making it safe and moving to subscription. April 3. Retrieved September 2, 2009 from http://www.virtualworldsnews.com/2008/04/virtual-worlds.html.

Part II

Virtual Literacies in Everyday Life

4 Multiliteracies in the Wild
Learning from Computer Games

Catherine Beavis

INTRODUCTION

In his now classic analysis of distributed cognition, based on his observations of naval navigation, Hutchins (1995) coined the term 'cognition in the wild.'[1] As Hutchins uses it, the phrase

> refers to human cognition in its natural habitat—that is, to naturally occurring culturally constituted human activity. . . . I have in mind the distinction between the laboratory, where cognition is studied in captivity, and the everyday world where human cognition adapts to its natural surroundings. I hope to evoke with this metaphor a sense of an ecology of thinking in which human cognition interacts with an environment rich in organizing resources. (Hutchins, 1995: xiii–xiv)

Research that addresses digital and multimodal literacies and their implications for literacy education is structured around an expanded view of literacy that recognizes the changing and dynamic nature of text and textual forms, and draws particularly on studies of the textual, communicative, and cultural practices of young people as they engage with online popular culture and the digital world. Among the most popular and pervasive of these new textual forms are video or computer games, with vast numbers of players playing alone or in combination, with multiple genres and variants, with new games or new iterations of existing games continually creating or capitalizing on new and hybrid forms of representation. Following Hutchins' notion of situated and distributed cognition as 'cognition in the wild,' video games and gameplay might be said to epitomize multiliteracies 'in the wild.'

COMPUTER GAMES: MULTILITERACIES IN THE WILD

Central to the concepts of multiliteracies, digital literacies, and new media is the view of literacy as design. In games, "learning about and coming to appreciate design and design principles is core to the learning experience . . . [where] (l)earning about and coming to appreciate interrelations within and across multiple sign systems (images, words, actions, symbols, artifacts, etc.) as a complex system is core to the learning experience" (Gee, 2003: 49). Gee characterizes games as "semiotic domains"—little universes of meaning— where all elements have a part to play in constructing the knowledge domain. Managing gameplay also requires players to be reflective: "Learning involves active and critical thinking about the relationships of the semiotic domain being learned to other semiotic domains" (Gee, 2003: 50).

As they play computer games, alone or with others, and in physical and/ or virtual locations, young people are engaged in a mix of emergent textual forms and new and familiar forms of literacy and literacy practices. Games provide examples par excellence of the ways in which literacy is recon-figured and redesigned in digital times, and of intersections between tex-tual experience, meaning-making, and the socially situated nature of play. Games utilize and work at the boundaries of the affordances of the tech-nologies on which they are played, largely unconstrained by institutional parameters or surveillance. They reinvent narrative structures and forms of engagement, and push constructions of literacy as design to the point where literacy and action blur, and where boundaries between players and machine, and between time, place, and space, struggle to be seen as fixed and knowable. Analogies between the structures and narratives of game-play with film, literature, art, and media offer valuable lenses on the nature of games and gameplay, as do multimodal conceptions of literacy. How-ever, these parallels and lenses approximate but do not fully address the multidimensionality of games and gameplay. Seeing games exclusively in terms of literacy, or as forms of textual practice, tells only half the story in relation to literacy and games. More is needed to take into account interac-tions between players, games, and technology, and the active nature of play. Successful gameplay also pivots on action. In exploring games as exemplars of multiliteracies, in the wild, these literacies need to be seen as part and parcel also of the action dimension of games. An approach that sees games and games literacy in terms of both text and action is required.

This chapter draws on the experience of a three-year project in the Australian state of Victoria that set out to explore the nature of computer games as text, and as embodiments of multimodal digital literacies; and to investigate the possibilities and implications of incorporating computer games into English and literacy curriculum.[2] The focus of the project was on understanding more about the nature of computer games (initially con-ceived primarily as texts): the kinds of literacies and literacy practices in which young people are engaged as they play; the role of games in young people's lives; and the implications for teachers and curriculum of bringing the study of computer games into English and literacy curriculum. This chapter focuses on the last of these, and on the model for conceiving of games as both text and action developed over the three years.

THE WILDNESS OF COMPUTER GAMES

The project brought a diverse set of perspectives and understandings to bear on what constituted games and gameplay; gaming, digital culture, and identity work within young people's 'life worlds'; and the ways in which games expand and rewrite conceptions of literacy as they are co-created within parameters of time and space. While an important part of the project was to explore whether, and if so how, computer or video games might be incorporated into English as exemplars of digital cultural forms and multimodal literacies, this was always in the full consciousness that what characterizes successful commercial games is their *difference* from school-based texts, with respect to their out-of-school habitus, pleasures, and purposes.

From the outset we were conscious of the wildness of games. Games cannot be contained or fully accounted for even 'in the wild,' let alone within the formal parameters of school. Games are undomesticated and untamable with respect to the ways in which they inhabit and are shaped by the out-of-school, leisure-time contexts in which they are played. Games and game players are in turn part of a broader global context, and as such are subject to a wealth of influences and pressures, ranging from competitive market drives to increase market share, develop new products, and win new audiences, through to the effect of economic downturns, political turmoil, natural disasters, and the like; or more narrowly, interactions with other players in different cultural, geographic, and temporal locations, and the world of games culture, paratexts, and gaming capital (Consalvo, 2007) that surround each game.

When considered in the context of the classroom, games are dangerously wild in comparison to more familiar forms of texts and literacies. In addition to the variability of game experience and the multiple combinations of character, circumstance, weapons, timing, and the like that constitute individual instances of gameplay, the scale of most games and the many hours required to play mean that for most teachers, games cannot be fully 'known' as 'complete' texts in the ways expected of other genres studied as textual forms. Further, there is little apparent correlation between the 'age appropriateness' indicated by games ratings and what young people actually play. Most commercially successful games draw an audience of players that includes some much younger than those indicated by the rating of the game. Among other things, this means that introducing computer games in school can become a fraught endeavor, where the games studied may be popular and actually played by students out of school, but have age-related ratings that reflect community norms about content and concerns deemed appropriate to young people with varying degrees of experience and maturity. Finally, as part of young people's out-of-school digital cultural worlds, games are read, played, and shaped by a host of fluid, anarchic, and 'private' social experiences, relationships, and connections.

It was not at all clear how games brought into the classroom would survive the almost inevitable 'flattening' that takes place when popular culture texts are treated as objects of study. Nonetheless, we believed there was much to gain from bringing these immensely popular cultural forms into the spectrum of texts and literacies encompassed by contemporary literacy and English curriculum.

When it comes to the structure and narrative of the game, as these might be understood in terms of text and literacy, games are 'untamable' too, in the evanescent and changing nature of each iteration of the game as it is played, and the embodied experience and knowledge players bring to bear as a game is played. As is the case with any text, the game itself comes into existence only through being read (or played), and the presence of the reader/player is fundamental to the constructed meaning of the text. In the case of games, however, unlike more familiar forms like poetry or the novel, this given of literary theory is unambiguously manifest. Similarly, the reader/player literally constructs the text, bringing it into existence through his or her engagement and the act of play. Each game, while powerfully governed by the game algorithm and design, narrative structures, and generic features, differs from player to player, from occasion to occasion, and as players progress through set stages to the completion of game; or in the case of more open-ended forms such as massively multiplayer games, as they interact within defined parameters to create their own iterations and variants of the game. Acknowledging debates about the nature of games as primarily play or narrative that characterized the early study of play (Aarseth, 1997; Juul, 2001; Frasca, 2003), team member Clare Bradford described games as "hybrid products which incorporated narrative and game elements while engaging players in energetic action and (in many cases) interpersonal and social processes" (Bradford, 2010: 54). Context and embodiment are fundamental. "When young people play video games they do as embodied subjects whose identities are shaped by the cultures in which they are situated, the circumstances of their lived experience, and the particularities of their dispositions, abilities and interests" (54).

The project encompassed a range of activities. Team members themselves played games—in some instances for the first time—to learn more about games in general and some specific games in greater detail, and to reflect on their own experiences as game players. Teachers in the project schools undertook individual research within their classrooms, developing a variety of curriculum units centered on computer games. The units explored intersections between the literate and textual characteristics of games, the literacy practices in evidence as students played games, the prior knowledge of games and more familiar forms of text and narrative they brought to bear, and the requirements of state-based English curriculum requirements about print-based and digital literacies. Students were interviewed about their experiences with video or computer games, how they saw themselves as game players, and how games fitted into the everyday business of their out-of-school lives. Teachers brought groups of students into the Australian Centre for the Moving Image, where they were videoed as they played games in groups of two or three, and interviewed again in focus groups in debriefing sessions afterwards.

COMPUTER GAMES IN THE CLASSROOM: FOUR VIGNETTES

Literary Framing: Archetypes and Narrative in Games

At one school, Lisa McNeice and her colleagues drew on literary perspectives with Year 9 students, to explore connections between games and other textual forms, the ways in which narrative features and generic conventions were represented in different genres, and how they were called upon to contribute meaning, in this instance in relation to quest narratives. Drawing on the knowledge they had developed in their out-of-school participation in gameplay, and their experience of epic films and literature, at the completion of a unit of work on Tolkein's *Fellowship of the Ring*, students were asked to consider the ways in which common generic elements were transformed and utilized in different textual forms. As part of their study, students were presented with an account of the hero's journey broken into 12 stages, based on the work of Joseph Campbell (McNeice, Smith, & Robison, in press). From there, they examined and reported their findings on two narrative-based computer games. They covered narrative, characters, setting, and aims, while exploring how game designers chose to employ, exclude, or transgress archetypal characters and the quest narrative. Students reflected on and wrote about the differences between print texts and digital texts, commenting on their similarities and differences.

After investigating their own digital text, students interviewed a classmate about their (different) game, examining essential elements such as setting and plot and the use of archetypes and the quest narrative. Students finished their report with a compare/contrast section, for which they were asked to explore how the digital worlds they examined differed from the world J. R. R. Tolkien created in his novel *The Fellowship of the Ring*. The students examined how the texts were different or alike and commented on the devices each creator used to construct his or her world.

Units like the one developed by Lisa and her colleagues capitalized on the knowledge students had consciously or unconsciously gained about the qualities and characteristics of hero figures in film, literature, and computer games, bringing them to conscious attention both to make them more available for reflection, and to extend students' awareness and understanding of how such archetypes were represented and used in literary forms beyond computer games.

Literacy Framings: Building New and
Traditional Literacies around Games

Other units took more literacy-based approaches, looking at the range of literacy skills and knowledge about literacy and multiliteracy elements required to play, and at the capacity of games to strengthen students' capabilities as both analysts and users of multimodal forms. Paul Byrne used the occasion of the *Game On* history of games exhibition hosted at the Australian Centre for the Moving Image in 2008 to develop a literacy unit around computer games. With Christopher Walsh, he planned a two-pronged unit to capitalize on students' considerable interest and expertise in computer games and gameplay. Following a highly successful excursion to the exhibition, students were given two tasks. First, they were required to give a presentation back in class about a game of their choice—initially, PC-based games, DS and PSP games only, but this was quickly extended to also include console games. Second, he adapted the four-resources model developed by Freebody and Luke (1990) to the digital context and asked students to use this framework as the basis of the written part of their assignment (Byrne, in press). Students worked well, quickly settling into their tasks and working cooperatively in their groups. In the first year, Paul asked them to use PowerPoint as the basis for their presentations, but extended this to Photo Story in the following year. This was more challenging, and made a greater call on students' literacy abilities. Yet, as Paul writes, this too worked effectively to build new and traditional literacy skills and abilities:

> With the next year came a new group of underachieving students. This time I was even more excited to run the computer games unit again. The chief difference this time would be that the students would not use PowerPoint to give their presentations; they would present using Photo Story. I told them this time that they would have to put in spoken narrative with their presentation. This was a lot more for the students (and me) to coordinate.
>
> The chief difficulty this time was getting the students to write this narrative. And when it came to them actually recording their narratives we had problems with the computers. The computers could not pick up some of the students' words as there were faulty sound cards in some of the computers.
>
> However, the results were much the same as the previous year. Students were enthusiastic and involved. Writing for them became less of a chore because it involved writing about something they didn't see as work but as play (Byrne, in press).

A reminder of the 'wildness' of games is in Paul's cautionary tale of what he saw when he glimpsed what the boys 'so engaged' in a group of girls' presentation of a fashion dress-up game were actually doing with their own dress-up version of the model in the game! Nothing that Paul could not handle, but a salutary reminder of the 'wildness' not only of games, but also of many classrooms and the rambunctious, unruly nature of students'—and teachers'—lives.

Gaming Capital and the Negotiation of Diverse Texts and Literacies

A different classroom approach to multiliteracies in the wild that students were negotiating out of school was taken by Joel Keane. As part of a unit exploring the concept of media convergence, Joel introduced the popular fantasy football game *AFL SuperCoach* to his Year 11 media studies students. Playing and reflecting on the game, which was already familiar to many students, provided the opportunity to explore issues around media convergence, the ways in which popular culture and fan culture were closely intertwined, and the continuing presence of different iterations of related textual forms (from footy cards to gameplay) as part of popular culture over time. Observing students' gameplay and their evident expertise, and the ways in which this online expertise translated effortlessly into increased status among peers in everyday home and school worlds, also gave us, as researchers, the chance to explore notions of 'gaming capital' (Consalvo, 2007), and the crossovers between on- and offline 'real-world' identity and play. Further, it provided insights into the ways in which students read across and analyzed a wide range of information presented in different forms, in order to successfully play—TV coverage of the games themselves, after-game commentaries, interviews, newspaper reports, posters, stills, games shows, predictions, and more, including opinions offered by relatives and friends. Their own emotional preferences and loyalties also had to be negotiated, to make astute decisions about which players to include in their team. Successful play depended crucially on making informed decisions, which in turn required the capacity to seek out, read, and evaluate advice proffered in these many forms—all taking place out of school, unrequested by any teacher, and not required for any purposes other than their own. Assessment, such as it was, came quickly and unambiguously as the effectiveness of their decisions each week about who to include was measured against the actual success of chosen team members on the muddy football fields of the weekend's play (Gutierrez & Beavis, 2010).

Exploring Gameplay Issues through Role Play

In another school, Belinda Lees and Joanne O'Mara used drama workshops with Year 8 students to explore and play with ideas about video games and fears and moral panics in the community, game characters, the ways in which characters viewed are conceptualized, and what might happen should they come to life. As they describe it:

The drama workshop was designed to co-construct with the students some creative data about their understandings of games and to enable them to playfully explore some of the issues around the place of computer games in their lives. We decided to run a drama workshop so that we could provide creative opportunities to extend their ideas into a range of "what if . . ." speculations. We were particularly interested in:

- their perceptions of the real world as opposed to the gaming world,
- their perceptions of their parents fears' and insecurities relating to their hobby as a gamer,
- their perceptions and experiences of the virtual worlds, and if there is any distortion of reality when they re-enter the non-virtual world. (O'Mara & Lees, in press)

Students discussed favorite characters, and the roles and characteristics of characters in video games. They launched into a Super Mario role play, where Luigi comes to visit on Christmas day, jumping out of the screen, and coming out for Christmas lunch, while adults and family members faint in shock. In other role plays, they parodied stereotypical parental actions and fears. Drama provided a context for wit and humor, and an informed and skeptical stance on moral panics and community discourses and attitudes. The workshops:

mirrored what we found through our interviews with the boys—they knew what they were doing in the game world, and they were aware of what the alarmist view was. The drama world enabled them to both exploit and subvert their positions and the world's perceptions of adolescent boys. (O'Mara & Lees, in press)

A MODEL FOR VIDEO GAMES LITERACY: GAMES AS TEXT, GAMES AS ACTION

A major 'deliverable' from the project was the development of a model for games and literacy that could be used as the basis for planning curriculum, pedagogy, and assessment. Finding a way to account for the wildness of games, and to learn from and about the multiliteracies entailed, required the development of a framework that could take account of games understood as both text and action, and the situated nature of gameplay.

The central challenge in developing such a model lay in relation to games' double-sided nature as both text and action. While in many respects games as cultural artifacts might be characterized as having family resemblances with other textual forms—film, television, literature, painting (Bolter & Grusin, 2000)—they are clearly different in a number of ways, in particular in the role of the player in bringing the game into being, and the role of the other elements—for example, the software or other players—in shaping how the game is played and the meanings that are made. Similarly, while computer games 'as texts,' and the literacies entailed in playing them, exemplify multiliteracies, multimodality, and understandings of literacy as design, the role of context, the situatedness of the game, and the effect and influence of technology, algorithms, and the like also play a powerful role. Considering games as actions entails understanding how play occurs in the context of other games, in the context of video game histories, and of other media. Situation, design, and actions work together to create a coherent experience. A model for games and literacy needed to include considerations of how these contexts and elements influence each other, how design influences action, how actions influence situations, how situations influence design, and vice versa. Similarly, considering games as text needed to reflect rich conceptions of multimodal textual forms, literacies and literacy practices, the role of intertextual knowledge and knowledge about form and ideology that shapes readings/play, reflective insights into the roles of players and the way they are positioned, and the kinds of learning that can take place through games—that is, learning through games.

To account for these multiple dimensions, and the ways in which literacy and textual aspects are integrally bound up with action, we developed a model for games and literacy that addresses games as text and action, and incorporates attention to such elements as design, situatedness, intertextual knowledge, reflexive awareness, and so on (Beavis & Apperley, in press). Led by Tom Apperley and myself, the model grew out of the team's experience in literacy and English curriculum and games studies; our reading of relevant research and literature in the fields of literary theory, new literacies and games studies, observations of our own and students' gameplay, interviews with students about their in- and out-of-school game playing practices, and the work of the teachers in designing and teaching curriculum units on and around literacy and computer games. The model is intended both as a map of these intersecting dimensions of video or computer games (i.e., as a research mapping tool) and as a framework for curriculum planning entailing the use and study of games.

Games as Action

The model has two layers with dimensions of each intersecting with, overlapping, or duplicating each other at various points. The first, Games as Action, draws on the work of theorists such as Aarseth (1997), Bogost (2007), Galloway (2006), and Stevens, Satwicz, and McCarthy (2008), and doctoral research undertaken by Apperley (2010). In this layer, dimensions of situation, action, and design are foregrounded.

The *Situations* sector includes such matters as the input of players, non-players, and technologies, and the interactions between them. It draws attention to the ways in which physical contexts and contexts of time and space color or inflect the experience of gameplay, with resulting influence on games iterations and the ways in which they are played. A further set of 'contexts' is provided by the network of intertextual referencing surrounding games, including paratexts (Genette, 1997; Consalvo, 2007) generated by and around the games. Issues of status are also recognized in this sector, with status in the 'in-game' world seen as washing back into the 'offline' world for young players (Walsh & Apperley, 2008; Walsh, 2010). This was evident, for example, among the *SuperCoach* players in Joel's class, and among Paul's students and the authority on which they drew in presenting their digital games.

The *Actions* sector encompasses such matters as the interactions between players and other players, and between players and the machine. It encompasses actions taken within the game world, as players progress through the game, and the consequences of these actions for the ways in which the game in play is shaped and developed. The use of knowledge gleaned from previous play is also included in this sector, as players activate this knowledge to further progress the game. Players are also active in this sector,

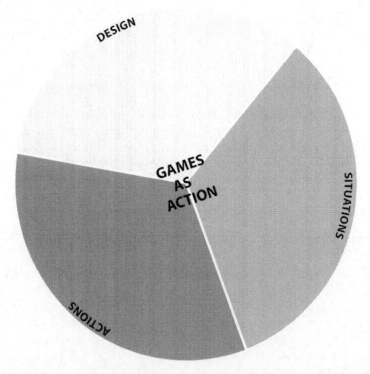

Figure 4.1   Games as Action—outline.

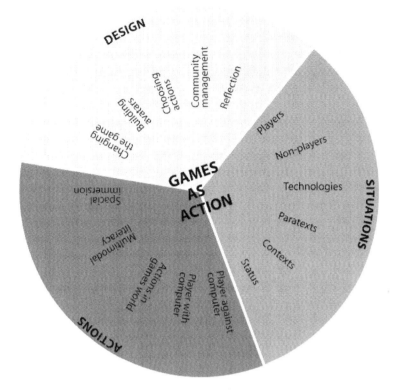

Figure 4.2   Games as Action—elaborated.

using their knowledge of the multiple semiotic forms that constitute games as 'multiliteracies in the wild' to create and negotiate play.

The *Design* sector, consistent with the 'Action' focus of this layer, provides for the player's active agency in design. It includes both the creation of tailored choices within the game and opportunities for sub-version or extension going beyond the apparent boundaries of the game. This sector includes changing the game, building avatars, choosing actions, building objects, designing spaces/levels, community manage-ment, and reflection. The Games as Action layer of the model might be represented as follows:

Games as Text

The second layer of the model, Games as Text, draws on work in the areas of new literacies, digital media, and contemporary childhood (Alvermann, 2010; Willett, Robinson, and Marsh, 2009), multiliteracies (New Lon-don Group, 1996), and literacy and computer games (Gee, 2003; Carr, Buckingham, Burn, & Schott, 2006; Buckingham & Burn, 2007; Pelletier, 2005; Steinkuehler, 2007). This layer is organized into four sectors, with the player understood to be at the center. The four attend to knowledge about the game, learning through games, the world around the game, and me as game player.

The *Knowledge about Games* sector attends to both the players' knowledge of related games and the characteristic features and generic elements of games of the kind they are playing, including how to play; and to their knowledge of a wider sweep of related texts, including literary, filmic, visual, and oral forms, particularly with respect to narrative structures and features. This sector is analogous in some ways to the 'knowledge about language' strand of the tripartite model of language development developed by Halliday (1993: 112): "Learning language, learning through language and learning about language." It includes attention to the construction of ideology and subject positioning, how games structure knowledge and participation, and developing critical perspectives on games.

The *Learning through Games* sector is similarly analogous to Halliday's tripartite model and to overtly didactic approaches within drama and drama education. It explores the ways in which games are used to teach explicitly, through 'Serious Games' or through the use of commercial, off-the-shelf games, in curriculum content areas, and invites reflection on the workings of "procedural logic" (Bogost, 2007), and the consequences of using or experiencing games in this way. It includes attention to metacognition and metacognitive strategies, with respect to games, critiquing games, and developing critical perspectives about and through games.

The *World around the Game* sector includes attention to the literacy practices surrounding games, including both those entailed in 'reading/ playing' games, discussion and problem solving around games, reading and analyzing the wealth of texts of different kinds and literate forms that surround games, through to the creation of texts of their own related to their gameplay—all paratexts of a kind. This sector also foregrounds situated contexts for gameplay and their effects, including both specific and broad global contexts for play and games location within the military entertainment complex. This section also attends to gaming capital, Consalvo's adaptation of Bourdieu's notion of social capital, to describe the ways in which in game success and achievement result in increased status both within and outside the game (Consalvo, 2007).

The sector *Me as Games Player* extends reflexive awareness of the player's positioning within the broader context of gameplay to attend specifically to issues of engagement and reflection. It draws attention to the nature of players' interactions with other players, both within the game and 'outside' it, whether physically present or absent, and known or unknown; and issues surrounding the textual representation and interpretation of self and others. The Games as Text layer might be represented this way:

Collectively, the model is envisaged as two superimposed spinning wheels, enabling multiple combinations of elements from both layers to be in interaction at any time.

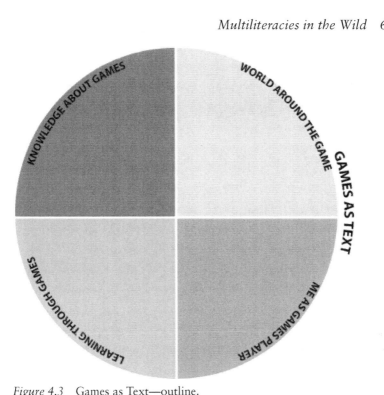

Figure 4.3   Games as Text—outline.

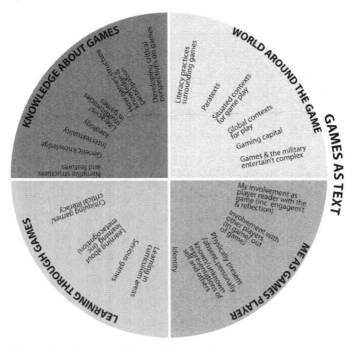

Figure 4.4   Games as Text—elaborated.

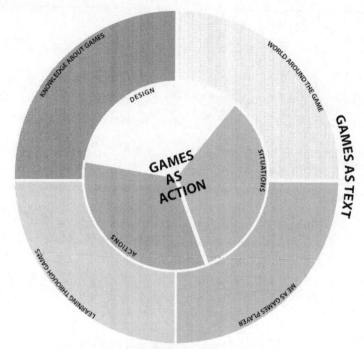

Figure 4.5   Games as Action, Games as Text—outline.

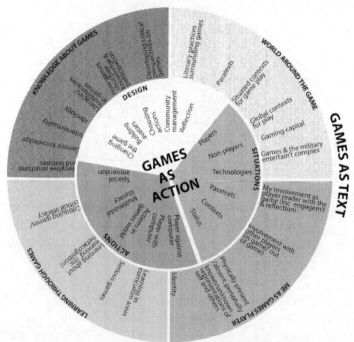

Figure 4.6   Games as Action, Games as Text—elaborated.

The Model in Practice

How does the model work in practice? The model has two aspects: one concerned with mapping what players do as they engage with games, functioning primarily as an observation tool and a heuristic for research. The second is its use as a basis for curriculum planning and design, reflecting the dual nature of games as text and action, where different sectors of each layer are drawn upon in accordance with the curriculum and learning focus of the units taught. Specific sectors of each layer are foregrounded differently according to context and need. In the description that follows, the model is used to identify and foreground the action and literacy-based dimensions of gameplay, and to highlight elements of the curriculum unit that connected with these—in this instance, in Year 11 Media.

In the case of Joel's unit on Convergence, centered on *SuperCoach*, the layers of the model of particular relevance might be represented as follows:

In this particular alignment between the Games as Text and Games as Action layers, there are close parallels and overlaps in a number of areas. Starting with the Games as Action layer, Situation was fundamental to the ways the game was played. As always, *context* powerfully influences meaning and the nature and purpose of play. Recognition of the importance of situated contexts for gameplay figures also in the Games as Text layer, in the World around the Game sector called upon here. *SuperCoach* is played by

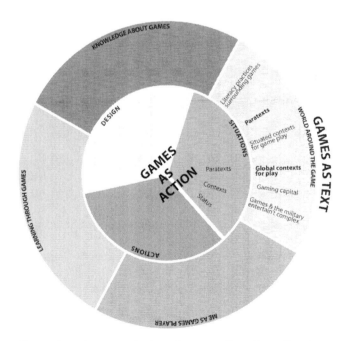

Figure 4.7   Games as Action, Games as Text: *SuperCoach*.

students in their leisure time out of school but also, in this instance, within the classroom, and among not just other *SuperCoach* players but also other classmates, teachers, and peers. Understood more broadly, the context of *SuperCoach* also included star footballers' performance in the 'real-life' world of the AFL football game to which it refers, and the weekly games played on sports fields across Australia as part of the national league. More broadly again, the context of the game includes those things that players draw upon in order to make judgments about the game—their own knowledge of the game and how it is played, and the wealth of commentary and information—*paratexts*—that surrounded the 'real-life' game. Players need to establish and develop their status as game players from the outset of any form of public play. Players' success or otherwise in making wise choices, picking winners, and acting strategically affects their standing within the world of the game, not only within the fantasy football games world composed of other *SuperCoach* players but also with material crossover effects into the 'real-life' world of family, friends, and school, through the increase in gaming capital, picked up further in the Games as Text layer similarly. The Games as Text layer also foregrounds the *literacy practices surrounding games* and entailed in play—in this instance including the capacity to read and judge information presented in multiple forms, ranging from newspaper commentaries, game replays, and footy show experts through to the views of friends and family, online commentary on specific games, and statistical and visual representations of various aspects of play. As a fantasy sports game *SuperCoach* is linked both to the immensely popular Australian League Football and to a major media empire—the game is hosted by the Melbourne tabloid *Herald Sun*, a subsidiary of News Limited as part of Rupert Murdoch's News Corporation.

CONCLUSIONS

As extreme cases of the wildness of digital literacies, video games and game playing practices resist domestication. They do not fit readily either into available definitions of literacy or into subject-specific parameters within the school. Nonetheless, they exemplify the ways in which literacy is evolving in the direction of design. Driven by economic imperatives as much as by technological innovation, new generations of games across multiple platforms continue to stretch boundaries in the mix of meaning-making elements on which they call, and the new combinations and iterations brought into being. To learn more about the changing nature of literacy and about students' textual experiences and orientations out of school, and to consider how schools can address twenty-first-century literacies, the study of video games and game playing practices provides rich opportunities to extend understandings, and develop pedagogical approaches to them, as multiliteracies in the wild.

ACKNOWLEDGMENTS

The model shown in these images was developed by Tom Apperley and myself in the course of our ARC project: Literacy in the Digital World of the Twenty First Century: learning from computer games, first published by the Australian Association for the Teaching of English/Wakefield Press.

NOTES

1. I am grateful to Robert Fitzgerald of Canberra University for drawing my attention to Hutchins' work.
2. Beavis, C., Bradford, C., O'Mara, J., & Walsh, C. (2007–2009). Literacy in the digital world of the 21st century: Learning from computer games. Australian Research Council. Industry partners: The Australian Centre for the Moving Image, The Victorian Association for the Teaching of English, The Department of Education and Early Childhood Development, Victoria. Research fellow: Thomas Apperley. Research assistant: Amanda Gutierrez.

REFERENCES

Aarseth, E. (1997). *Cybertext: Perspectives on Ergodic Literature.* Baltimore: John Hopkins University Press.

Alvermann, D. (ed.). (2010). *Connecting Classrooms: Digital Media and Popular Culture.* New York: Peter Lang.

Apperley, T. (2010). *Gaming Rhythms: Play and Counterplay from the Situated and the Global.* Amsterdam: Institute of Network Cultures.

Beavis, C. & Apperley, T. (in press). A model for games literacy. In C. Beavis, J. O'Mara, & L. McNeice (eds.), *Digital Games: Literacy in Action.* Adelaide: Australian Association for the Teaching of English/Wakefield Press.

Bogost, I. (2007). *Persuasive Games: The Expressive Power of Video Games.* Cambridge: MIT Press.

Bolter, J. & Grusin, R. (2000). *Remediation: Understanding New Media.* Cambridge: MIT Press.

Bradford, C. (2010). Looking for my corpse: Video games and player positioning. *Australian Journal of Language and Literacy* 33(1): 54–64.

Buckingham, D. & Burn, A. (2007). Game literacy in theory and practice. *Journal of Educational Multimedia and Hypermedia* 16(3): 323–349.

Byrne, P. (in press). In C. Beavis, J. O'Mara, & L. McNeice (eds.), *Digital Games: Literacy in Action.* Adelaide: Australian Association for the Teaching of English/Wakefield Press.

Carr, D., Buckingham, D., Burn, A., & Schott, G. (2006). *Computer Games: Text, Narrative and Play.* Malden: Polity Press.

Consalvo, M. (2007). *Cheating: Gaining Advantage in Videogames.* Cambridge: MIT Press.

Frasca, G. (2003) Ludologists love stories too: Notes from a debate that never took place. Conference Proceedings: *Level Up: Digital Games Research Association Conference 2003*, 4–6 November, University of Utrecht, the Netherlands pp. 92–97. Retrieved May 25, 2011 from http://www.digra.org/dl/search_results?general_search_index=frasca&SUBMIT=Search

Freebody, P. & Luke, A. (1990). Literacies programs: Debates & demands in cultural context. *Prospect: Australian Journal of TESOL* 5(7): 7–16.
Galloway, A. (2006). *Gaming: Essays on Algorithmic Culture.* Minneapolis: University of Minnesota Press.
Gee, J. P. (2003). *What Video Games Have to Teach Us about Learning and Literacy.* New York: Palgrave.
Genette, G. (1997). *Paratexts: Thresholds of Interpretation.* London: Cambridge University Press.
Gutierrez, A. & Beavis, C. (2010). 'Experts on the field': Redefining literacy boundaries. In D. Alvermann (ed.), *Adolescents' Online Literacies: Connecting Classrooms, Digital Media, and Popular Culture.* New York: Peter Lang.
Halliday, M. A. K. (1981–1982). Three aspects of children's language development: Learning language, learning through language, learning about language. In Y. Goodman, M. Haussler, & D. Strickland (eds.), *Oral and Written Language Development: Impact on Schools.* Urbana, IL: National Council of Teachers of English.
Halliday, M.A.K. (1993) Towards a Language-Based Theory of Learning. *Linguistics and Education* 5, 93–116
Herald Sun TAC (2008). *SuperCoach.* Retrieved October 20, 2011 from http://supercoach.heraldsun.com.au/.
Hutchins, E. (1995). *Cognition in the Wild.* Cambridge, MA: MIT Press.
Juul, J. (2001). Games telling stories?—A brief note on games and narratives. *Games Studies* 1(1). Retrieved October 25, 2011 from http://www.gamestudies.org/0101/juul-gts/.
McNeice, L., Smith, A., & Robison, T. (in press). Computer games, archetypes and the quest narrative: Computer games as texts in the Year 9 English classroom. In C. Beavis, J. O'Mara, & L. McNeice (eds.), *Digital Games: Literacy in Action.* Adelaide: Australian Association for the Teaching of English/Wakefield Press.
New London Group (1996). A pedagogy of multiliteracies: Designing social futures. *Harvard Educational Review* 66(1). Retrieved May 25, 2011 from http://www-static.kern.org/filer/blogWrite44ManilaWebsite/paul/articles/A_Pedagogy_of_Multiliteracies_Designing_Social_Futures.htm.
O'Mara, J. & Lees, B. (in press). Breaking through the fourth wall: Invitation from an avatar. In C. Beavis, J. O'Mara, & L. McNeice (eds.), *Digital Games: Literacy in Action.* Adelaide: Australian Association for the Teaching of English/Wakefield Press.
Pelletier, C. (2005) The uses of literacy in studying computer games: comparing students' oral and visual representation of games. *English Teaching Practice and Critique* 4(1) 40–59
Steinkuehler, C. (2007). Massively multiplayer online games as a constellation of literacy practices. *E-Learning* 4(3): 297–318. Retrieved May 25, 2011 from http://dx.doi.org/10.2304/elea.2007.4.3.297.
Stevens, R., Satwicz, T., & McCarthy, L. (2008). In-game, in-room, in-world: Reconnecting videogames to the rest of kids' lives. In K. Salen (ed.), *The Ecology of Games: Reconnecting Youth, Games and Learning.* Cambridge: MIT Press.
Walsh, C. S. (2010). Systems-based literacy practices: Digital games research, game play and design. *Australian Journal of Language and Literacy* 33(1): 24–40.
Walsh, C. and Apperley, T. (2008) Gaming capital: Rethinking literacy. *Changing Climates: Education for Sustainable Futures. Proceedings of the 2008 Australian Association for Research in Education International Education Research Conference,* http://ocs.sfu.ca/aare/index.php/AARE_2008/AARE/paper/viewFile/101/200 Downloaded 6 May 2012
Willett, R., Robinson, M., & Marsh, J. (Eds.). (2009). *Play, Creativity and Digital Cultures.* New York: Routledge.

5 Countering Chaos in *Club Penguin*
Young Children's Literacy Practices in a Virtual World

Jackie Marsh

INTRODUCTION

In this chapter, I examine the literacy practices of children aged from 5 to 11 as they engage in out-of-school use of virtual worlds. There is now extensive evidence that many children in developed societies have access to a range of technological hardware and, in the course of using this, participate in multiple digital practices (Blanchard & Moore, 2010; Ofcom, 2010; Rideout, Foehr, & Roberts, 2010). These include activities such as watching television and films, playing with console games, using computers, and using a range of technological hardware such as karaoke and dance machines. Increasingly, online activities are prevalent in the out-of-school activities of children and young people. Patterns of access and use with regard to children and the Internet appear to be specific to context, however. In a study of 189 sixth and seventh graders' use of computers in the U.S., Agee and Altarriba (2009) reported that the sixth graders they surveyed appeared to be largely uninterested in computers, but the seventh graders were more likely to express an interest in gaming and instant messaging. This contrasts somewhat with large-scale research conducted within the UK, which indicates that 84% of 9–19-year-olds in the UK access the Internet at least weekly (Livingstone & Bober, 2005) and 75% of children aged 8–11 report playing games (Ofcom, 2010). Socio-economic status and ethnicity map onto access and use (Moje, Overby, Tysvaer, & Morris, 2008), although it is clear that other factors also impact on children's use of online sites, such as established family practices (Marsh, Brooks, Hughes, Ritchie, & Roberts, 2005). This varied picture does indicate that many children have regular access to the Internet outside of school and there is growing evidence that they are engaged in a range of interactive practices, including the use of social networking sites (SNS), such as Facebook and Myspace (Lenhart, Madden, & Hitlin, 2005), and sites that facilitate online networking, such as virtual worlds (Marsh, 2010). While virtual worlds do not fit the criteria of SNSs as defined by Merchant (2009), they do include elements that enable social interaction, such as chat facilities and collaborative games.

This chapter is focused on young children's (aged 5–11) use of one virtual world and explores the ways in which literacy is embedded within the use of this site. While studies of literacy practices in virtual worlds are limited in number, emergent work in this area indicates that literacy is central to online interactions in these spaces and that there are numerous opportunities for reading and writing in the worlds (Gillen, 2009; Merchant, 2009). The chapter outlines the range of literacy practices that took place in the virtual world and suggests that a key function of these practices was to make order out of chaos. This stance starts with the premise that virtual environments can appear to be chaotic. It is possible to draw from both chaos theory and complexity theory in developing an understanding of this phenomenon. Chaos theory was initially developed in the sciences where mathematical modeling was used to develop theories about apparently chaotic systems. Gregerson and Sailer (1993) suggest that such theories can be applied in the social sciences, as these mathematical models have identified that chaotic systems are "iterative recursive systems that can exhibit discontinuous change over time" (Gregerson & Sailer, 1993: 792). There are obvious limitations to applying this theory to social systems, but it is possible to identify the differences between complex and chaotic social systems by drawing on the literature in this field. While chaos is typified by unpredictable behavior, complex systems exhibit patterns in which creativity can emerge from self-organization and the formation of ad hoc groups that work "at the edge of chaos" (Waldrop, 1992). Complexity studies identify "the inescapability of indeterminacy and nonlinearity in partially predictable and partially unpredictable environments" (Morrison, 2010: 378). It would seem that many online environments have characteristics that would align them along the complex-chaotic end of the order-complexity-chaos spectrum. For example, some are iterative, recursive systems that can allow for creativity through the self-organization of groups. An example of this would be the website Flickr, which allows users to share photographs and create dynamic groups that share similar lines of interest. From this example of a complex system, we can move to a more chaotic environment exemplified by the social networking site Chat Roulette, which offers users the chance to interact with random strangers across the Internet. Virtual worlds may offer opportunities to move across the complex–ordered continuum dependent upon the activities undertaken, as I explore in this chapter. A key argument made is that literacy may offer children opportunities to construct and maintain a social order in a somewhat random and chaotic virtual world.

LITERACY AND THE SOCIAL ORDER

Social order is constructed through the beliefs and value systems of different groups who work together to achieve social cohesion in society (Durkheim,

1964 [1893]). Inevitably, literacy is fundamental to the construction and maintenance of social order and has been found to be integral to the functions of nation-states over centuries (Cressy, 2006; Graff, 1987). Durkheim emphasized the role of language in the construction and maintenance of a social order, but it is also the case that literacy permeates social and cultural life. Barton (2000), when describing the findings of the 'Local Literacies' study (Barton & Hamilton, 1998), an ethnographic study of literacy in the lives of a community in northern England, suggests that we live "textually-mediated" lives:

> We found that in the various areas of everyday life which we studied, such as communication, organising life, leisure activities and social participation, people's activities were mediated by literacy. We found that we had been studying a textually mediated everyday life, not one held together solely by spoken language. We concluded that nearly all everyday activities in the contemporary world are mediated by literacy and that people act within a textually mediated social world. (Barton, 2000: 100)

The relationship between literacy and the social order is one that has seen radical transformations in the digital age. Urry (2000: 195) reminds us that the construction of social order has always depended upon extrasomatic elements, and in contemporary society, technologies intersect with humans in complex and dynamic ways. The literacy practices that emerge in these intersections are key to the construction and maintenance of a social order. This has not been subject to extensive empirical interrogation in relation to young children as yet, although the work of Steinkuehler (2007, 2008) does indicate how literacy underpins social exchanges between young people and adults in the MMOG *World of Warcraft*. The study reported in this chapter contributes to this emergent area by outlining how children using a virtual world utilized literacy in the building of an online social order, a social order that connected to children's offline lifeworlds.

The work of Leander (2003, 2007) and Bulfin (2009) in particular has informed our understanding of how literacy practices circulate across online and offline spaces. Leander, Phillips, and Headrick Taylor (2010), in a recent review of the spatiality of learning, point to the way in which online and offline spaces are mutually constitutive in children's lives and confirm that it is important to look at children's literacy practices across virtual and offline spaces. Children and young people themselves treat boundaries between spaces as permeable, as Bulfin's (2009) study of Australian teenagers indicates. His work explicates how young people "import and insinuate" out-of-school texts and practices in schools' proscribed technologies and ICT curriculum, such as in the way in which they bring unsanctioned texts into school on memory sticks. Thus, it is important to acknowledge the way in which literacy moves across spaces, both virtual and non-virtual, and consider what else traverses alongside these practices and how they may be transformed in the process.

CHILDREN'S VIRTUAL WORLDS

Boellstorff (2008) traces the origins of virtual worlds back to antiquity, to Plato's allegory of the cave in Book 7 of *The Republic* (Plato, 1991) (which depicts the actual world as a mere shadow of a non-physical world of ideas) and he moves on to outline how virtual worlds as we currently know them, in the form of sites such as *Second Life*, began to emerge in the 1970s with the development of the first video games and multiplayer dungeons (MUDS). The burgeoning of the children's virtual world market began around the mid-point of the first decade of the twenty-first century, with some of the current major players, such as Ganz's *Webkinz* and Viacom's *Neopets* beginning to attract large numbers of users around that time. Since then, this has been an area of rapid development, with some reports that the fastest growing demographic of virtual world users is children between the ages of five and nine, a group that will see 27% growth in the use of these sites over the next five years (Gilbert, 2009). The majority of children's virtual worlds involve playing games as a major activity. This is not to suggest, however, that the worlds should be categorized primarily as games. As Meyers (2009) argues, the activities undertaken in what he terms 'shared virtual environments' (SVEs) have more in common with virtual worlds for adults, such as *Second Life*, than other online game sites. Many of the sites enable users to manage an avatar (clothe and manipulate an online representation of themselves), create home environments, chat to others through the use of instant messaging, and engage in shopping for virtual artifacts. These virtual worlds promote a range of types of play from the more restricted rule-bound play involved in games constructed by the site producers to imaginative play, which can involve fantasy and sociodramatic play (Marsh, 2010). There are few studies of children's use of virtual worlds. The most comprehensive so far, the American study of tweens' (aged 10–12) use of *Whyville*, has focused on social interaction and learning in a site that was developed to promote learning (Kafai, 2010). Kafai (2010) and colleagues, in a special issue of the journal *Games and Culture* (5,1) devoted to their project, offer a wealth of information on how the tweens they studied interacted with each other in *Whyville* and how they engaged in the investigations and games embodied into that virtual world narrative. The study outlined in this chapter focuses on one of the commercially based virtual worlds for children, *Club Penguin*.

Club Penguin was developed by the media company New Horizon Interactive in Canada and opened to public use in October 2005 with approximately 25,000 users. In 2007, there were more than 12 million registered accounts and the world was subsequently acquired by Disney Inc. for $350 million. *Club Penguin* is currently reported to have 32 million registered accounts.[1] The virtual world consists of an arctic environment in which avatars are penguins. Each penguin has an igloo home. There are numerous games in *Club Penguin* in which users earn coins and also games that can be played for sport—e.g., swimming, ice hockey. Users can buy clothes and artifacts for their avatars and igloos.

Text is kept to a minimum throughout the virtual environment and is used primarily to identify the use of buildings. Symbols, such as arrows, are used throughout the world to guide penguins and every page contains the icons that link to a map of the world, the newspaper *Club Penguin Times*, and a 'Moderator,' who can be contacted if penguins wish to complain about the behavior of others in the world. The navigation bar at the bottom of the screen contains icons that enable children to engage in chat with other penguins, to use emoticons, to throw snowballs, to contact other penguins in order to request that they become friends, and to navigate to their avatar's home, their igloo. Chat appears in speech bubbles above the heads of avatars, similar to the placement of speech in comics. This limited use of text and extensive use of icons and symbols mean that very young children find it relatively straightforward to navigate *Club Penguin*. Some of the servers enable 'safe chat' mode, which means that users choose from a set of words and phrases in order to communicate with each other, again enabling children who are not fluent writers to engage in communication with other avatars. *Club Penguin* contains texts that are more extensive in nature for those who wish to access them. The newspaper, for example, includes puzzles, jokes, and stories and there is a library that contains books, including interactive books, for longer reads. In addition, the editors of the *Club Penguin Times* do invite users to submit pictures and articles.

Club Penguin, therefore, contains many of the features of other virtual worlds for children, such as the use of a market-based system in which shopping is a key activity and the tight control of user engagement through the design of the site, but it also has distinct features, such as the lack of in-world marketing and the provision of a range of written texts beyond game instructions and shopping resources. Virtual worlds for children have been the focus of a range of critique, not least because the producers often embed sophisticated data-mining software, which enables surreptitious surveillance of users' online practices (Chung & Grimes, 2005) and also because they are embedded within a complex, multimedia world of commercial products aimed at children and parents. Further, *Club Penguin* itself is now a part of Disney, a longstanding focus for critical analysis by political economists and cultural theorists who point to its corporate manufacture of imperialist fantasy (Wasko, 2001). Notwithstanding these concerns, it would seem important to understand the kinds of literacy practices that are undertaken on these sites and the purposes for these practices, given the extent to which virtual worlds such as *Club Penguin* are used by young children. In addition, literacy educators need to be aware of the out-of-school literacy practices of young children in order to build on them in an appropriate manner in the classroom. In particular, the ways in which children use literacy in online spaces in order to create social groups are of interest, given that there is little research in this field. We know much about the way in which written texts are central to children's social practices (Dyson, 2003, 2010; Wohlwend, 2009); there is now a need to extend this understanding to online spaces.

The study was undertaken in a primary school in a large city in northern England, which was involved in ongoing projects with a local university. The school serves a primarily white, working-class community located on a housing estate, in an area of significant economic deprivation. The ICT teacher in the school, who taught every class during the course of a week, was involved in the study as he wanted to initiate work in the ICT curriculum on virtual worlds and so felt that he would find it valuable to know about children's engagement with virtual worlds outside of school. An online survey was set up using 'Google Docs.' Children were asked a range of questions relating to their Internet use, including a request to identify if they used virtual worlds outside of school and, if so, how often. Questions also focused on the nature of children's activities when using virtual worlds—i.e., if they shopped, played games, read the in-world texts, and chatted to friends. A total of 175 children across all year groups (ages 5–11) completed the survey. Following the completion of the survey, 26 children were interviewed about their use of virtual worlds. In the third stage of the study, three children, Emily, John, and Sally, were filmed in their homes using the virtual world *Club Penguin* over the period of a month. All were aged 11 when the filming took place.

THE VIRTUAL SOCIAL ORDER

In total, 52% (n=91) of the 175 children aged 5–11 surveyed stated that they used virtual worlds on a regular basis, 53% (n=49) of whom were girls. The most frequently used virtual world was *Club Penguin*. It is a central argument of this chapter that one of the key functions of the literacy practices within *Club Penguin* was to establish and maintain social interaction. When first logging on to this virtual world, one is struck by the apparent chaos that operates in it, as indicated in my field notes from the first observation of John:

> *John moves his avatar to the town centre using the map. I cannot see his avatar as it has landed on top of a large number of avatars in the centre of the town. He presses the arrow key and his avatar moves across the town square into a space. There are lots of avatars in this small space. Movement appears to be spontaneous and quite chaotic— some avatars are moving at speed, others are still in one space and occasionally speech appears above avatars' heads in a bubble as they*

appear to be addressing the crowd. For example, one penguin shouts "pool zoo dance party at coolies on map." John leaves his avatar here for 8 minutes, during which time I observe a lot of apparently random behaviour. (Fieldnotes, August 5, 2008)

The ability to navigate a complex, multimodal screen was a primary skill required to engage in *Club Penguin*. Literacy was a significant element of movement through the bounded space of the virtual world environment in that there was extensive use by children of environmental print in order to find their way about—for example, by following signs or using maps.

Both verbal and non-verbal communication are central to social exchanges in public life. In virtual worlds that are not voice-enabled, written communication is used to interact with others and the written text becomes close to speech, as is the case with other forms of online communication, such as texting on mobile phones (Baron, 2008; Crystal, 2008). Reading and writing were integral to the practice of establishing or fostering relationships in *Club Penguin* and the creation and maintenance of an interaction order. I observed the way in which children used a series of literacy practices in order to communicate with other users and begin to move towards a more ordered sense of social interaction, as indicated in these fieldnotes:

Emily clicks onto an avatar and looks at its profile. She then chooses a postcard to send. It states "Be my friend!" I have noticed that this is a regular pattern in the children's use of Club Penguin. They identify potential new friends and then send them postcards in order to invite friendships, rather than approaching them directly. Perhaps this offers them a safety-net if the other user chooses not to respond to their request. (Fieldnotes, August 19, 2008)

One of the first activities children undertook when they encountered an avatar who either interested them or who had approached them with a request for friendship was to click on their avatar profile to read them. If this reading of the data led them to feel comfortable about the avatar, the next step would be to send a postcard inviting friendship. As Misztal (2001) suggests, a sense of 'normality' and trust in social interactions is built through routines and rituals and the sending and receiving of postcards, messages, and emoticons appeared to have this effect in *Club Penguin*. In this way, literacy was central to the construction and maintenance of friendships. In interviews, children reported sending others postcards as an expression of friendship and writing and reading messages to and from other penguins:

I like reading messages and falling in love with girl penguins. I have got about five girlfriends. You have to win a loveheart and then you can send them to them. (Billy, aged 7)

> *I read them letters what tell you if they are your buddies or not and when they send you postcards and things.* (Lisa, aged 7)

Communication was undertaken with both known and unknown interlocutors. For example, children wrote messages to unknown avatars present in the same space in attempts to communicate. These attempts to initiate interaction were not always successful. Direct questions to other penguin avatars that belonged to users not known in the offline world were frequently not answered. For example, in one episode, Emily wished to find out how her flat television screen could display pictures. She entered an igloo in which three avatars were engaged in a game of imaginary football. They did not have a (virtual) ball to play with, but used the chat facility to outline their imaginary actions as they raced around the igloo.

Emily entered an igloo to face three avatars that were running around. The users were using the chat facility to signal their footballing moves:

> *Avatar 1:* Misses
> *Avatar 2:* U better
> *Avatar 1:* Takes shoot
> *Avatar 3:* Whacks round hed
> *Avatar 1:* Heart stops
> *Avatar 2:* Hands up
> *Avatar 3:* Good
> *Emily's avatar:* How did you turn on your TV?
> *Avatar 1:* Falls
> *Avatar 2:* Waaaaaaaaa
> *Avatar 3:* Catches
> *Avatar 2:* I weaving

Eventually, Emily gave up her attempt to obtain information and left the igloo, moving on to another igloo to ask the same question. Boellstorff (2008: 187) points out that, "It has long been noted that persons involved in virtual worlds (and other forms of online interaction, from email to blogs) can experience forms of 'disinhibition.'" This disinhibition enabled users of *Club Penguin* to flout offline social rules and ignore approaches from other avatars when they were unwelcome, as in the foregoing example. Other examples included throwing snowballs at unknown avatars, or telling other avatars to "Go away." There was no evidence from the interviews or the observations that children found this upsetting, although as the children were regular users of virtual worlds, it may have been the case that they had become used to such practices.

Ritual is an important part of establishing and maintaining social order, as Habermas has suggested. As in the offline world, literacy served to establish and maintain social networks between groups of children in *Club*

Penguin in ritualistic ways. At times, the children engaged in ritualistic play (Marsh, 2010). These patterns of behavior sometimes involved groups of users typing in the same or similar phrases as they joined in the ritualistic play. For example, a frequent activity in *Club Penguin* is for avatars to gather on an iceberg and attempt to tip it by jumping up or down, or drilling. Sometimes one avatar uses a particular phrase during this activity (such as "Tip it!") and then all avatars use this phrase. These 'interaction ritual chains' (Collins, 2004) serve to develop the 'emotional energy' (Collins, 2004) that can be gained from membership of a group. This pattern has been documented in older children and young people's use of social networking sites (Davies and Merchant, 2009; Dowdall, 2009) and adults' use of massively multiplayer online games (MMOGs) (Steinkuehler, 2008). Children in this study reported using a variety of literacy practices that facilitated this kind of social networking. In addition to text chat, they also used emoticons to give specific messages to others. For example, Sally at one point animated her avatar so that it appeared to be clapping at a group of penguins on a stage. She commented:

> I'm just applausing people that's on stage, just to be friendly with them. You can, whatever you feel like, you can click the emotions. So I feel like happy today so [she clicks on the smiley face emoticon] and then everybody knows you're happy and want to come play with me.

Literacy and multimodal communicative practices were thus a central element in making connections with others in the virtual world. As outlined earlier, these practices became ritualized in many instances, with the children developing an understanding of the place these rituals played in online interaction.

The beginning and end of social interaction turns were different in *Club Penguin* than in both offline contexts and other virtual worlds. In some other virtual world environments, such as *Second Life*, it is possible to discern when another user is typing text into the chat box, as her or his avatar makes automated movements that replicate hands typing on a keyboard. It is commonplace, therefore, in dyad or small group communication for other users to wait for this user to type in her/his phrase before responding. There is no way to determine when another user is typing in *Club Penguin*. This means that frequently users begin to type in chat but then other users move their avatars away as they do not realize this. Sally suggested that she sometimes used the set phrases to communicate with other avatars, rather than type in her own text; otherwise they might not stay around to hear what she had to say:

> *Sally: I usually use these up here [she pulls down the set-phrase menu] because it's easier than writing. When you like someone to play with*

> *you, you ask them a question because they're your buddy you've got to like type it really quick before they run off . . . so it's just easier to click things so they don't run off or something.*

Nonetheless, patterns could be discerned in relation to conventions such as turn-taking or leave-taking. For example, some users used emoticons to signal welcomes or goodbyes, and at times avatars moved closer together or further apart to signal the beginning and the end of conversations. It is to be expected that there would be differences in offline and online system and ritual constraints, given the nature of both contexts. What is of note in this study is that the children constructed a social order by both drawing on offline ritualized practices and abandoning those when they did not meet their needs. There was no evidence, across all interviews and the observations, that children were disconcerted or upset by what might be considered abrupt or confusing exchanges with others. This online resilience is important and thus play in virtual worlds can be viewed as a significant context in which children can experience both continuous and discontinuous social engagement.

An overall analysis of the video and interview data suggests that literacy was central to the construction and maintenance of a social order in a variety of ways, which are detailed in Table 5.1.

Literacy enabled the children to engage productively in this online environment, to make friends, to express themselves and to engage in pleasurable interactions with a variety of multimodal texts on a regular basis.

Table 5.1   The Role of Literacy in the Construction and Maintenance of an Online Social Order

Literacy practice	Contribution to construction and maintenance of social order
Reading of environmental print e.g. signs/ maps	Enabled users to navigate the virtual world
Reading of in world texts e.g. newspaper/ library books	These were stable texts in a changing environment, which users returned to on recurrent basis over time
Use of synchronous chat facility to send messages to other users	Enabled users to communicate with each other and participate in extended social discourse
Sending and receiving of asynchronous messages/ postcards to other users	Enabled users to communicate with each other and to establish and maintain friendships
Use of ritualised literacy practices e.g. users gathering together and chanting the same phrase, or using the same emoticon	Enabled users to construct social cohesion through community practices

CONCLUSIONS

As the foregoing data indicate, literacy is an essential element in the 'media ecologies' (Ito et al., 2009) of young children as it acts as a social glue and creates connections in a networked environment that might otherwise be daunting for individuals. It was clear from this study that virtual worlds such as *Club Penguin* are stimulating environments for young children. They also consist of complex and even chaotic social systems. Complexity theory suggests that complex systems are partly predictable and partly unpredictable and at this 'edge of chaos' (Waldrop, 1992) self-organized groups can be highly creative and productive. However, once systems move towards the chaotic, there can be a breakdown of order and small changes can have large and unpredictable outcomes. In the children's reports of their engagement in the virtual world, there was evidence of both complexity and chaos. Ultimately, Disney has control of the site and can impose some kind of order (which they do through moderators, who can ban users who are particularly disruptive), but there are numerous opportunities for chaotic interactions to occur even within these constraints. The data illustrate how the children created a social order as a means of making sense of this virtual environment. Literacy and multimodal communication were significant elements in the creation of a sense of 'normality' and effective social functioning. Online spaces offer opportunities for engagement with both known and unknown interlocutors, and with people who are located locally and globally. Literacy as a social and cultural practice as experienced in virtual worlds offers young children the opportunity to engage in authentic activities that provide an induction into social networking and develop the skills and understanding they will require as they move further into their digital lifeworlds. The children are learning much more than how to read and write in online spaces as they use virtual worlds; they are learning what it means to be a member of an online community and a participant in collaborative networks, valuable learning opportunities in this twenty-first-century 'participatory culture' (Jenkins, 2009).

The implications of the analysis undertaken here are numerous. First is the implication that engaging in social discourse in virtual worlds can be valuable in terms of developing children's understanding of online interaction. What this study has highlighted is the way in which these children's use of one virtual world was dependent upon literacy practices for a sense of coherence and purpose. Too often, activities in online forums can be branded as mundane or trivial pursuits by commentators who do not consider the underlying reasons for these exchanges. To some, the apparent chaotic nature of activity in *Club Penguin* might indicate that users are not engaged in meaningful interactions with others, yet analysis of the data in this study indicates that the children were involved in a range of social encounters, some of which held significance for them. Investigations such as this highlight the way in which there are both continuities and discontinuities in social interaction in online and offline spaces. If children are not familiar with this, then the behavior of online users of a specific environment could become very off-putting and even upsetting. Children's online resilience and their sensitivity to other web users could be enhanced through an examination of this phenomenon.

Second, the study indicates that we must pay attention to the types of literacy practices in which children engage in their out-of-school lives if we are going to be able to build a curriculum that is relevant to their interests and expertise. Utilizing children's interest in virtual worlds in the classroom could lead to innovative practices that engage pupils and replicate out-of-school purposes for literacy. The data indicate that the children were engaged in a rich range of literacy and multimodal activities in the virtual world and that these practices were fostering numerous skills and competences. As Black and Steinkuehler (2009: 283) argue, in their analysis of the online literacy practices of teenagers and young people, "many such practices are perfectly within the realm of what various national standards and other policy documents indicate that we, as a society, value and ought to foster in our youth." The potential benefits for literacy development in the use of such environments are overlooked, unfortunately, in the emphasis on online safety, or the concern that such online activities preclude children from playing outside (Palmer, 2006). Finally, there are implications of this study for further research into young children's use of virtual worlds. It would be valuable, for example, to identify how far such environments can impact positively upon children's offline literacy practices. Do interest and engagement in these worlds lead to reading and writing off-screen that is related to their onscreen interests? There is a need to examine in further detail the relationship between online and offline literacy practices in the years ahead, as these two domains become increasingly blurred.

NOTES

1. Kzero research, reported in February 2010 at http://www.kzero.co.uk/.

REFERENCES

Agee, J. & Altarriba, J. (2009). Changing conceptions and uses of computer technologies in the everyday literacy practices of sixth and seventh graders. *Research in the Teaching of English* 43(4): 363–397.
Baron, N. S. (2008). *Always On: Language in an Online and Mobile World*. New York: Oxford University Press.
Barton, D. (2000). Directions for literacy research: Analysing language and social practices in a textually mediated world. *Language and Education* 15(2): 92–104.
Barton, D. & Hamilton, H. (1998). *Local Literacies: Reading and Writing in One Community*. London: Routledge.

Black, R. W. & Steinkuehler, C. (2009). Literacy in virtual worlds. In L. Christen-bury, R. Bomer, & P. Smagorinsky (eds.), *Handbook of Adolescent Literacy Research*. New York: Guilford.

Blanchard, J. & Moore, T. (2010). *The Digital World of Young Children: Impact on Emergent Literacy*. Pearson Foundation White Chapter. Retrieved March 20, 2010 from http//www.pearsonfoundation.org/PDF/EmergentLiteracy-WhiteChapter.pdf.

Boellstorff, T. (2008). *Coming of Age in Second Life: An Anthropologist Explores the Virtually Human*. Princeton: Princeton University Press.

Bulfin, S. (2009). *Literacies, New Technologies and Young People: Negotiating the Interface in Secondary School*. (Unpublished doctoral dissertation). Monash University, Melbourne.

Chung, G. & Grimes, S. M. (2005). Cool hunting the kids' digital culture: Data mining and the privacy debates in children's online entertainment sites. *Canadian Journal of Communication* 30(4): 527–548.

Collins, R. (2004). *Interaction Ritual Chains*. Princeton: Princeton University Press.

Cressy, D. (2006). *Literacy and the Social Order*. Cambridge: Cambridge University Press.

Crystal, D. (2008). *Txting: The gr8 db8*. Oxford: Oxford University Press.

Davies, J. & Merchant, G. (2009). *Web 2.0 for Schools: Learning and Social Participation*. New York: Peter Lang.

Dowdall, C. (2009). The texts of me and the texts of us: Improvisation and polished performance in social networking sites. In R. Willett, M. Robinson, & J. Marsh (eds.), *Play, Creativities and Digital Cultures*. New York: Routledge.

Durkheim, E. (1964 [1893]). *The Division of Labor in Society* (G. Simpson, Trans.). New York: Free Press.

Dyson, A. H. (2010). Writing childhoods under construction: Re-visioning "copying" in early childhood. *Journal of Early Childhood Literacy*. Vol. 10 (1) pp7–31.

Dyson, A. H. (2003). *Brothers and Sisters Learn to Write: Popular Literacies in Childhood and School Cultures*. New York: Teachers College Press.

Gilbert, B. (2009). *Virtual Worlds Market Forecast 2009–2015*. Strategyanalytics. Retrieved March 2010 from http://www.strategyanalytics.com/default.aspx?m od=ReportAbstractViewer&a0=4779.

Gillen, J. (2009). Literacy practices in Schome Park: A virtual literacy ethnography. *Journal of Research in Reading* 32(1): 57–74.

Giroux, H. A. (2001). *The Mouse That Roared: Disney and the End of Innocence*. New York: Rowman & Littlefield.

Graff, H. J. (1987). *The Labyrinth of Literacy*. London: Falmer Press.

Gregerson, H. & Sailer, L. (1993). Chaos theory and its implications for social science research. *Human Relations* 46(7): 777–802.

Ito, M., Baumer, S., Bittanti, M., Boyd, D., Cody, R., Herr-Stephenson, B., Horst, H. A., & Tripp, L. (2009). *Hanging Out, Messing Around, and Geeking Out: Kids Living and Learning with New Media*. Cambridge, MA: MIT Press.

Jenkins, H. (2009). *Confronting the Challenges of Participatory Culture: Media Education for the 21st Century*. Cambridge, MA: MIT Press.

Kafai, Y. (2010). World of Whyville: An introduction to tween virtual life. *Games and Culture* 5(3): 3–22.

Leander, K. (2007). "You won't be needing your laptops today": Wired bodies in the wireless classroom. In C. Lankshear & M. Knobel (eds.), *A New Literacies Sampler*. New York: Peter Lang.

Leander, K. (2003). Writing travellers' tales on new literacyscapes. *Reading Research Quarterly* 38(3): 392–397.

Leander, K., Phillips, N. C., & Headrick Taylor, K. (2010). The changing social spaces of learning: Mapping new mobilities. *Review of Research in Education* 34(1): 329–394.

Lenhart, A., Madden, M., & Hitlin, P. (2005). *Teens and Technology*. Washington, DC: Report to the Pew Internet and American Life Project.

Livingstone, S. & Bober, M. (2005). *UK Children Go Online: Final Report of Key Project Findings*. April. London: London School of Economics. Retrieved June 6, 2009 from *http://www.children-go-online.net*.

Marsh, J. (2010). Young children's play in online virtual worlds. *Journal of Early Childhood Research* 8(1): 23–39.

Marsh, J., Brooks, G., Hughes, J., Ritchie, L., & Roberts, S. (2005). *Digital Beginnings: Young Children's Use of Popular Culture, Media and New Technologies*. Sheffield, UK: University of Sheffield. Retrieved November 2011 from http://www.digitalbeginings.shef.ac.uk/.

Merchant, G. (2009). Literacy in virtual worlds. *Journal of Research in Reading* 32(1): 38–56.

Meyers, E. (2009, January 20). Tip of the iceberg: Meaning, identity, and literacy in preteen virtual worlds. Paper presented at the Association for Library and Information Science Education Conference, Denver, Colorado. Retrieved January 8, 2010 from http://blogs.iis.syr.edu/alise/archives/71.

Misztal, B. A. (2001). Normality and trust in Goffman's theory of interaction order. *Sociological Theory* 19(2): 312–324.

Moje, E., Overby, M., Tysvaer, N., & Morris, K. (2008). The complex world of adolescent literacy: Myths, motivations, and mysteries. *Harvard Educational Review* 78(1): 107–154.

Morrison, K. (2010). Complexity theory, school leadership and management: Questions for theory and practice. *Educational Management Administration and Leadership* 38(3): 374–393.

Ofcom (2010). UK children's media literacy. Retrieved March 27, 2010 from http://www.ofcom.org.uk/advice/media_literacy/medlitpub/medlitpubrss/ukchildrensml/.

Palmer, S. (2006). *Toxic Childhood*. London: Orion Press.

Plato (1991). *The Republic: The Complete and Unabridged Jowett Translation*. New York: Vintage Books.

Rideout, V. J., Foehr, U. G., & Roberts, D. F. (2010). *Generation M2: Media in the Lives of 8–19-Year-Olds*. Menlo Park, California: Kaiser Family Foundation. Retrieved February 2, 2010 from http://www.kff.org/entmedia/mh012010pkg.cfm.

Steinkuehler, C. A. (2008). Cognition and literacy in massively multiplayer online games. In J. Coiro, M. Knobel, C. Lankshear, & D. Leu (eds.), *Handbook of Research on New Literacies*. Mahwah, NJ: Erlbaum.

Steinkuehler, C. (2007). Massively multiplayer online gaming as a constellation of literacy practices. *eLearning* 4(3): 297–318.

Urry, J. (2000). Mobile sociology. *The British Journal of Sociology* 51(1): 185–203.

Waldrop, M. (1992). *Complexity: The Emerging Science at the Edge of Order and Chaos*. New York: Simon & Schuster.

Wasko, J. (2001). *Understanding Disney: The Manufacture of Fantasy*. Cambridge: Polity Press.

Wohlwend, K. (2009). Damsels in discourse: Girls consuming and producing identity texts through Disney princess play. *Reading Research Quarterly* 44(1): 57–83.

6 Telling Stories Out of School
Young Male Gamers Talk about Literacies

Alex Kendall and Julian McDougall

INTRODUCTION

In this chapter we consider how post-structuralist troublings of traditional educational research orthodoxies might raise important questions about the way literacy and media literacy curricula are conceived and enacted. Focusing particularly on the performative (after Butler, 1990) dimension of young people's literacy practices, which are very often absent from discussions of literacy pedagogy, we illustrate, through an analysis of young men's participation in online technologies, how central the performance of identity is to the dynamic of a literacy event and make the case that pedagogy needs to take account of literacies as 'ways of *being* with others.' Such an emphasis demands a reconfiguration of literacy curricula to reposition teachers and young people as co-investigators of the dynamic and rituals (Marsh, 2004) of *being* with others and enables/facilitates the exploration and problematization of the boundaries between the different modalities within which performances of self are played out and/or given. By drawing attention to the rituals (Marsh, 2004; and see Marsh, this volume) of young people's cultural practices this kind of praxis may mobilize more nuanced understandings of the sense of displacement young people experience as they transgress heavily insulated (Bernstein, 1996) domain boundaries— for example, between their lifeworld experiences and schooled experience.

This approach seeks a more 'honest' account of young people's literacy practices—that is not to say more 'truthful' but in the sense of bringing to the fore the illusory nature of playing at being. Such accounts may facilitate new insights that inform the fields of literacy and game studies as well as for the emerging field of 'media literacy.'

CONTEXT

This chapter draws on a study that emerged from the outcomes of previous work (Kendall, 2008; McDougall & O'Brien, 2008) that has illuminated young adult males' preferences for gaming over 'reading.' A regional study

(Kendall, 2008a) of the leisure reading habits of 16–19-year-olds found that when the range of leisure activities that participants engaged in was analysed, statistically significant differences emerged between the time male and female participants reported playing sport and computer games. Males in the study commented

> A: It [a game] can challenge you, yeah, it's not boring, sometimes you get bored of newspaper reading and reading like, and computer games you've got like more games to do they don't get boring.

> B: You've got control over it; whereas the book it just takes you in a straight line from start to finish, whereas a game you can take it your own way.

> C: You can choose your own path in a game. (Kendall, 2008a)

As readers of books these male readers seemed to feel 'subject to' particular ways of being that encouraged an organized, linear response and deprived them of agency and choice; as players of games they felt licensed to be creative and innovative. As gamers they are perhaps more enabled to "accept risks, and choose possible future actions by anticipating outcomes" (Gauntlett, 2002: 98), behaviors that Gauntlett associates with Giddens' (1991) notion of late modernity. As such we considered whether the practice of gaming offers these students a more tentative, provisional framing for textual experience within which the relationship between reader and text (player/game) is differently mediated so that the 'player as reader' of the 'game as text' is "positioned as an agent in knowledge making practice rather than a recipient of 'knowledge'" (Kendall, 2008b: 18). This kind of questioning resonates with the call for broader understandings of the social practices of gaming made by those in gaming studies (Crawford & Gosling, 2009).

Concurrently we were interested in the emerging policy agenda for media literacy in the UK context and it is important to explain briefly at this point what we mean by this. In the UK, Ofcom (the independent regulator and competition authority for the UK communications industries) has given hitherto-absent credence to media education through the development of a media literacy strategy (Ofcom, 2010), created in collaboration with academics and industry professionals and disseminated through the convening of regional 'Media Literacy Task Force' groups. This national body liaises with European media literacy groups, UNESCO, and, through international media literacy research seminars (at which we have presented our work) academics from New Zealand, the U.S., Canada, and Australia. Our sense that the media literacy agenda is fraught with confusion and a reluctance to adequately 'theorize' media literacy *as* literacy is twofold. First, the structural arrangement of the agenda by a regulatory body inevitably provides, intentionally or not, a protectionist agenda. Second, this protectionist impulse is amplified by the dialogue with international groups for whom such a 'risk reduction' approach is unproblematic, with an assumed connection made to the Byron report (Byron, 2009). This was a government-commissioned investigation into a 'problem' lacking a precise definition in which video games and virtual world experiences were 'lumped together' with cyber-bullying and online pedophile grooming. The voices from research into how digital literacies are developed from early ages—for example, Marsh (2004) and Livingstone (2008)—are insufficiently heard in the development of an overly pragmatic agenda, as is evidenced by the framing statements by Ofcom's Head of Media Literacy, Robin Blake (2010). Our intention here, then, is to inform the media literacy agenda by offering data that might lead to a more discursive, complex, and theoretically grounded phase of 'the project.'

METHOD

The research discussed in this chapter was conducted in two stages. Eight 16–17-year-olds were recruited to the project from two further (tertiary) education colleges in England, one in the West Midlands and one in the South East. The colleges were chosen entirely contingently and the project did not aim to look at geographical or contextual issues. Although this might have yielded further interesting data it was beyond the scope of the study. Research focused on the young male players' interactions with games.

The participants, all male and following academic programs in media studies that include the exploration and analysis of a broad range of 'textual products' including video games, were self-identifying as keen players of computer games. They had already been playing our chosen game *GTA4* (Grand Theft Auto IV). We had chosen this game for a number of reasons. First, we felt that it would be good to agree on some common territory for our players to discuss. Second, *GTA4*, part of a series of very popular GTA games, had recently been released in a wave of media hype so we felt it would be relatively easy to find young people who were already playing it. Third, the GTA series is seen as groundbreaking among many gamers and while online elements increasingly come as standard for video games, *GTA4* represents the most significant example to date of a mass market, narrative-based game with a detailed, complex, and open-ended location to explore online alongside or even outside the mission-based storyline. Our interest in the game lies explicitly in this interrelationship of progression through (and thus determination by) a textual experience and agency— 'being with others' in a virtual space—and in the dynamics of this duality in relation to the attribution of meaning in literacy practices. Finally *GTA4* is the kind of game that is the focus of 'moral panic' in the United Kingdom (see, for example, Greenhill & Koster, 2008) and so it was felt it would offer an additional opportunity to contribute to the debates around protectionist accounts of media literacy.

Talking to 17–19-year-olds about the game called for careful consideration of ethical issues as in the UK *GTA4* is classified as unsuitable for players under 18. However, in reality 16- and 17-year-olds are playing the game. A key priority was not to introduce players to the game but to work with those who were already playing it. Therefore as a condition of participating participants were required to return signed parental consent forms to confirm that they had already purchased and were permitted to play *GTA4*. Participants then joined a Facebook group established exclusively for the project and were asked to submit regular playblog accounts as they moved through the game over a two-week period. The Facebook group enabled a space for the gaming talk to occur but also, we recognize, frames the interactions in particular ways. We have to be careful to take these into account.

Participants were given plenty of guidance on the technicalities of how to participate: how to join the group, how often to contribute and when, etc. However, the only guidance about what to contribute was that they should write about their playing experiences in each case. They were free to respond to each other's postings, or to ignore them as they preferred. On several occasions reminder messages were sent to the whole group but these reminders did not include any prompts regarding content or structure of postings. Individual students were never contacted by us and we did not comment on any postings. The postings, perhaps unusually for a social networking site, were referred to as 'blogs' within the project.

The second stage was a semi-structured interview with each player. This followed a standard pattern of questioning, referring to postings as prompts—either directly with regard to the participant (e.g., "*I noticed you gave an example of . . . ,*") or more generally (e.g., "*towards the end of the two weeks the postings became more . . .*"). The rationale for the use of the Facebook group was threefold. First, using a Web 2.0 context with which all the participants were already familiar avoided some of the potentially awkward dynamics of this kind of research. Second, it allowed the participants to take responsibility for the nature of their own literacy practices. Third, it offered a 'transliteracy' bridge from playing to talking.

The range of stories that emerged from the data about playing and telling has been reported elsewhere (Kendall & McDougall, 2009). In this chapter we want to focus on two areas for further discussion: weblog 'talk' about being in the game and the 'talk about the weblog talk' captured in the interviews.

WAYS OF TELLING . . .

Last night I began the story of Nico Bellic . . . (Bill)

Like many of our bloggers, Bill quickly settled into the role of storyteller, recounting dramatic tales of his adventures in Liberty City. Often postings were woven together through a loose, yet traditional, narrative thread. This kind of opening is argued by Crawford and Gosling (2009) to be typical of out-of-game storytelling:

> A long night in liberty city, it seems for Nico Bellic and his cousin Roman. After the mass bloodbath, which we created last night's wild antics at the splitsides comedy club in central liberty city, before the face off with police. (Justin)

'Grand finales' are clearly gestured towards:

> So this is my last post, so i thought therefore i should go on a truly world class killing rampage . . . this is how I got on. (Justin)

> I decided to go out with a bang. (Ben)

> OK, its here. The fifth and final hour, the big one . . . oh yes, you know what I'm talking about . . . (Sunny)

In the last of these examples Sunny feels the proximity of his onlookers and addresses 'us' directly. Similarly self-conscious of audience, Andy, perhaps our most accomplished storyteller, rejects the simple past tense in favor of an invitation to the reader to share his 'present' and so to experience his journey through Liberty City more immediately:

> I hit the gas and aim my car at their wreckage, when i hit full speed i leap out the vehicle and watch it carrear into the mess. With the remaining bullets i have i pump the gas tank full of lead and gaze at the explosions as one of the flaming carcasses of my enemies falls to my feet. (Andy)

The 'in-between' action was for Ben and Justin and their fellow bloggers a fast-paced pastiche of the action-movie genre, a melodrama of "mass bloodbaths" (Justin), "killing sprees" (Justin & Dean), "guns blazing" (Andy), and "mini riots" (Ben). The writers were taking up—and savoring—the position of the excessive action hero posturing at the center of the narrative—unnerved, amoral, fearless, and bloodthirsty:

> i decided to do the impossible spawn a bike on the top of the building and try the craziest jump i have ever performed on the game . . . (Justin)

> I conveniently snatch a woman out of her car and when the male passenger challenges my antics i make him run by pointing a gun at him and then shoot the back of his knees making him slide across the pavement. I then approach him like a stereotypical Russian gangster and stand over him whining and put him out of his misery with a single head shot (oh so delightful!!). (Dean)

And there were moments of mock-chilling detail resonant of the Tarantino oeuvre:

> i thort i would change my clothes for a killing spree a nice new suit.
> black with a red tie. (Simon)

There is something of the cartoonish 'baroque showman' about these descriptions. They are self-conscious, outrageous, carnivalesque 'performances' to the wider blog community, an overlay of friends, college peers, and Facebook contact trails:

> . . . before I posted my first blog I did read what everyone else had written and I tried to write in my own style, I did kind of stick to the same structure as other people. (Ben)

> I tried to stick to my own sort of style of writing and keep it sort of close to that but I noticed a few of the blogs were out there. (Dean)

Of course they are performed also to 'us'—the researchers (outsiders?)—not blogging but almost palpably listening to these wild adventures played out vicariously. Telling the story of playing for these participants is an act of playful artistry, as Dean summarizes in his interview:

> I think to a certain extent there was a kind of competition because everybody wants their blog to be read and everyone wants people to laugh at their blog and they just want a chance to shine.

This is at its most explicit when the gamers tell of performing against others in the multiplayer online modes. Here are Dean and Bill pitted against a group of American gamers:

> However I was subjected to being in a team of 4 with 3 Americans who were useless at the game but talked like they were professors of super bowl. This resulted on us arguing about what's better rugby and American football after them saying rugby is a girl's sport in which I jumped out the car and sent 4 single bullets into the windscreen and windows hoping they change their thoughts on rugby. (Dean)

> After shooting a few people down and evading various 1/2 wanted star levels, I get an invite to play online, fun. With the invite accepted I found myself in a lobby full of rowdy Americans wanting to kill me (in the game of course), the game mode is GTA Race meaning you race but can get out of your car at any point, picking up weapons along your way. Just as the game started I heard an overly-enthused American shout the words, "Holy shit, here we go!" (Bill)

This more immediate, live audience offers both Bill and Dean the opportunity to perform their gaming selves.

GAMING SELVES

This version of the macho male protagonist the bloggers play out for us, themselves, and each other in the game and in their telling of the game is, they suggested in their interviews, remote from their everyday sense and expression of self, agency, and the 'real.' Rather than the projection of any deeper aspiration they described *GTA4* as:

> a fun thing to play with no restrictions. It's just like a different world really which makes it fun and interesting to play. (Andy)

> a sick and twisted fantasy really and it's down to the human psychic really. People wouldn't actually go out and, get in a car and run over thirty people and jump out and it on the body and do things like that. (Sunny)

This is contrasted with their sense of 'real life,' where:

> running away from the police often ends with you getting caught in real life. Somehow you can end up like having a helicopter following you and just magically happen to have a grenade launcher which can blow up the helicopter so that things are great. I could never imagine doing that in real life. At least I hope not! (Dean)

And this playing at the 'other' within the 'unreal' provides a source of enjoyment and pleasure:

> What appeals to me about it? I think it's just real light-hearted fun and you can get a good laugh out of it even though it's crime and it's probably not morally correct, you know there's not really that much of a consequence, you know? You just get to have a little bit of fun and have a little joke with your mates when you're playing it. (Dean)

This playfulness is observable throughout the blogs, which show a constant fracturing of the in-game narrative with out-of-game observations and critiques prompted, for example, by moments of intertextual signification, 'moral' compromise, or technical novelty. Some of our players described themselves as immersed in their game character's 'time'/'reality,'—for example:

> I just put myself in the character. You are Nico. (Justin)

I do get pretty involved when I play games and when I do get into the cover thing I don't actually notice myself kind of ducking into cover when I'm actually playing the game yes so you can get really involved and think that you are Nico. (Sunny)

The blog entries offer less resolved narratives. Peppered by moments of internal, meta-aware commentary, they play out instead a more complex plurality. At times this meta-awareness is prompted by a sense of 'wonder' at what's new. Here, for example, Justin describes his first encounter with an in-game 'sensation':

After collecting him, I then took my eastern European cousin for a drink in Blarneys Irish pub, before a game of darts, where I participated in a sensation, which I have never discovered before on a video game, my character being drunk. Whilst walking around the beer garden of the pub I found another feature which makes GTA a favourite of mine, not just due to the revolutionary aspects of gameplay, but the humour, as I chuckled to myself while reading a umbrella on one of the tables with a sign for a mock German beer, Pißwasser, GTA never ceases to amaze me, or to make me laugh. (Justin)

This intertextual moment adds a further fracturing layer. Luke shares a similar moment of surprise, enjoyment, and reflection as he marvels at the incidental but closely observed, and, to him, fascinating detail of the animated cup:

One particular sad thing to do is knock a cup out of someone's hand on a hill and watch the cup gain momentum and speed down the hill, a tribute to the physics engine. (Luke)

Similarly Dean contemplates the introduction of 'consequences,' which he seems to appreciate as a sort of maturation' of the *GTA* series:

Finally they have built in the concept of consequences into GTA. I had to step out and face the music . . . (Dean)

At other times it is an emotional—even moral—challenge that prompts critique, as Ben's tendency to acknowledge the innocence of his victims to a perhaps judgmental audience might suggest:

Despite being briefly distracted by the lure of slaughtering innocent bystanders. (Ben)

I passed the time by climbing onto a high surface and taking pot shots at innocent civilians. (Ben)

Equally Justin's revoke in the codicil here—which seems to begin with a silent "don't worry" to his audience—perhaps indicates a gentle slippage from his otherwise bravado-fuelled narrative:

> I decide to leave him to his watery grave (he will be fine next time i get wasted or busted, I hope!). (Justin)

However, the moments of disruption are most apparent when the in-game male characters interact with female characters. It is at these moments that many of the bloggers express either comedy bravado, like Justin, that plays to the blog audience:

> After this i was distracted by my in game relationship with the character Michelle, like a real girlfriend she clearly only wanted to drain my patience as well as my wallet. (Justin)

. . . or a more self-conscious tentativeness, like Ben here, that may be more 'out of game':

> The date looked to be ending in disaster when the taxi drivers erratic driving upset her stomach, but she seemed to enjoy the burgers and I managed to get invited inside. (Ben)

> A hectic nights drinking led to me surprisingly leading Michelle back to her flat unscathed, although after my embarrassing behaviour I didn't even ask to go inside. (Ben)

Ben is surprised by his success with in-game girlfriend Michelle as he 'manages' to get invited inside, while his embarrassment at his behavior in front of her would seem to play against the direction of the moral framework of the game. What we do see here is that for these young men, as for the young children in Marsh's (2004) study of popular culture, gaming does not provide a "parallel reality but, rather, interact[s] with daily individual and social practices in complex and significant ways" (Marsh, 2004: 45).

RECLAIMING PLAY

Play here becomes a very 'grown-up' pursuit. Rather than merely ludic, play is concerned with the brokering of particular ways of being in different modalities of practice. Participants play with the game, against and through the game for multiple audiences (us, each other, the online community), performing and re-performing versions of their (male) selves. In relation to young children's lives Marsh pays attention to ritual practices as processes of assimilation and accommodation of new learning and goes on to suggest that "this kind of performance is not just about re-telling the narrative as a multi-modal form of reader-response . . . it is also about performing a particular kind of ritual that can be used to establish social practices and identities" (2004: 42). To rethink young men's participation in online cultures as ritualized performance opens up new possibilities for re-reading gaming (and indeed the social networking spaces that frame such pursuits) as performing useful functions—what Bean (1999) calls 'functionality'—in young people's lives.

Drawing on post-structuralist understandings of self, Gauntlett reminds us that "we do not face a choice of *whether* to give a performance. The self is always being made and re-made in daily interactions" (2002: 141). It is this peformativity, argues Butler (1990), that is central to constructions of gender. What becomes interesting here is that our participants, although on the surface interacting with a text that has been described in the *Daily Mail* and *The Sun* as 'morally dubious,' are contemporaneously playing with identities in ways that might be described, in MacLure's terms, as 'frivolous.' MacLure (2006: 1) understands frivolity as "to be whatever threatens the serious business of establishing foundations, frames, boundaries, generalities or principles. Frivolity is what interferes with the disciplining of the world." It is precisely this kind of posturing that Butler advocates in her incitement to make "gender trouble":

> through the possibility of subverting and displacing those naturalized and reified notions of gender that support masculine hegemony and heterosexist power, to make gender trouble, not through the strategies that figure a utopian beyond, but through the mobilization, subversive confusion, and proliferation of precisely those constitutive categories that seek to keep gender in its place by posturing as the foundational illusions of identity. (Butler, 1990: 33–34)

Perhaps unexpectedly then it is possible to understand our participants as engaged in radical moves that threaten the stability of the binaries around which moral panic discourses converge.

The participants shared an explicit meta-awareness of how to play against, with, or despite the narrative that resonates with Gauntlett's (2002) idea of the postmodern 'pick and mix' reader of magazines. In Gauntlett's study female readers did not read magazines as 'blueprints' for authoring identity. Rather, magazines seemed to offer possibilities for 'being' that might be engaged with dialogically; the reader is invited to "play with different types of imagery" (Gauntlett, 2002: 206). Such clearly understood 'parology' (Lyotard & Thebaud, 1985)—new moves in the game that disrupt orthodox analyses of 'effects' and of reading itself—is perhaps our most compelling evidence that there is no singular 'way of being' in a game.

Such playfulness around identity resonates strongly with those calling for re-reading of masculinities as a way of repositioning young men in relation to literacy practices. Rejecting the kinds of school effectiveness discourses that position boys as 'victims' and 'losers' in terms of achievement in literacy, critics such as Jackson (1998) and Kehler and Greig (2005) call for "acknowledgment and unpacking [of] the overlapping and competing ways that boys enact or perform what it means to be a man." This, they argue will "evolve much more complex and messier understandings of masculinities underscored by competing sets of understandings" (Kehler & Greig, 2005: 360). Drawing on the outcomes of their small-scale ethnographic research into young men's literacy practices, these writers argue for much more "nuanced readings of boys who themselves are sophisticated readers of particular texts, namely the most authorial and widely read text they know and understand, that of their bodies" (Kehler & Greig, 2005: 366).

A further reading of the data might see the 'baroque showman' as an act of *desistance*—that is, resistance to becoming the object of study, as any single truth of identity is eluded and eclipsed by the camp humor of the interplay. MacLure et al urge that research methods must find

> more nuanced and less forensic attitude[s] to humour [that] might allow us to recognise its productive role in maintaining solidarity and identity, and to respect its value for marginalised groups as a form of resistance to power and inequality—even where this resistance manifests itself uncomfortably in the research/intervention situation as also a resistance to analysis. This would not mean endorsing or overlooking the misogyny and prejudice that is often coded into such humour. But it would mean also considering the positive qualities that humour involves—such as skill, timing, collaboration and quick-wittedness. Humour also relies on a kind of "double vision"—the ability to see the absurdity, irony or double meanings in social situations. (2007: 8)

Drawing on the findings of a study of young men's attitudes and practices around health, MacLure et al further note that

> Much of the joking that circulates in young men's talk shows an astute, if often jaundiced, understanding of their own and others' social roles and status. It is not surprising that humour, silence and the ambivalent respect of mimicry have been identified as the strategies of subaltern subjects faced with disciplinary power (cf Bhabha, 1994). Lies, secrets, silences and deflections of all sorts are routes taken by voices or messages not granted full legitimacy in order not to be altogether lost. (2007: 9)

This kind of posturing 'queers,' in Butler's sense, what it is possible to 'know,' in the sense of 'grasp,' about young people's engagement with popular textualities. And MacLure would have us know such shortcomings as intrinsic to, indeed of, the very fabric of social interaction. In relation to research methodologies MacLure calls alternatively for 'baroque' approaches that might begin to

. . . consider the possibility that jokes, masks, camp performance, secrets, lies, uncertainties about who is fooling whom, or even about whether one is fooling oneself, are routine aspects of social interaction that can never be fully eliminated from interview encounters in the interests of disclosure. A baroque method of analysis would also be radically undecided about the questions of mastery and surrender that have troubled qualitative research. It would recognise that analysis is always *both* an aggressive act that does violence to the realities of research subjects, and a submissive act of surrender to their persuasions. (MacLure, 2006b: 13)

MacLure's 'baroque' favors a fragmented, dislocated undoing characterized by movement over composure, estrangement of the familiar, disorientation, and loss of mastery (MacLure, 2006a: 8) towards a frivolity (2006b) that undoes and is undone. And it occurs to us that this type of approach might usefully form the basis of curriculum and pedagogies that seek to re-inscribe teacher/student relations and the subject/object of study towards a seriously frivolous pedagogy, which "postures 'new imaginaries' for the relation of the researcher to the object" and imagining with MacLure a peepshow that

. . . brings the viewer into an intimate relation with the object, one into which desire, wonder and Otherness are folded, and out of which something might issue that would never be seen by shining a bright light upon the object in the empty space of reason and looking at it as hard as possible. But the peepshow also calls attention to the compromised, voyeuristic nature of the researcher gaze and the unavoidable absurdity of the research posture. To view the delights of the peepshow you have to bend down, present your backside to public view, put yourself at risk. (2006a: 18)

CONCLUSIONS

Towards a conclusion, however unfrivolous and un-McClurian that might be, we argue that social practice in this emerging field, whether mobilized through research, curriculum, or pedagogy, must bear witness to forms of literacy as difference. In *Just Gaming*, Lyotard conceives multiplicity, itself an inevitable paradox (along with postmodernity); hence, in keeping with Lyotard's ethics, we wish to offer a set of conclusions that resist reducing these multiple ways of reading *GTA4* to a set of competences or 'levels' of critical engagement with the text. Instead we seek to bear witness to the various ways that the young men participating in our research attribute meaning to the game. In so doing we suggest that media literacy, as practiced in educational contexts, ought to be concerned with discovering and exploring local practices in reading, telling, and meaning-making without recourse to a principle of literacy, or media literacy, as a regulatory idea.

We propose that paying attention to these local practices as not only the starting point for but also the *substance* of learning enacts a pedagogical shift that revises the idea of where expertise is located in the classroom. This "pedagogy of the inexpert" (Bennett, Kendall, & McDougall, 2011) repositions teachers and young people as co-investigators in the dynamic and rituals of *being* with others through textual practice and facilitates the exploration and problematization of the boundaries between the different modalities within which performances of self are given.

Enacting this kind of pedagogical practice requires a reading of teacher identity against the grain to accept our awareness of but unfamiliarity with and *inexpertise* in the particular textual fields of learners and the ways they make texts matter. The role of the teacher in this dynamic is to facilitate and scaffold the auto-ethnographic storytelling of learners and to accept and embrace the more unchartered, unknowable learning spaces that emerge, learning spaces that, we assert, are charged with productive possibility. This will better enable the taking up of MacLure's challenge "to seek out [frivolity] and help to set in motion" (2006b: 2) 'baroque' accounts of young people's engagement with popular textualities that support young people, in Kehler's and Greig's (2005: 367) words, to (re)read the "textualized stories of their lives."

REFERENCES

Bean, T. (1999). Intergenerational conversations and two adolescents' multiple literacies: Implications for redefining content area literacy. *Journal of Adolescent & Adult Literacy* 42(6): 438–449.

Bennett, P., Kendall, A., & McDougall, J. (2011). *After the Media: Culture and Identity in the 21st Century*. London: Routledge.

Bernstein, B. (1996) *Pedagogy, Symbolic Control and Identity: Theory, Research, Critique*. London: Taylor & Francis.

Blake, R, 2010. 'OFCOM and Media Literacy' at *Our Digital Futures* conference Retrieved 20.5.11 from http://www.youtube.com/watch?v=WWLLChzRLLI

Butler, J. (1990). *Gender Trouble: Feminisms and the Subversion of Identity*. Routledge: London.

Byron, T. (2009) *Safer Children in a Digital World*. London: DCMS.

Crawford, G. & Gosling, V. (2009). More than a game: Sports-themed video games and player narratives. *Sociology of Sport Journal* 26: 50–66.

Gauntlett, D. (2002). *Media, Gender, Identity*. London: Routledge.

Giddens, A. (1991). *Modernity and Self-Identity: Self and Society in the Late Modern Age*. Cambridge: Polity.

Greenhill, S. & Koster, O. (2008). Man stabbed queueing for midnight launch of ultra-violent video game Grand Theft Auto IV. *Daily Mail Online*. Retrieved April 10, 2008 from http://www.dailymail.co.uk/news/article-562729/Man-stabbed-queueing-midnight-launch-ultra-violent-video-game-Grand-Theft-Auto-IV.html#ixzz0bwcefeAD.

Jackson, D. (1998). Breaking out of the binary trap: Boys' underachievement, schooling and gender relations. In D. Epstein, J. Elwood, V. Hey, & J. Maw (eds.), *Failing Boys?: Issues in Gender and Achievement*. Buckingham: Open University.

Kehler, M. & Greig, C. (2005). Reading masculinities: Exploring the socially literate practices of high school young men. *International Journal of Inclusive Education* 9(4): 351–370.

Kendall, A. (2008a). '*Giving up*' reading: Re-imagining reading with young adult readers. *Journal of Research and Practice in Adult Literacy* 65(Spring/Summer): 14–22.

Kendall, A. (2008b). Playing and resisting: Rethinking young people's reading cultures. *Literacy* 42(3): 123–130.

Kendall, A. & McDougall, J. (2009). Just gaming: On being differently literate. *E-ludamos: Journal for Computer Game Culture* 3(2): 245–260.

Livingstone, S. (2008). Engaging with media—A matter of literacy? *Communication, Culture & Critique* 1(1): 51–62.

Lyotard, J. with Thebaud, J. (1985). *Just Gaming*. Minnesota: Minnesota University Press.

MacLure, M. (2006a, November 27). The bone in the throat: Some thoughts on baroque method. Keynote to Annual Conference of the Australian Association for Research in Education, Adelaide.

MacLure, M. (2006b). Entertaining doubts: On frivolity as resistance. In J. Satterthwaite, W. Martin, & L. Roberts (eds.), *Discourse, Resistance and Identity Formation*. London: Trentham.

MacLure, M. (2005). 'Clarity bordering on stupidity': Where's the quality in systematic review? *Journal of Education Policy* 20(4): 393–416. Reprinted in B. Somekh & T. Schwandt (eds.), *Knowledge Production: Research Work in Interesting Times*. London: Routledge.

MacLure, M., Holmes, R., Jones, L., & MacRae, C. (2007, April 10). Silence and humour as resistance to analysis. Paper presented to American Educational Research Association Conference, Chicago.

Marsh, J. (2004). Ritual, performance and identity construction: Young children's engagement with popular cultural and media texts. In J. Marsh (ed.), *Popular Culture, New Media and Digital Literacy in Early Childhood*. London: RoutledgeFalmer.

McDougall, J. (2007). What do we learn in Smethwick Village. *Learning, Media, Technology* 32(2): 121–133.

McDougall, J. & O'Brien, W. (2008). *Studying Videogames*. Leighton-Buzzard: Auteur.

Ofcom (2010). Children's media strategy. *Ofcom*. Retrieved January 11, 2012 from http://stakeholders.ofcom.org.uk/binaries/research/media-literacy/ukchildrensml1.pdf.

Part III

School Innovations

7 'What Is the MFC?'
Making and Shaping Meaning in Alternate Reality Games

Angela Colvert

"hi we have a lots more we no a abot 😊😮🐾🖼️we will find it there are2m"

INTRODUCTION

Alternate reality games (ARGs) differ topologically from the virtual worlds represented by computer games and other online spaces. In ARGs, the construction of fictional worlds and of spaces for play involves a combination of everyday technologies such as websites, films, and artifacts, and therefore incorporates a range of modes and media. Additionally, the everyday environments of participants may also form key parts in gameplay. Typically ARGs present players with complex mysteries to be solved, requiring that they collaborate with other players, collating and interpreting trails of clues that have been dispersed and distributed both online and offline. The designers may respond to players' contributions and manage the content of games both before and during play; message boards, webcams, and letters can all be used to provide valuable feedback loops, enabling designers and players to shape the fiction and gameplay together through imaginative dialogue. However, although some ARGs have been designed by adults for children and young people, there has been little investigation into the skills, knowledge, and understanding that children might develop if given the opportunity to design and play ARGs with and for their peers. This chapter explores and describes the dynamic and distinctive process of ARG authorship, and the complex ways in which a group of 10–11-year-old children made, shaped, and negotiated the meaning of texts with their 9–10-year-old peers in order to perpetuate play, in an ARG they had designed and produced themselves.

THE PROJECT DESIGN: A CASE STUDY

This chapter draws on the findings of a two-year ethnographic study that forms part of ongoing research into alternate reality gaming in educational settings. The project was undertaken in a large South London primary school with a class of Year 6 (ten- and eleven-year-old) children, aiming to investigate the ways in which they would develop their understanding of authorship through designing and participating in an ARG with and for their Year 5 (nine- and ten-year-old) peers. The ARG design was a collaborative endeavor between the children and me (their teacher), and regular whole class project meetings ensured that there was flexibility and reflexivity built into the planning, enabling the children to build on and develop each other's ideas. Since the project would take almost a year to complete, it needed to meet the requirements of the National Curriculum as well as the research objectives, and although it was primarily a multimedia, multimodal literacy project, it was also cross-curricular.

The Design Challenge

The ARG was based on a novel by Philip Ridley, *The Mighty Fizz Chilla* (2002). The Year 6 children, as designers, were challenged to 'bring the story to life' and create a game that would involve the Year 5 children, as players, following a 'trail of clues' to find the creature at the center of Ridley's novel—the 'Mighty Fizz Chilla' or 'MFC'—before it reached the school! This brief gave the designers scope to respond to and develop Ridley's multithreaded narrative across a range of modes and media, and also to consider aspects of game design, creating rules that would shape player engagement. The novel features many memorable characters, but among the most significant are Cressida Bell, Dee Dee 6, Milo Kick, Mr. Chimera, and the Captain. Designers were divided into six working groups, each of which was responsible for communicating as one of the characters in the game. Each group was instructed to provide information and artifacts that would help the players to capture the beast.

In response to the brief, the designers chose to gradually distribute clues about the whereabouts and appearance of the creature online and offline over the course of a week, and created websites, films, and artifacts that could be revealed to players over time. These included personal and business websites for the characters (which served to introduce the characters to the players) and message boards that would enable dialogue between players and characters. The designers also created webcam 'diary entries' that appeared to have been recorded by the characters, and handmade books and maps that would be posted to the players if they asked the characters to send them. In addition to producing a range of text types for the game, which included news articles, character webpages, recipes for potions, letters, and information texts about monsters (included in a tome about 'Creatures of the Deep'), the designers also created puzzles such as codes for the players to crack. In this way they succeeded in creating an engaging quest that would require the players to solve the mystery at the center of the game: what is (and where is) the MFC?

Constructing a Game World: The Quest for the MFC

The fictional world of the ARG was defined by the quest: the search for the beast. This was the playful social context in which the texts produced by the designers, and the actions and interpretations of the players, would become meaningful. The representations of the Mighty Fizz Chilla (MFC) were essential to the construction of the game world as the successful completion of the quest would require the players to correctly identify and locate the beast. The MFC served an essential ludic function, as catching it was the aim of the game, in addition to a narrative function: helping to frame play as a fantasy quest. The players' shared understandings of the appearance and whereabouts of the creature were therefore key to gameplay, and this information needed to be effectively communicated to the players. However, the designers understood that in order for the quest to feel authentic, the information could not be revealed all at once, since this was supposed to feel like a 'hunt for the beast.' Like the consumers of transmedia stories produced by large franchises and media companies described by Jenkins (2006: 21), the players would need to "assume the role of hunters and gatherers, chasing down bits of the story across media channels, comparing notes with each other via online discussion groups" and collaborate with each other "to ensure that everyone who invests time and effort comes away with a richer entertainment experience." In order to position the players as active participants in the quest, the designers distributed clues about the creature's whereabouts and appearance to be uncovered and discovered during play. Players' actions would be rewarded with new revelations: pieces of evidence that would help them catch the beast.

Discovering the meaning and relevance of the multiple texts in the ARG was part of gameplay, but the designers realized that in order to experience a sense of agency within it, players would need to feel as if they were instigating and controlling events. The ARG's ludic elements—the rule systems that shaped player engagements—therefore needed to be planned prior to play. The players would be required not only to collate, configure, and interpret information, but also to act upon it and produce texts and artifacts during the game—for example, by writing to characters on the message boards, or making potions to catch the creature.

The ARG as an Act of Communication

Authorship of the ARG was an act of communication in which meaning was shaped though discourse, design, production, and distribution: the four communicative strata described by Kress and van Leeuwen (2001). Therefore, in order to develop an appreciation and nuanced understanding of the process over time, empirical data were collected throughout the planning, making, and playing stages of the project. These data included semi-structured interviews with the players and designers, the texts that the children produced, and teacher observations. At each stage of the project, the children needed to decide which resources they would use to construct messages about the creature, and how they might disseminate them during gameplay. According to Kress (2010), the affordances of modes and the facilities of media are central to any communicative act as is "social interaction and interchange around meaning, orientated to the processes of *making* and *remaking* meaning through the making of signs—simple or complex—in *representation*" (p. 34). In the ARG, the designers created representations of the MFC but during play these were remade in the minds of players and transformed through the imaginative dialogue between the players and designers on the message boards.

The designers distributed representations of the MFC across a variety of modes, across a range of text types, across media, and across the matrix of texts created by the other groups in order to form a logically structured game world, within which the players could verify and cross-reference information. In this, they considered the impact of the game's temporal structure on the players' ability to perceive the game as a meaningful, coherent whole. When tracing the ways in which the ARG was designed and structured, it is perhaps useful to draw upon and adapt concepts developed by linguists Halliday and Hassan (1985), who define coherence as the reader or listener's perception of the text's unity (1985: 52;94), a judgment which is informed by the contextual and linguistic cues she receives. They explain that "a text is characterised by coherence; it hangs together" (1985: 48) and suggest that if a reader recognises the relations of meaning between groups of utterances or sentences they may consider these to constitute a text. Halliday and Hasan posit that "in certain types of narrative, where the continuity is provided by the doings or the personality of one individual, it would be interesting to know whether this is reflected in a predominance of reference to that individual as a cohesive device" (1976: 332). Despite the structural complexity of the ARG, because of its multimodal organization and multimedia distribution, tracing linguistic cohesive ties created by the references to the MFC offers a valuable insight into the way the designers hoped to manage the players' perception of coherence. References to and representations of the MFC helped to shape and define the game world.

Hasan and Halliday's concepts refer to linguistic texts, rather than multimodal and multimedia structures. However, Lemke has argued that because the cohesive relations they define "are all essentially *binary*," they can therefore "make local linkages of meaning without depending on the existence of larger structures" (2002: 307). Thus they can be usefully used to examine the ways in which ties can function in hypermedia, across hypertextual links on websites. This chapter extends this idea and demonstrates the ways in which 'linkages of meaning' functioned in the ARG, both online and offline over time.

PRIOR TO PLAY: SETTING THE TRAIL

The following sections in this chapter present an analysis of the texts produced by three children—Marcy, Rebecca, and Jermaine—who were part of a group representing the character of the Captain. The game designers had decided that websites would be presented to players first, followed by webcam footage, before finally the artifacts would be revealed. This sequence was planned prior to play. The designers in the Captain's group had decided not to simply repeat the same information on each day, but considered how it might be distributed gradually over time in order to guide the players' interpretations. The group considered the directional relations between ties, and demonstrated an implicit understanding that the references to the MFC needed to function both anaphorically (referring back to a previous reference) and cataphorically (linking to a future reference), depending on the reading pathway chosen by the players and the order in which the information was distributed. Here, I present the texts chronologically in the order in which they were revealed to players, and analyze them within a social semiotic framework.

The Email and the Ocean Estate Webpage: "There's a Beast on the Loose"

The first representation of the MFC was in an email that signaled the start of play. It was sent by a resident of Ocean Estate (the setting for Ridley's novel) and announced that "a beast was on the loose" and that it was "heading towards London." However, the message provided little other information about the monster's appearance or whereabouts, beyond stating that there had been "trouble at Ocean Estate because of this creature" and that it needed to be caught. These references to the 'beast' and 'creature' functioned cataphorically, pointing forward towards an explicit (or simple) reference to the MFC that had yet to be revealed. In order to complete the quest successfully, the players needed to find further information and follow a link at the bottom of the email to the Ocean Estate website (Figure 7.1).

The Ocean Estate website was created using a London Grid for Learning (LGfL) account and 'Digital Brain' platform, which made it possible to easily set up password-protected access to areas of the site, and to upload the children's webpages, which they had produced using Microsoft Publisher. The designers decided that the Ocean Estate homepage should feature a number of links to their webpages. These included links to the

Figure 7.1   The Ocean Estate homepage designed by the class. Source: Editure Education Services UK Ltd., Learning Manager

'community pages,' which featured characters' personal webpages, and 'ocean news,' which contained a series of reports about unusual events and happenings in the area. The Ocean Estate homepage also provided links to webcam footage and message boards, to which only the designers and players had access.

The Captain's Webpage: "Everything Ye Need to Know about the Cursed Creature"

If the players clicked on the link to the community pages on the Ocean Estate homepage, they would discover the personal sites of the residents, including two of the Captain's webpages, one designed by students Marcy and Rebecca, the other by Jermaine. The designers ensured that the information they provided was consistent across both of the Captain's websites, each of which was designed to support the players in understanding the name of the beast mentioned in the email. The Captain's homepage (Figure 7.2) that had been designed by Marcy and Rebecca greeted players with the following message:

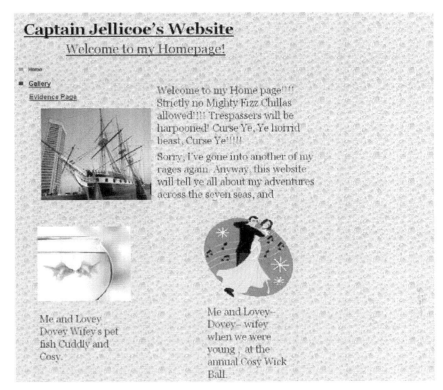

Figure 7.2 The Captain's homepage produced by Marcy and Rebecca.

Welcome to my Home page!!!! Strictly no Mighty Fizz Chillas allowed!!!!
Trespassers will be harpooned! Curse Ye, Ye horrid beast, Curse Ye!!!!!
    Sorry, I've gone into another of my rages again. Anyway, this web-
site will tell ye all about my adventures across the seven seas, and everything ye need to know about the cursed creature!!!! Ye know what I'm
talking about, right? Ye don't know?! It's the Mighty Fizz Chilla!!!!
Arghhh!!!!!

This passage presents repetition of the name Mighty Fizz Chilla and
co-references in the form of synonyms: beast and creature. The character addresses the players directly and, by reiterating the creature's name,
attempts to reduce ambiguity, which, as Halliday and Hasan (1985) suggest, can occur when the referent can signify more than one thing. "An
ambiguous grammatical cohesive device," they note, "is one that could be
interpreted in more than one way given the frame of the particular text"
(p. 89). Here, through lexical reiteration, the designers try to ensure that
references to the 'horrid beast' and 'accursed creature' on the homepage
can be interpreted only as references to the Mighty Fizz Chilla. In doing

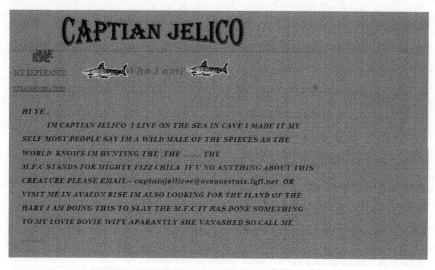

Figure 7.3   The Captain's homepage produced by Jermaine.

so, these designers hoped that the players would understand that the name of the Mighty Fizz Chilla is also an anaphoric reference to the 'beast' and 'creature' mentioned in the email. On the Captain's homepage (Figure 7.3) designed by Jermaine, both the full name and the acronym for the Mighty Fizz Chilla are introduced, thereby establishing them as co-referents. Jermaine's Captain states, "AS THE WORLD KNOWS IM HUNTING THE, THE . . . . THE MFC STAND FOR MIGHTY FIZZ CHILLA."

In addition to introducing the name of the creature, both character websites also alluded to its whereabouts. In Ridley's novel the Captain explains why it is such a challenge to find the MFC: its habitat is 'The Floating Island of the Heart,' which "is always moving, ye see. One day here, the next day there" (p. 144). In the ARG, the Captain's group developed this idea, and on the Captain's webpage Marcy and Rebecca included a small image of an island, the shape of which was not clearly discernible, with a caption explaining its significance and noting its proximity to the UK (Figure 7.4). Jermaine's page also offered clues to the creature's whereabouts. On a page entitled 'strange creature' (Figure 2.2), he inverted the initials of the MFC so they appeared to read '2FW' and added a caption suggesting that these marks were found in the sea. Jermaine later reflected on his design decisions and during a project meeting explained his reasons for including the initials:

> I did the MFC backwards so it says 2FW [. . .] I just wanted to give them like a hint so like if they if they went on this page first they'd like know about it and if they were clever enough to work it out they'd, they

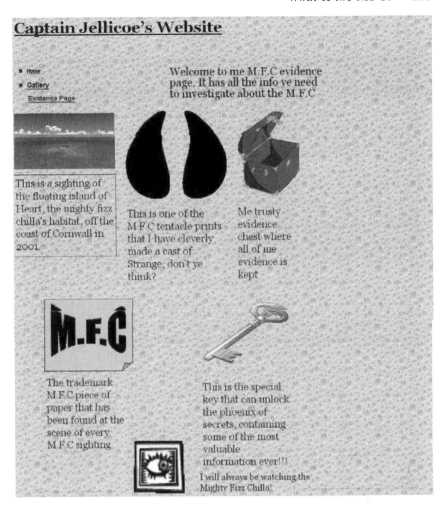

Figure 7.4   The Captain's webpage produced by Marcy and Rebecca.

could know [. . .] yeah that erm that the MFC was floating across the ocean.

Interestingly, Jermaine was aware that players might not read his pages first, but he designed the hyperlinks on the Captain's webpage in such a way that players would have visited the homepage before seeing the code, thus supporting the players in deciphering the cryptic message. If correctly interpreted by players, the writing was a recognizable reiteration of the creature's name; '2FW' functions anaphorically, referring back to the reference to the MFC on the Captain's homepage. Jermaine's use of the word 'hint' is also interesting, suggesting that he aimed to guide the players

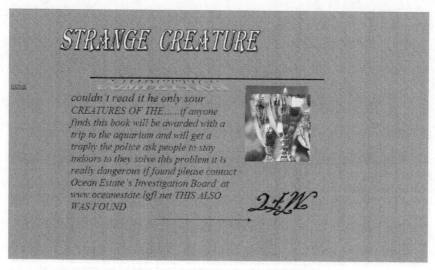

Figure 7.5   The Captain's webpage produced by Jermaine.

without revealing too much, too soon, encouraging them to investigate and discover more. Similarly, although Marcy and Rebecca's site claimed to contain "everything ye need to know about the creature," it contained very little visual or linguistic information about the creature's appearance. This would be disclosed elsewhere.

Newspaper Articles: "Strange Creature Sighted"

In addition to the characters' webpages, the Ocean Estate homepage also provided a link to a newspaper account created by Marcy and another member of the Captain's group. This report did not simply repeat the information contained on the Captain's webpages, but aimed to further the players' understanding of the creature's appearance and whereabouts. The designers demonstrated their ability to produce consistent information across the range of text types they produced, without simply replicating their representations of the creature. A news report created by Marcy entitled "Strange Creature Sighted" added important and *new* details to the trail of clues. It incorporated two witness accounts, which provided corroborating evidence about the appearance of the MFC, and a quote from the Captain revealed that the creature had a horn:

> "I was collecting driftwood on the beach when I noticed something large moving in the water. I saw a unicorn's horn stick out of the water. I said to myself 'What kind of creature could this be?' But as the beast turned round, I realized this was no ordinary sea dweller," the Captain told reporters.

In the same article, the creature's appearance was confirmed by another witness's recollection:

> "I was walking along the road with my grocery bags when I saw an unusually large bite mark on the railings lining the river Thames. The metal was still warm from the biter's breath, so I looked down into the river to see if I could glimpse the creature. As I looked down, I saw a vast, dark shape swimming away. Suddenly, what looked like a giant unicorn's horn protruded from the water. I was terrified!" she told reporters.

Here, the designers created a cohesive tie between the reference to the terms 'creature' and 'beast' and the 'unicorn's horn.' They also skillfully tied the two locations together: Cornwall, the setting of the novel, and London, the location of the gameplay, by suggesting that the MFC has been sighted in London, near the Thames, as well as in Cornwall (where the Floating Island of the Heart was situated). The designers implied that the creature had been present in the vicinity, although it was not described fully either in words or through imagery. By choosing not to include an image of the creature at this stage, the designers left gaps for player interpretation (Iser, 1978) and hoped the players would begin to imagine and visualize the creature; both witnesses cited in the newspaper report referred to the large size of the creature, and both drew attention to its horn. However, Marcy's article is careful to withhold any mention of the creature's name.

In fact, reports produced by designers across the class as a whole demonstrated a collective refusal to explicitly name MFC. Instead, the designers included references to the 'creature,' the 'beast,' and the 'monster.' The designers understood that they needed to support the players' appreciation of the coherence of the ARG and to prompt them to make conceptual links between references to the 'beast' in the newspaper articles and the 'beast' mentioned on the Captain's webpages. Unless the players were able to understand the co-referential nature of these terms, and that they were all hypernyms for the MFC, they would not appreciate the relevance of the information they were being given and would not be able use the clues in the articles to catch the creature. The designers could not determine whether the players would view the newspapers before the Captain's webpage, and therefore attempted to establish semantic relations between the name 'Mighty Fizz Chilla' and its characteristics. When designing the Captain's webpage, Rebecca and Marcy had tried to ensure that it included a cohesive tie between the term 'MFC' and mention of 'tentacle prints.' Similarly, their newspaper account also included a linguistic and visual reference to 'tentacle prints' (Figure 7.6). In this they hoped to support the players in understanding that the term 'beast' in the article also referred to the creature named on the Captain's webpage, since in both the creature appears to have tentacles.

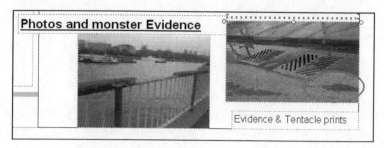

Figure 7.6   Part of the news article 'Strange Creatures Sighted,' produced by Marcy and Charlotte.

The Webcams: "They've Stolen My Chest!"

Webcam footage produced by this group included the Captain's 'diary entry' performed by Jermaine (Figure 7.7). When producing the films, the designers in the Captain's group had collaborated with those representing Milo in the game in order to develop a storyline about vital evidence going missing. This demonstrated the children's ability to produce consistent information across the matrix of text types produced by each group. The films were not designed to reveal information about the creature but to prompt players to act and contact the Captain for help. In the Captain's diary entry he explained that his maps had been stolen:

> Curse these scallywags. They've stolen my chest. I wake up at dawn and I come back and and all of my maps have gone and now there's no way for me to go to the Island of the Heart but I still have the chosen one [. . .] maybe he will know where they've gone.

A designer playing the character of Milo (the Captain's 'chosen one') recorded a separate diary entry in which he is seen to examine an ancient

Figure 7.7   The Captain's webcam.

Figure 7.8   Milo's webcam.

map (Figure 7.8), explaining that, "I was on this cliff top and I found this amazing map. Look at it; innit cool innit. It looks like it's a thousand years old. I wonder who it belonged to [. . .] Wow Looks cool come on [. . .] I wonder what it's for?" The child playing Milo indicates the map's significance by holding it up in front of the camera while staring at it in awe, examining it closely and asking a series of questions intended to pique the players' interest. At this stage in the game the designers continued to withhold any further information about the appearance or whereabouts of the beast until the players asked for the items featured in the film footage. The players would need to contact Milo and the Captain to ask for important maps in order to locate the MFC.

The Artifacts: "With This Guide . . . Learn EVERYTHING about the MFC"

Once the players had asked Milo for the map to be sent to them, it appeared to arrive in the post. The players were also sent a parcel of artifacts (Figure 7.9), produced by the Captain's group, containing a map of the Floating Island of the Heart (Figure 7.10) and a handwritten 'Mighty Fizz Chilla Route' (Figure 7.11), which claimed that "with this guide you'll be able to learn EVERYTHING about the MFC." However, although the route indicated that the Island of the Heart was near the UK, the players also needed the maps of the Thames and sewers that Milo had in his possession (Figure 7.12) in order to locate the creature. The parcel from the Captain also contained a 'wanted' poster of the MFC, the first full image of the MFC to be revealed to players (Figure 7.13).

The image of the MFC on the poster was consistent with previous linguistic descriptions of the beast in the ARG, and was closely modeled on illustrations from Ridley's novel. Until the artifacts arrived, the designers had attempted to communicate a coherent but partial account of the beast's appearance, reiterating its description in Ridley's novel as a sea creature with a shark's head, a tiger's body, an alicorn (unicorn's horn), octopus

Figure 7.9   The Captain's artifacts.

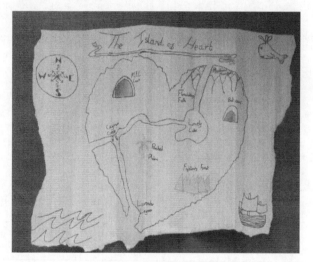

Figure 7.10   Map of the Island of the Heart.

tentacles, and wings. In the early stages of the game, the designers referred to parts of the creature, such as the tentacles and horn, but chose not to reveal any full images of the creature. Only when the artifacts arrived could the players get the full picture. The designers had decided that, in the last stages of play, visual images of the MFC should be released so there would be no doubt as to the identity of the creature and that these images should help the players confirm or adjust their ideas.

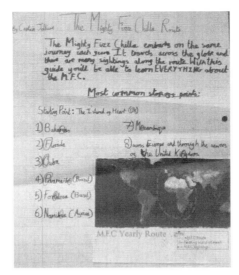

Figure 7.11 The MFC route.

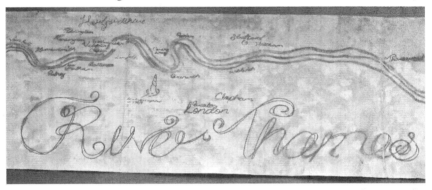

Figure 7.12 The map of the Thames.

Figure 7.13 MFC wanted poster.

SHAPING THE TEXT DURING PLAY: NEGOTIATING MEANING

It was necessary that evidence about the MFC be collated and interpreted correctly in order for the players to complete the quest, since they would need to name the beast in order to discover and make the correct potion to tame it! The designers had carefully constructed cohesive chains for the players to piece together and had left metaphorical conceptual 'gaps' (Iser, 1978) for the players to fill. The cohesive ties presupposed that the players were aware that the words 'beast' and 'creature' referred to the MFC. However, although the texts could guide players' interactions and understanding, the designers were, of course, never able to fully predict or control players' interpretations. Kress and van Leeuwen (2001) suggest that "communication depends on some 'interpretive community'" (p. 8), and that communication cannot be considered to have occurred until messages are interpreted. Indeed, Burn and Durran (2007) propose that interpretation is so key to meaning-making that it could be added as a fifth strand to Kress and van Leeuwen's concept of communicative strata (2001) mentioned earlier in this chapter.

Players' interpretations, constructed both internally and externally, were central to the meanings shaped in the ARG. The players needed to engage with the embedded narrative, that which Salen and Zimmerman (2004) call the "pre-generated narrative content that exists prior to a player's interaction with the game" (p. 383). But they were also partially responsible for the emergent narrative that, as Salen and Zimmerman note, arises "from the set of rules governing interaction with the game-system [where] unlike embedded narrative, emergent narrative elements arise during play" (p. 383). The message boards provided an invaluable feedback loop between players and designers where meanings could be negotiated, narrative developed, and play perpetuated. Players were required to share their findings online and contact characters to ask for help, and the designers responded to the players' contributions in role. However, during this playful dialogue, the designers needed to consider the agency of the players and how, when, or if they should assert their authority as designers of the experience. Although they built on and accepted many of the player's contributions and interpretations, occasionally they decided that they needed to contest and correct them.

The Message Boards and Phone Call: "They Was Getting Muddled Up"

There were several unexpected outcomes of gameplay that surprised the designers. For example, the players began to 'discover' multiple monsters. One player wrote in a forum thread entitled 'our threories'[sic]:

> hi we have a lots more we no a abott 🐱🐱💜⬛ we will find it there are2m

Here the player explains that he knows that there are '2m' or two monsters. As if this were not surprising enough, some of the players had decided that the character of Milo must be the monster! Another player summarized her findings on the message board:

> Sorry to tell you this but they're might be two monsters or even three! [. . .] I think that he [Milo] is the second monster fizzy wasp and that might help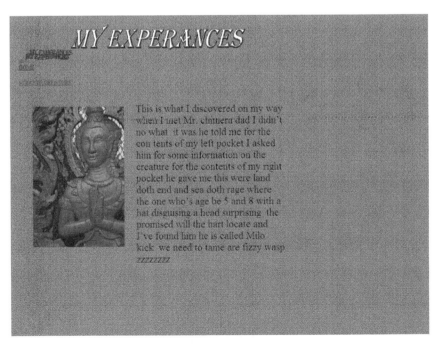

Why might the player think that Milo is the 'second monster' and what is the relevance of the phrase 'fizzy wasp'? A closer inspection of the Captain's website designed by Jermaine seems to suggest how the player's (mis)understandings may have occurred.

On Jermaine's website, the Captain explains that he had approached Mr. Chimera, "asked him for some information on the creature" (Figure 7.14), and had subsequently been told that:

> were [where] land doth end and sea doth rage where the one who's age be 5 and 8 with a hat disguising a head surprising the promised one will the hart locate and I've found him he is called Milo kick we need to tame are fizzy wasp zzzzzzzz

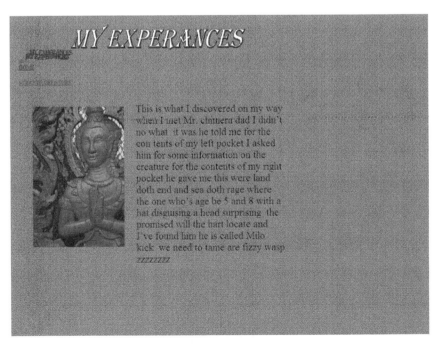

Figure 7.14 The Captain's webpage designed by Jermaine.

Here Jermaine includes a riddle from Ridley's novel that explains that only Milo (who wears a hat to cover his shocking hair style) can help the Captain find the Island of the Heart (and therefore the MFC). In Ridley's novel, 'fizzy wasps' is actually a metaphor for Milo's anger rather than a description of physical creatures. However, on Jermaine's webpage the reference to the 'creature' is followed by the statement "I've found him he is called Milo Kick" and therefore the term 'creature' could potentially be interpreted as a reference to Milo. The statement about 'fizzy wasps' is also ambiguous. Jermaine has a detailed and nuanced understanding of the language and themes in Ridley's novel, but because the players had not read the novel prior to play, they were unable to interpret the metaphorical reference to fizzy wasps in the way he had intended. During an end-of-project interview Jermaine explained that the players:

> knew that we knew that they was getting muddled up cause they was saying all this stuff on the website when they was sending the emails [. . .] saying all this stuff about three monsters like Fliss is a monster and after you have to correct one of them.

The message boards enabled Jermaine to enter into dialogue with the players as he wrote in role as the Captain to clarify the number of monsters and Milo's status as a human character in the game:

> no laddy there is only one creature milo is a human he is my chosen one he is trying to help me capture the beast and fliss is his mother <u>thanks laddy but you got it all wrong</u>

In this, Jermaine asserts his authority by 'correcting' the players and, because he recognizes that it is essential for the players to get things right at this point, his language is emphatic, direct, and unambiguous.

The designers felt that it was important that the players understood the relationship between the phrase 'fizzy wasps' and Milo's 'anger problems,' so a designer wrote to the players in role as the character of Cressida to explain:

> milo a monster? how dare you milo is a loving caring sweet little boy he just has anger problems and he calls them fizzy wasps you silly child! i love him very much and know him very well ok and i should know if he's a monster or not !!!

The metaphor of fizzy wasps might never have been understood by the players had the designers not intervened and elaborated on the message boards in this way.

Towards the end of the game, interestingly, the designers decided that the characters should contact the players by phone in order to answer any last-minute questions they might have. Tanskanen (2006) suggests that in spoken conversations "participants actively cooperate to achieve coherence" (p. 24) and explains that:

> Collaboration can be realised for example as feedback between participants in the form of completions, clarifying questions or other types of acknowledging that the participants have understood what their fellow communicators were saying. (p. 24)

Although the online communication on the message boards was asynchronous and not as immediate as spoken dialogue facilitated by phone calls, both helped the children when "collaborating towards coherence" (Tanskanen, 2006). The designers commented that they valued the 'thinking time' that the message boards provided as it gave them longer to respond to players' questions and suggestions, and they recognized that the feedback loop, made possible by the online discussion forum, was a powerful and essential part of the ARG. It was through these online interactions that the players were able to seek guidance and assistance, and through this they successfully completed the game, identifying and locating the MFC. Simultaneously, the designers gained insights into the players' experiences of gameplay.

CONCLUSION: EXPLORING THE DISTINCTIVE PROCESS OF ARG AUTHORSHIP

ARG authorship, the creation of a fictional world ripe with narrative and ludic possibilities, is a distinctive and challenging process. As the designers engaged in transmedia storytelling, which, as Jenkins (2006) argues, "unfolds across multiple media platforms, with each new text making a distinctive and valuable contribution to the whole" (pp. 95–96), they carefully considered the order in which they would distribute messages about the beast, not simply repeating information but instead creating a trail of information that needed to be collated by the players. In this they skillfully made decisions about when and how to communicate information about the creature across modes and media. In exploring the "affordances of modes" (Kress, 2010: 85) they considered the effect of revealing primarily linguistic references to the creature and withholding images of the beast in the early stages of play. When examining the "media and their facilities" (Kress, 2010: 194) they thought about how the media used might affect the experience and heighten the excitement of play, as demonstrated by their decision to send 'ancient'-looking maps through the post. However, the selection and appropriation of modes and media are only aspects of communication.

In the social semiotic model outlined by Kress (2010) "sign-makers and their agency as social actors are in the foreground and with them the social environments in which they make signs" (p. 34). The "*making* and *remaking*" (p.34) of meaning are therefore of central importance. In this ARG, the designers attempted to guide the players' interpretations through the organization of the game. However, through engaging in online dialogue with the players, they supported them in becoming significant participants in the meaning-making—negotiating and clarifying the answer to the question 'what is the MFC?' The designers provided opportunities for the players to act on the information they received, and attempted to respond to and incorporate the players' contributions into the game.

The project extended the repertoire of literacy practices that had previously been explored in the school setting. Examining transmedia practice undertaken by adult practitioners, Dena (2009) suggests that:

> Unlike the literacy involved in creating and experiencing multimedia within a media platform, these works require a different kind of knowledge and skill. A creator may be well-versed in writing novels and screenplays, but not necessarily skilled in writing stories that begin in a novel and continue in a film, in the rhetoric necessary to guide their reader to become a player, and even in understanding the combined effect these media platforms may have on the experience. Likewise, a person may be familiar with using a computer and reading a book, but unfamiliar with needing to attend to both in order to engage with the entire work. It is this phenomenon that is peculiar in ways that have not been deeply interrogated. (p. 5)

When producing this ARG, these young designers set an intriguing trail of clues across the websites, films, and artifacts that they had created and devised rules that enabled exciting ludic possibilities to develop and emerge as the players acted on the information they received during the quest. In addition to this, there were many occasions when the designers skillfully guided the players through their imaginative and inventive interactions online. This ARG project provided the designers with a playful context and purpose that shaped the way in which they engaged with their audience, and through the process of design the children developed their understanding of authorship as a communicative process.

Kress (2010) suggests that "the world of communication has changed and is changing still; and the reasons for that lie in a vast web of intertwined social, economic, cultural and technological changes." He argues that "'Authorship' in particular is in urgent need of theorising" (p. 21) in order that we avoid the "misconceived transfer of old conceptions of authorship to new conditions" (p. 21). In this project, the children demonstrated an extraordinary range of skills and knowledge, abilities and talents that I would have been unaware of had we not created the game together. The children tackled the distinctive challenge of ARG authorship with real enthusiasm, and in ways I could never have predicted, shaping with their peers, as I hope this chapter has demonstrated, a game of complexity and richness. That complexity, of course, lends itself towards further analysis, and in doing so my aim is to develop a model of ludic authorship, grounded in the exploration of the empirical data, through which I hope to suggest a framework within which the playful communicative practices of the children can be examined further.

REFERENCES

Burn, A. & Durran, J. (2007). *Media Literacy in Schools: Practice, Production and Progression*. London: Sage.

Colvert, A. (2009). Peer puppeteers: Alternate reality gaming in primary school settings. Paper presented at Breaking New Ground: Innovation in Games, Play, Practice and Theory: DiGRA, Brunel University, London. Retrieved from www.digra.org/dl/db/09287.19018.pdf. [Accessed 14/05/12]

Dena, C. (2009). *Transmedia Practice: Theorising the Practice of Expressing a Fictional World across Distinct Media and Environments*. (Unpublished doctoral dissertation). University of Sydney, Sydney. Retrieved from www.christydena.com. Also available at http://dl.dropbox.com/u/30158/DENA_TransmediaPractice.pdf [Accessed 14.05/12]

Halliday, M. A. K. & Hasan, R. (1985). *Language Context and Text: Aspects of Language in a Social-Semiotic Perspective*. Victoria: Deakin University Press.

Halliday, M. A. K. & Hasan, R. (1976). *Cohesion in English*. London: Longman.

Iser, W. (1978). *The Act of Reading: A Theory of Aesthetic Approach*. Baltimore: John Hopkins University Press.

Jenkins, H. (2006). *Convergence Culture*. New York: New York University Press.

Kress, G. R. (2010). *MultiModality: A Social Semiotic Approach to Contemporary Communication*. London: Routledge.

Kress, G. R. & van Leeuwen, T. (2001). *Multimodal Discourse: The Modes and Media of Contemporary Communication*. London: Arnold.

Lemke, J. L. (2002). Travels in hypermodality. *Visual Communication* 1(3): 299–325.

McGonigal, J. (2003). A Real Little Game: The Pinocchio Effect in Pervasive Play. Paper presented at Level Up: DiGRA,University of Utrecht, Utrecht. Retrieved from www.digra.org/dl/db/05097.11067.pdf. [Accessed 14/05/12]

Ridley, P. (2002). *Mighty Fizz Chilla*. London: Penguin.

Salen, K. & Zimmerman, E. (2004). *Rules of Play: Game Design Fundamentals*. Cambridge, MA: MIT Press.

Tanskanen, S. (2006). *Collaborating Towards Coherence: Lexical Cohesion in English Discourse*. Amsterdam: John Benjamins.

8 More Than Tweets
Developing the 'New' and 'Old' through Online Social Networking

Martin Waller

INTRODUCTION

Social networking sites have fundamentally changed the areas of social participation and communication for many people in today's society. School use of such systems tends to confine communication and networking to tightly controlled virtual learning environments (VLEs), while out-of-school use is characterized by global networks where identity is affirmed within an online community of practice. This suggests a dissonance between home and school literacy practices. However, this chapter explores how a real social networking site (Twitter) can be used in a safe way to support the development of both traditional and digital writing in classrooms. This Twitter project (@ClassroomTweets) started as a short-term classroom experiment but has now blossomed into a contextually driven way for children to make meaning within a living and breathing social network.

The interactional nature of Twitter facilitated communication beyond the classroom walls, even of a global nature, so that they were able to learn competencies not only around meaning-making, but also around e-safety. The children were able to participate in intergenerational interactions, sometimes with people known to them in face-to-face situations, but who sometimes 'found them' via online networks. They were thus able to benefit from authentic activities that opened out participative possibilities in their learning, but in a safe, controlled environment.

The world has changed. It continues to change at an unprecedented pace and impact the ways in which we live and work. Many of our old centralities are now defunct and we live in a world where the ability to access and transform information with speed and ease is central to everyday life (Lankshear & Knobel, 2006). Digital technologies are increasingly permeating nearly every aspect of our lives and have been instrumental in many of the changes in our society—not just in recent dramatic political uprisings of the so-called 'Arab Spring' or 'Occupy Wall Street' movements but also, perhaps more crucially, in more mundane ways that integrate into the daily practices of our everyday lives. We are now able to communicate and manage our lives through online services such as calendars, email, documents, social networks, and e-commerce. As a result such technologies have become more than a matter of 'information technology' and are becoming a dominant means of entertainment, communication, and cultural expression in our lives (Buckingham, 2002: 7). Since new technologies have been instrumental in developing and facilitating new meaning-making systems and the creation of new types of texts, they have become implicated with what it means to be 'literate' in our society (New London Group, 1996; Prestridge, 2005).

New social technologies have altered the underlying architecture of how many people communicate. Despite this fact, many conservative educators view social technologies in a negative way and fail to let go of pre-existing assumptions about how the world works (boyd, 2007). Education needs to reflect the way in which technologies are used beyond the walls of educational institutions to ensure that teaching and learning genuinely prepare pupils for the future so that they can think critically about the ways technologies are shaping our society and social relationships (Lankshear & Knobel, 2006; New London Group, 1996; O'Rourke, 2001). Such a shift ensures that pupils can become active and participatory citizens in a world with constantly evolving communicative architectures.

In this chapter I therefore explore the implications of social networking technologies on children's literate lives and the resulting implications for education. My aim is to explore the context in which these systems are embedded in our society and then move onto how educators may wish to address this issue. First, I briefly outline some of the theoretical standpoints about social media in education and then move onto a case study of the way I have used Twitter as a social networking system for documenting and reflecting on learning with my Year 2 class.

WEB 2.0 AND POPULAR CULTURE

Barton (2007) suggests that different literacies are associated with different domains of life such as home, school, and work. Within such domains people act and use language differently (Barton, 2007: 39). Pahl and Rowsell suggest:

> There is a clear gap between the way we are teaching reading and writing in school and the sophisticated set of practices students use outside school. Covering language as a skill in the curriculum speaks to a fraction of the skills children actually make meaning in the world. (2005: 3)

This suggests that there is a mismatch between the diverse domains children move within and the schooled curriculum. Millard (2003) suggests that such literacy practices are implicated in popular culture through multiple representations as disparate cultures meet and co-mingle. The New London Group (1996) promotes the need to adapt pedagogy to take account of the cultural differences and the fluidity of movement between multimodal representations and literacy. The education system therefore has the responsibility to provide children with the skills and understanding necessary for interpreting the constructed nature of popular culture (Merchant, 2007: 15). However, the pedagogization of literacy sometimes means that this is not the case and literacy is presented as a discrete set of skills to be mastered, regardless of culture or context (Street, 1997; Pahl & Rowsell, 2005).

SOCIAL NETWORKING SITES

Platforms such as blogs, wikis, and instant messengers have allowed international construction of discussion, debate, and collaboration across cultures (Alexander, 2008). Social network sites (SNS) such as Facebook and Myspace allow users to present themselves, articulate their social networks, and establish connections with others within different contexts (Ellison, Steinfield, & Lampe, 2007). boyd and Ellison define SNS as:

> Web-based services that allow individuals to (1) construct a public profile or semi-public profile within a bounded system, (2) articulate a list of other users within whom they share a connection, and (3) view and traverse their list of connections and those made by others within the system. (2008: 221)

In this sense literacy practices are encoded in the construction of personal profiles and forging of friendship links across the social networks. However, the symbol systems within online social networks are highly complex in contrast to unitary symbol systems like alphabetic print. SNS employ a mix of symbol systems and modes rendered seamless in digital code (Lankshear & Knobel, 2008: 256).

Ellison et al. (2007) and boyd and Ellison (2008) suggest that social networks such as Facebook are unique in the sense that they are used primarily not to meet strangers, but rather enable users to articulate and publish their existing social networks. As boyd (2007) suggests:

> People join the sites with their friends and use the different messaging tools to hang out, share cultural artefacts and ideas, and communicate with one another. (2007: 2)

Within such a fluid and dynamic space the interface between audio, visual, and print technology constantly shifts (Millard, 2003). The audience therefore decides which media better gratify their needs and motives when creating discourses (Lee & Lee, 2010: 716). It is also evident that social networking systems can become embedded in participants' lives. Ellison et al. (2007) report that in their sample members of Facebook, users spent between 10 and 30 minutes each day on Facebook.

As a result of their popularity, new social networks continue to be developed and used by different communities. One such SNS that has received an influx in media attention is Twitter. This SNS takes a different approach to other, more established networks since it limits communication to 140 characters. This has led to the term 'micro-blogging,' in which users create a limited profile and begin sending short messages known as tweets (Galagan, 2009: 28). Twitter incorporates the direct friendship model of choosing accounts to 'follow' and receiving 'followers' in return in a similar nature to Facebook. It also borrows features from blogging platforms in that it allows dynamic, interactive identity presentation to unknown audiences through ongoing tweets and conversations with others, rather than static profiles. It is through the ongoing tweets that self-presentation takes place on Twitter (Marwick & boyd, 2010: 3). Individuals work together within the SNS to uphold preferred self-images and collectively encourage group dynamics and social norms. A large proportion of Twitter accounts are available for any Internet user to see (without a Twitter account); hence there is a potential disconnect between followers and audience (Marwick & boyd, 2010). This contrasts with Facebook, where the audience is more precise and articulated by the user. The wide and unknown audience ultimately affects the content of tweets. As Goffman (1959, cited by Marwick & boyd, 2010: 10) suggests, within any situation people navigate 'frontstage' and 'backstage' areas. While Facebook could be seen as the 'backstage,' where existing offline ties are strengthened (Ellison et al., 2007), Twitter can be seen as the 'frontstage,' with self-censorship used in the face of an imagined audience that includes parents, employees, and significant others. Tweets are therefore formulated based partially on a social context constructed from the tweets of the people a user follows (Marwick & boyd, 2010). This has therefore led to the creation of niche networks operating within the Twitter social networking system with the careful selection of followed users. Such networks link with Gee's (2004) concept of affinity spaces, where various members of the network adopt particular roles according to their interests and experiences within the online network. Such affinities can, for example, support teachers in their own professional development where skills are developed through collaborative debate, discussion, and activities. It is therefore evident that literacy is embodied in the constructions and interactions of users of the site (Waller, 2010: 14).

MORAL PANICS, E-SAFETY, AND SCHOOLING

The rise of social networking systems such as Facebook and Bebo has attracted increased scrutiny from the press and privacy advocates, primarily focused on the safety of school-aged users (boyd & Ellison, 2008; Rose, 2010). As Davies and Merchant (2009) suggest:

> Much of the moral panic around new media focuses on the idea that they distract the attention of children and young people from engaging with print literacy practices and are a causal factor in falling standards in literacy in schools. (2009: 111)

However, there is little evidence to suggest that children's reading of print has actually declined when using digital technologies (Buckingham, 2002: 8). boyd (2007) also suggests that a large proportion of adults are panicking and simply do not understand the shifts in terms of the changing communication landscape. Furthermore parents are sometimes anxious about the online networks they believe their children are participating in, which may also be coupled with insecurities about a 'digital divide' in knowledge and understanding. They may also have a different mindset in comparison to how their children view the Internet and digital technologies (Lankshear & Knobel, 2006). What is clear is that just like the offline world there are dangers and risks that cannot be completely eliminated (Byron, 2008). boyd (2007) also suggests that if a teen is engaged in risky behavior online then it is typically a sign that they are engaged in risky behavior offline. She argues that the technology is too often blamed for what it reveals and suggests destroying the technology will not solve the underlying problems that are made visible through mediated spaces like SNS (boyd, 2007: 5). In contrast Rose (2010) highlights that a common problem with social media such as SNS is that there is the tendency to 'over-share' information, such as their exact location. He suggests that:

> Sharing location-based information just means there is another layer of personal information exposed which, in most cases, is not really necessary. (Rose, 2010: 810)

Despite this, location-based social networks such as Foursquare have seen membership rise significantly in recent months (Beaumont, 2010). Such services allow users to 'check-in' at certain locations and gain experience points and badges as well as the title of 'Mayor' if they check-in most frequently at a particular venue. This location-based news stream is posted onto the Foursquare website for any user of the SNS to read. This essentially creates an online digital footprint of a user's offline activities and, as Rose (2010) suggests, is seen by many as unnecessary. However, Davies and Merchant (2009: 112) suggest that real experiences of Web 2.0 technology within the education system are likely to be more effective than applying blocks, filters, and other controls. Embedding a Web 2.0 system into the everyday practices would allow pupils the opportunity to learn safe practices within online mediated spaces within a real and meaningful context. Despite this fact, all of the previous research studies cited in this chapter have focused primarily on the use of SNS in home settings as opposed to the classroom. While research such as Dowdall's (2006) has demonstrated that social networks have blurred the boundaries between online and offline social practices, there are very few models of practice to suggest how online social networks can be integrated in a meaningful and relevant way into classrooms.

SOCIAL NETWORKS IN THE CLASSROOM

As well as privacy fears, one of the barriers to the implementation of SNS systems within education systems is that the emergence of Web 2.0 coincided with the adoption of course management systems (CMS) also known as virtual learning environments (VLEs) and commonly referred to as learning platforms in the United Kingdom (Alexander, 2008: 157). While Web 2.0 systems promote social participation and publication on a global scale (Davies & Merchant, 2009), VLEs are primarily closed systems with inbound links blocked and communication usually restricted to single class instances (Alexander, 2008). Alexander also asks this important question:

> How does one maintain conversations on either side of a password barrier? (2008: 158)

While boyd (2007), Ellison et al. (2007), and boyd and Ellison (2008) have argued that one of the most prominent aspects of identity construction within Web 2.0 systems is the creation of friendship links, profiles, and the creation of discourses, it is difficult to see how a VLE could develop literacies more effectively than a Web 2.0 service such as an SNS. Marsh (2010) argues that using SNS in classrooms provides a context for reading through the construction of social networks where knowledge is co-constructed and distributed through social practices (29). This has significant challenges for educators who are trying to provide real-world opportunities for children to engage in meaningful literacy practices. While privacy advocates (Rose, 2010) argue the case against social networks in any setting and local education authorities promote VLEs, implementing any open Web 2.0 system becomes problematic, despite the cited benefits. However, some educators are working with their children to experiment with SNS in their classrooms. I have previously documented how I have used Twitter with my Year 2 class at the beginning of the project (Waller, 2010, 2011). I am now able to reflect more fully on the benefits and implications of embedding such Web 2.0 systems into the culture of my classroom.

TWITTER IN THE PRIMARY CLASSROOM

Many of the children in my class had an awareness of SNS from their experiences of using it at home. In their home uses of SNS the children used a range of multimodal forms of representation such as interactive games and some limited use of hypertext. They could still be described as emergent literacy learners because their experience of literacy was through playful activities rather than regimented experiences, which focused on traditional writing skills with pen and paper. This is a contrast to the way many children traditionally experience literacy in schools (Millard, 2003). As such I was keen to build on the children's experience of multimodal and digital literacies to support them in developing safe practices with new technologies.

Twitter is quick, free, and easy to join using an email address and password to create a unique username. When a user account is set up, this is represented through an online profile from which you tweet. This profile can be minimalistic and does not need to include detailed information. Other users then choose to follow your account and vice versa, which means that online ties are developed through a direct friendship model. In addition you can set two levels of privacy so that your tweets are either open for all to see or private so that only those who you approve may view. The SNS simply asks "What's happening?" and allows only 140 characters to be typed as a "tweet." This offered the ideal rubric for emerging writers to engage in text creation. From experience I have found that young learners find a page of blank paper very daunting when beginning to write, whereas a small box with a 140-character limit is less so. I set up a single anonymous account (@ClassroomTweets) for the children to use from the classroom computer. This meant that children's identities would not be exposed and privacy issues could be addressed. Furthermore, as the account was set to 'private' Twitter allowed me to approve followers to our online social network before they could view any tweets from the account.

I decided that adults would not correct the children's spelling. Since self-presentation on Twitter is created through tweets, it would be inappropriate for an adult to intervene in this process and I wanted the children's tweets to express their own literate identity. However, this did not deter the children from asking for support from their peers, or indeed from adults within the classroom. Marsh (2010) suggests that:

> Reading in this context means not simply decoding, but involves the taking part in the construction of social networks in which knowledge is co-constructed and distributed. (Marsh, 2010: 29)

Within this context the children feel comfortable at experimenting with language meaning-making, the stigma of getting something wrong is removed, and the encouragement the children receive when tweeting from their peers promotes a culture of collaboration and reflection (Waller, 2011). Indeed, our profile clearly states that we use Twitter to document, share, and reflect on our learning and the children's tweets clearly reflect this. As Gee (1996) suggests such discourses can always be traced back to the identity of the author and the context in which they were created.

I am little.I have courls like a parrot. What am i?
10.33 AM Apr 28ᵗʰ via blu

I am smaller than your hand but bigger than a tiny seed. The famers hate it when I go and eat there cabbige. I start of like an agg

Figure 8.1   Butterfly riddle (Waller, 2011: 101).

It is evident that children like to share their work, experiences, and interests with any audience. Twitter in this sense allows the children to project their interests to a dynamic and global audience and engage in powerful writing, driven by the potency of immediate publication (Davies, 2006: 60). The children are not fully aware of who their audience actually is but they have created their own imagined audience (boyd, 2007). Such an audience is ambiguous (but still exists) and different children choose to use Twitter in different ways and share different information with their audience. For example, some children enjoy demonstrating their understanding of topics covered in class to solidify their understanding and receive feedback from the social network (Waller, 2010).

In the foregoing two tweets (Figure 8.1), one of the children, after learning about riddles in class, decided to tweet a new riddle onto the Twitter stream to demonstrate his or her understanding. The fact that the child used two tweets shows that the 140-character limit does not hinder the child's meaning-making as he or she simply creates a second tweet and follows the conventions of the SNS. Furthermore, the child is reaching out to the social network and the imagined audience to answer the riddle, which would subsequently demonstrate the effectiveness of the work. As a result the child received many responses, most of which included the correct answer to the riddle. Twitter in this context allows the child not only to communicate with a community that extends beyond the classroom walls but also to share and celebrate his or her own learning and understanding (Waller, 2010).

Other children in the class chose to tweet about areas that interested them. Such areas link directly to the children's popular culture and show that their own interests are embedded within the school day. For example, Figure 8.2 includes a tweet from a child who enjoys collecting 'Match Attaxs' football stickers.

we have been swapted match attaxs
Tue May 18 2010 09:00:04 (BST) via blu

Figure 8.2   Swapping stickers.

Such a tweet demonstrates not only the literacy identity of the child but also his or her interests, priorities, and social participation within offline social networks. Such practices of communicating and exchanging football cards are integral in the child's life and the child has used the social network to further thicken offline practices (boyd, 2007) and communicate aspects of his or her own popular culture to the imagined audience. This links with the work of Dowdall (2006), who suggests that real and digital spaces can be mutually dependent upon one another.

As the children continued to tweet about their work, interests, and popular cultures they began to receive replies to their writing. Audience participation works on many levels, with most followers choosing to simply read the children's Twitter stream. However, while using Twitter the children developed a network within their imagined audience, which included people with whom they communicated on a regular basis and whom the children class as online 'friends' (Waller, 2011). The children chose to communicate with such followers and in this sense were shaping and creating their own personal network—a model many users of Twitter choose to adopt. As I was able to connect some of our followers outside the Twitter network (through professional contacts), it was possible to invite some of the contacts into our classroom to meet the children. This helped them to experience the power of written texts and meant that online ties have been thickened with offline visits to our classroom. Figure 8.3 shows an adult's tweet about her visit to the classroom.

This is a contrast to the model Ellison et al. (2007) suggest, in which online social networks thicken existing offline ties, as in this case the online SNS has instigated and facilitated social ties in the real world as well as simply thickening offline ties (boyd, 2007).

Some of the members of the children's social network chose to interact with them to begin a dialogue to facilitate the development of their literacy skills. For example, in Figure 8.4 one of the followers has asked the children what the weather is like. However, from the children's previous tweets they recall that they have been learning about describing words in their writing. Hence, the follower decided to include detailed descriptions in his or her tweets.

The children were then able to respond to the tweet and share information with a member of their network who lives in a different country. This exchange not only helped the children with their learning but also meant that the follower enjoyed the interaction too. Other followers took

> Spent a lovely afternoon with Mr Waller and @ClassroomTweets. Came back with lots of veg for my tea! Worth a follow on Twitter.

Figure 8.3   Visitor's tweet.

Good Morning @classroomtweets! I am in Madrid, Spain and it's a very
warm, sunny, blue-sky day here! What is your weather like today?
11:00 AM Apr 26th via web

Figure 8.4   Holiday message from a class friend (Waller, 2011: 102).

an interest in the children's work by asking them to describe and elaborate
on their learning. In Figure 8.5 one of our followers has used the convention of beginning a message with the '@' symbol before our username to
show they are responding to a tweet about finding a treasure chest.

Such a response can be classed as a literacy event (Heath, 1983) as it
instigated a discussion as to what words such as 'ancient' actually meant
and what Roman remains were. The fact that the follower also prompted
the children to 'Tell me more' led to the children creating a more detailed
account, which was emailed to the follower. The children understood that
Twitter was not the best medium to send a more detailed reply and that an
email was more appropriate (Waller, 2011). This experience also helped
facilitate the understanding that system and choice of modes require consideration of audience and purpose (Kress, 2003). Such exchanges with
members of the children's social network not only involved social participation but also exemplified what Marsh (2010) suggests:

> Reading is, in this example, a social practice that extends beyond the
> walls of the classroom and enables children to engage in forums in
> which inter-generational literacy is commonplace. (30)

Within this context children are not patronized or treated as inferior to
the adults in their social network; rather they are recognized as interlocutors in genuine communication and information exchange. There is mutual
respect between the children and their followers (for example, see Figure
8.3). Furthermore when the children engage in conversation with such users
to exchange ideas it mirrors the uses of technology they will encounter in
both leisure and employment in future years (Marsh, 2010: 30). This links
with Street's (1984) ideological view of literacy, in which meaning-making
is situated within a context of cultural values and practices of society.

@ClassroomTweets How exciting about that treasure chest. I live on an

ancient mound which people think has Roman remains. Tell me more

Figure 8.5   A reply from a @ClassroomTweets follower (Waller, 2011: 102).

@ClassroomTweets great fish! Can you twitpic one of your drawings?

1:56 PM Oct 14th from web in reply to ClassroomTweets

Figure 8.6   A response to children's work (Waller, 2010: 16).

Twitter was also instrumental in developing other practices with digital technologies. For example, when the children were learning how to draw pictures of fish in a lesson they tweeted about the activity and received the following reply (shown in Figure 8.6).

This literacy event (Heath, 1983) led to the children taking a photograph of one of their drawings, uploading it to the Twitpic service (http://www.twitpic.com) and then adding it to the Twitter stream. Twitpic can be described as a wrap-around service to Twitter that allows users to upload pictures, which are linked to their Twitter account and then automatically published within their Twitter stream.

They then received feedback on their learning from the original tweeter:

This exchange not only engaged the children in their work and allowed them to share it with a global audience, but also allowed the children develop digital literacy skills linked to photography and uploading of content to the Internet. This was an authentic assessment practice where the children demonstrated that they had met the objectives and received feedback from an independent user. It was also exciting and engaging for the children as they were keen to read the follower's response.

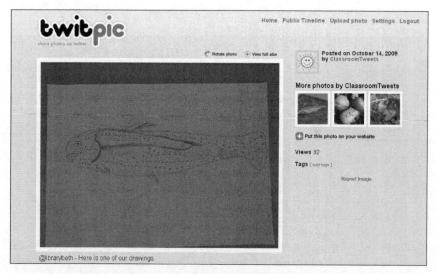

Figure 8.7   A screenshot from TwitPic (Waller, 2010: 16).

> @ClassroomTweets what a wonderful drawing! I love all the spots. Thank you for sharing that with me! Your tweets make me smile.
>
> 2:17 PM Oct 14th from web in reply to ClassroomTweets

Figure 8.8   Response to children's drawing (Waller, 2010: 16).

E-SAFETY ISSUES

Since e-safety and privacy have been highlighted as issues regarding young people's use of online social networks (Rose, 2010), this was carefully considered before Twitter was used with the children. The fact that Twitter is open and accessible to anybody with an Internet connection means that the safety implications and rules needed to be addressed with the children. We discussed these in an open and contextually driven manner (Davies & Merchant, 2009), with the children realizing why such precautions were needed when they started using the SNS. Three primary rules (Waller, 2010) were discussed with the children:

1. Children must not mention their names or any of their friends by name in tweets under any circumstances.
2. Children must not check for replies or messages (this prevents the possibility of them seeing any inappropriate material that may be viewable).
3. Children must not navigate away from our Twitter stream page and look at other people's profiles (in case of inappropriate content or language use).

As these rules were discussed in the context of real-world use with the children, they have always been followed. The children know the e-safety implications of not following them. Replies are always checked by adults before they are discussed with the children as there is always the possibility of inappropriate messages being sent due to the open nature of Twitter (Waller, 2010). As a result children are not able to engage in 'private' discussion with any members of the social networking system.

IMPLICATIONS

Web 2.0 systems and social networking sites such as Twitter and Facebook have fundamentally changed areas of social participation and communication. Such systems have been primarily used in personal domains and used as a means to thicken offline ties (Dowdall, 2006; boyd, 2007; Ellison et al., 2007).

The use of Twitter in the foregoing case study with Year 2 children does not necessarily reflect the way the children may choose to use such systems in the real world. The children did not create their own profiles, use their real names, or engage in 'private' discussions. However, through a managed and controlled environment the children are able to learn the competencies of such multimodal social media platforms in a meaningful and collaborative way. As such the children realized that there was a certain amount of structuring during the project in the sense that some of the interactions were managed by myself but were still authentic and spontaneous. Furthermore since good practice in relation to privacy and e-safety is embedded in the approach to using the SNS, children learn such skills in context—rather than through the consequences of moral panics (Davies & Merchant, 2009). In addition, such use of online social networks allows the children to experience literacy through collaboration and communication with participants from across the globe. Such experiences reflect the way that meaning is made in the real-world world, as opposed to the 'bubble' of a classroom, and reflect the ethos of ideological literacy (Street, 1984).

CONCLUSIONS

It is clear that digital technologies such as social networking systems have fundamentally changed the way we communicate in the world. It is also evident that such technologies will continue to feature in more areas of life, becoming even more closely interwoven with the way we get things done (Merchant, 2007: 126). The increasing convergence of media across multiple channels and networks presents a unique challenge to educators required to address such competencies and multiple literacies (Buckingham, 2002: 12). Street (1997) suggests that language and literacy should be studied as they occur naturally in everyday life and take account of context. However, new literacy practices in the classroom contrast with the educational routines of predefined classroom literacy routines, as well as with the dominant ICT pedagogies that often support the maintenance of teacher control (Davies & Merchant, 2009). Social networking systems that enable users to create, collaborate, and shape identities and networks online are now embedded in children's lives (Dowdall, 2006; boyd, 2007: Ellison et al., 2007). Such online activity encourages children to contribute rather than merely consume. However, this is often denied to them in school (Buckingham, 2002: 15).

As Davies and Merchant (2009) suggest, embedding Web 2.0 practices in school involves a focused look at how different kinds of services relate to educational objectives. However, moral panic over privacy concerns and online predators (Rose, 2010) creates a dissonance between education and Web 2.0 technologies. Such factors have resulted in many schools choosing to embed VLEs, which are closed systems where users cannot construct an audience. As Davies and Merchant (2009) suggest, teachers have sometimes found it difficult to create a relevant audience for whom their children can write and VLEs further complicate this matter. While Facebook or Twitter users do not know explicitly who makes up their audience, they have a mental picture of who they are writing or speaking to—the audience evoked (Marwick & boyd, 2010). Projects such as @ClassroomTweets, explored in this chapter, show that meaningful engagement in the construction of social networks can support children in their literacy development. Furthermore such SNSs support both the maintenance of existing social ties and the formation of new connections through the active co-construction of social networks (Ellison et al., 2007; Marsh, 2010).

The use of online social networks also supports an understanding of how different discourses can be constructed and how these are created effectively by means of various modes and meaning-making systems (Gee, 1996; Kress, 2003; Lankshear & Knobel, 2006). At a time when many educators are concerned about a so-called digital divide (Lankshear & Knobel, 2006) some simply choose to ignore such systems and hope they will disappear (boyd, 2007: 1). However, it is foolish and misguided to think that such meaning-making systems, which are becoming part and parcel of everyday life for many people, can be ignored in the education system. Teachers need to work with their classes to develop a critical understanding of how appropriate practice within such networks can be developed in classroom contexts. Getting the detail right is essential if educators are to help children develop a critical understanding of communication and meaning-making in our society. Social networking systems are developing at a critical pace and are here to stay. It is now time for educators to harness such technology in meaningful ways before the "awesome disconnect" (Genishi & Dyson, 2009: 4) between home and school widens further.

REFERENCES

Alexander, B. (2008). Web 2.0 and emergent multiliteracies. *Theory into Practice* 47(2): 150–160.

Barton, D. (2007). *Literacy: An Introduction to the Ecology of Written Language.* Oxford: Blackwell.

Beaumont, C. (2010). Foursquare enjoys surge in popularity. *The Guardian.* February 5. Retrieved August 29, 2010 from http://www.telegraph.co.uk/technology/social-media/7165699/Foursquare-enjoys-surge-of-popularity.html.

boyd, d. (2007). Social network sites: Public, private, or what? *Knowledge Tree* 13(May). Retrieved May 19, 2012 from http://www.danah.org/papers/KnowledgeTree.pdf.

boyd, d. & Ellison, N. (2008). Social network sites, definition, history, and scholarship. *Journal of Computer-Mediated Communication* 13: 210–230.

Buckingham, D. (2002). New media literacies: Informal learning, digital technologies and education. In D. Buckingham & A. McFarlane (eds.), *A Digitally Driven Curriculum?* London: IPPR. Retrieved May 19, 2012 from http://www.ippr.org/uploadedFiles/projects/digital_curriculum.pdf.

Byron, T. (2008). *The Byron Review: Safer Children in a Digital World*. Nottingham: Department for Children, Schools and Families and Department for Culture, Media and Sport.

Davies, J. (2006). Escaping to the borderlands: An exploration of the Internet as cultural space for teenage Wiccan girls. In K. Pahl & J. Rowsell (eds.), *Travel Notes from the New Literacy Studies: Instances of Practice*. Clevedon, UK: Multilingual Matters.

Davies, J. & Merchant, G. (2009). *Web 2.0 for Schools: Learning and Social Participation*. New York: Peter Lang.

Donath, J. & boyd, d. (2004). Public displays of connection. *BT Technology Journal* 22(4): 71–82.

Dowdall, C. (2006). Dissonance between the digital created worlds of school and home. *Literacy* 40(3): 153–163.

Ellison, N., Steinfield, C., & Lampe, C. (2007). The benefits of Facebook "friends": Social capital and college students' use of online social network sites. *Journal of Computer-Mediated Communication* 12(4): 1143–1168.

Galagan, P. (2009). Twitter as a learning tool. Really. *American Society for Training & Development* 63(2): 28–31.

Gee, J. P. (2004). *Situated Language and Learning: A Critique of Traditional Schooling*. London: Routledge.

Gee, J. P. (1996). *Social Linguistics and Literacies: Ideology in Discourses* (2nd ed.). London: Taylor Francis.

Genishi, C. & Dyson, A. H. (2009). *Children, Language and Literacy*. New York: Teachers College Press.

Heath, S. B. (1983). *Ways with Words: Language, Life, and Work in Communities and Classrooms*. Cambridge, UK: Cambridge University Press.

Kress, G. (2003). *Literacy in the New Media Age*. London: Routledge.

Lankshear, C. & Knobel, M. (2008). Digital literacy and participation in online social networking spaces. In C. Lankshear & M. Knobel (eds.), *Digital Literacies: Concepts, Policies and Practices*. New York: Peter Lang.

Lankshear, C. & Knobel, M. (2006). *New Literacies: Everyday Practices and Classroom Learning* (2nd ed.). Maidenhead, UK: Open University Press.

Lee, J. & Lee, H. (2010). The computer-mediated communication network: Exploring the linkage between the online community and social capital. *New Media & Society* 12(5): 711–727.

Marsh, J. (2010). The ghosts of reading past, present and future: The materiality of reading in homes and schools. In K. Hall, U. Goswami, C. Harrison, S. Ellis, & J. Soler (eds.), *Interdisciplinary Perspectives on Learning to Read: Culture, Cognition and Pedagogy*. Abingdon, UK: Routledge.

Marwick, A. E. & boyd, d. (2010). I tweet honestly, I tweet passionately: Twitter users, context collapse, and the imagined audience. *New Media & Society* (Online Early Edtion): 1–20: 13(1): 114-133.

Merchant, G. (2007). Writing the future in the digital age. *Literacy* 41(3): 118–128.

Millard, E. (2003). Towards a literacy of fusion: New times, new teaching and learning. *Reading, Literacy and Language* 37(1): 3–8.

New London Group (1996). A pedagogy of multiliteracies: Designing social futures. *Harvard Educational Review* 66(1): 60–92.

O'Rourke, M. (2001). Engaging students through ICT: A multiliteracies approach. *Teacher Learning Network Journal: Change, Growth and Innovation* 8(3): 12–13.

Pahl, K. & Rowsell, J. (2005). *Literacy and Education: Understanding New Literacies in the Classroom*. London: Paul Chapman.

Prestridge, S. (2005). Exploring the relationship between multiliteracies and ICT. Paper presented at the Pleasure, Passion, Provocation AATE/ALEA National Conference, Gold Coast Convention and Exhibition Centre, Brisbane, Australia.

Rose, C. (2010). The security implications of ubiquitous social media. Paper presented at the 2010 EABR & ETLC Conference. Dublin, Ireland. Retrieved August 28, 2010 from http://www.cluteinstitute.com/proceedings/2010_Dublin_EABR_Articles/Article%20535.pdf.

Street, B. (1997). The implications of the New Literacy Studies for education. *English in Education* 31(3): 45–59.

Street, B. (1984). *Literacy in Theory and Practice.* Cambridge, England: Cambridge University Press.

Waller, M. (2011). 'Everyone in the world can see it'—Developing pupil voice through online social networks. In G. Czerniawsku & W. Kidd (eds.), *The Student Voice Handbook: Bridging the Academic/Practitioner Divide.* London: Emerald.

Waller, M. (2010). It's very very fun and ecsting—Using Twitter in the primary classroom. *English Four to Eleven* 39: 14–16.

9 Children as Game Designers
New Narrative Opportunities

Cathrin Howells and Judy Robertson

INTRODUCTION

We are in a period of significant change in terms of writing; the supremacy of the written word for communication, which has held sway for centuries, is being challenged by multimodal forms of text, in particular the visual (Kress, 2003, Lankshear & Knobel, 2006, Jewitt, 2008). Children are surrounded by images that convey meaning in often powerful ways, ways that can complement words but that can also go beyond words, carrying their own meanings, meanings that are more open to interpretation. These images are strongly rooted in the cultures of the young, often produced, received, and exchanged by electronic means, making them less accessible to the older, more traditionally (typographic) text-orientated generation. The meaning-making processes that children use when working with new texts may also be less familiar to adults. Texts are more fluid and interwoven, and boundaries and roles begin to blur as digital opportunities facilitate collaboration and textual change (Merchant, 2009). Children often multitask with onscreen texts—several screens will be open at once, full of images as well as words, both moving and still; messaging flows alongside looking, reading, scrolling, hyperlinking, selecting, assembling, and creating new texts. The nature of composition has already changed from almost exclusively a process largely dependent on generating new typographic text from scratch, often emulating recognizable forms and formats, to the widespread practice of synthesis, fashioning text from words, images, and sounds from a variety of sources in a fluid and playful fashion. As new technologies emerge, so do new possibilities for communication; new composition practices and products evolve and our understandings of what constitutes 'text' must grow. A challenge for educators is to keep pace with learners as they increasingly draw on their own social (electronic) contexts for 'textual' inspiration.

Such challenges have been noted before. Kress (2000: 183) states that "we . . . find ourselves singularly ill-equipped in the new landscape of communication" (Kress, 2000;183) but Pahl and Rowsell (2005: 41) warn that "We cannot afford to ignore the communicational landscape our students find themselves in. If we harness it and tie it to literacy learning, its potential is huge . . . It is our challenge to capture its flows and ebbs, and to develop a dialogue with our students . . ." (Pahl & Rowsell, 2005: 41) And Jewitt (2008: 9) urges that it is necessary to reconceptualize literacy within education in the light of a strong "turn to the visual." To some degree, the new Curriculum for Excellence in Scotland (Education Scotland, 2010a) has responded to this twenty-first-century challenge in the literacy and English guidelines: "The definition of 'texts' also needs to be broad and future proof. Within the Curriculum for Excellence, a text is the medium through which ideas, experiences, opinions and information can be communicated" (Education Scotland, 2010a: 4). This is echoed in the technology curriculum (Education Scotland, 2010b), which specifies that children should become confident users of technology now and in the future, becoming informed users and producers; the outcomes expect the complex new media authoring task of game design to be part of the classroom experience at upper primary and lower secondary levels. These values to provide a relevant curriculum are also enshrined in the aims and values of the national curriculum in England (DfE, 2011).

Given these forward-looking aims, and the challenges that teachers face in implementing them in everyday classroom life, we argue that we need to better understand the literacy opportunities afforded by new media authoring environments. Further, we need to identify successful strategies that learners may use to create communicative artifacts that are of value to themselves, their teachers, and their peers. Pahl and Rowsell (2005) comment that in fact where new media is concerned, teachers should be prepared to learn from children, who may have different ways of knowing.

Our contribution in this chapter is to investigate one new media example: fictional, narrative, interactive, immersive 3D multimodal game texts created through computer game authoring. This is a challenging medium that offers learners powerful new opportunities to explore 3D spatial design as a method of telling stories. We make particular reference to how aspects of this medium extend Kress's notion of reading pathways, the routes that a reader will take through any text, be it conventional or multimodal (Kress & van Leeuwen, 2006). We also consider the role of new 'writing' elements we call 'story locations' and 'narrative vehicles.' This medium challenges learners by asking them to develop new techniques for conveying the story to the reader using largely the visual and spatial design of the storyworld, with typographic text playing only one part in the process of creating plot elements. The order in which players then encounter these plot elements depends on how they choose to explore the 3D spatial world. The choices players make will also alter their experience of the story, and the author must anticipate this.

As with any rapidly developing medium, it is hard to find an accessible source of practical knowledge on the authoring process that could apply to young learners. Indeed, Marsh and Singleton (2009) note that we are only just beginning to understand what virtual worlds of this kind might mean for literacy practices. We take advantage of the fact that young learners may in fact be more experienced consumers of new media than adults; our approach here is to analyze some strategies used by learners who have used game authoring tools to tell stories during a six-week classroom-based field study. Based on examination of the authoring process used by learners who appear to have a natural talent for making games, compared with those learners who were less successful, we can identify ways of working that may be useful to other learners in the future.

CREATIVITY IN WRITING

Grainger et al. (2005) stipulate that literacy learning should be highly motivating and interactive and build on the social context of learners. Sharples (1999) conceptualizes writing as a creative design process, while Kress (2003) talks of the concept of competence in language use giving way to that of interested design (Kress, 2003; 169). He suggests an approach to text creation that encourages and normalizes 'design' of text and views innovation and creativity as the norm that will equip learners and their teachers to respond to constant changes in media. Kress considers creativity an automatic consequence of a design-based approach to message creation: "Creativity becomes normal and unremarkable in every instance of sign-making" (Kress, 2003: 169). Grainger et al. agree that creativity has to be central to the writing process, facilitating not only children's growth as writers but also their self-esteem (Grainger et al., 2005: 13).

Kress foresees a new and more prominent role for imagination in literacy practices. He suggests that competence in one mode, with little place for imagination, will be replaced by the much more demanding tasks of "selection, arrangement and transformation, involving many modes, in always new environments, with their always changing demands" (Kress, 2003: 171). Grainger et al. (2005: 23) also stress the importance of imaginative and creative contexts for writing: "A creative context implies an environment of possibility, which offers choice and encourages children to experiment with ideas, take intellectual risks and find innovative ways forward with speech and writing. Such an environment is both supportive and challenging although is not without frames of reference."

NEW FORMS OF TEXT

Alphabetic text is rapidly becoming less dominant under the increasing influence of both the still and the moving image and the multimodal texts (employing pictures, sound, movement, color, texture) are becoming the norm (Kress, 2003; Lankshear & Knobel, 2006; Jewitt, 2008). In such texts, each mode influences the other and the result is often multilayered in meaning and non-linear in nature with the screen rather than the page providing the canvas (Kress, 2003, Merchant 2007). Such texts are certainly suitable vehicles for Kress's idea of 'interested design' and the 'future-proof' twenty-first-century texts of the *Curriculum for Excellence* (Education Scotland, 2010a). Both the reading and the writing of multimodal texts differ from the requirements for conventional texts.

Alphabetic, conventional text has a temporal, sequential logic, whereas the logic of image is spatial and simultaneous (Kress, 2003). In multimodal texts, the sequential and the spatial exist side by side and "the images often communicate different things from the words. And the combination of the two modes communicates things that neither of the modes does separately" (Gee, 2003: 14). No one mode carries the full meaning and children will experiment to create "a 'multimodally' conceived text, a semiotic play in which each mode, the verbal and the visual, is given a defined and equal role to play." (Gee, 2003: 19) (Kress & van Leeuwen, 2006: 113)

Kress stresses the importance of 'reading pathways,' the routes that a reader will take through any text, be it conventional or multimodal. These pathways are signposted and scaffolded to varying degrees, ranging from the provision of a firm hand to guide the reader (typical of conventional texts) to a few hints and suggestions (the semi-linear text) to texts where no one pathway is any more plausible than any other (Kress & van Leeuwen, 2006). In the medium of 3D computer games, on which this paper focuses, the reading pathways become far more complex and unpredictable than in a 2D text, not least because the reader (player) has the facility to take a 360-degree view of the world he or she is exploring, and is free to make many open-ended choices.

THE COMPUTER GAME AS TEXT

Compared with other multimodal texts, computer games offer added complexity for both designer and player, including the challenge that the player (anticipated by the designer) can move around inside the world of the text and experience it from more than one visual, spatial, and textual perspective. Other studies, including several reported in this book, have explored the potential literacy development benefits for players who take part in virtual worlds; this chapter moves beyond this to focus on the literacy opportunities for learners when they design their own games. From this point in the text we use the term 'designer' to refer to the learner who is creating a game, a role similar to that of the writer in conventional texts. The term 'player' is used to describe the role of the person who takes part in the game produced by the designer. This role encompasses the role of the reader of a conventional text.

Further, it is perhaps useful to mention that while previous researchers have made much of the conflict between narrative and gameplay, this theoretical debate does not have much bearing on the current discussion, as we are deliberately focusing on games authoring as a way of developing storytelling skills at the expense of developing skills in designing game mechanics.

Both game design and the playing of the finished game offer a highly interactive, spatial, and open-ended creative experience. The designer of the computer game must consider the creation and appearance of the world, the telling of the story, and the management of the player; the concept of salience (Kress & Van Leeuwen, 2006) is relevant here. Personal and cultural preferences come in to play as children decide where and how to place the key elements of their design and consider how to attract the player's attention to them and so to possible pathways through the 3D text. However, what might be salient to the designer is by no means guaranteed to carry the *same* weight of meaning for the player. Kress's more recent work acknowledges the need to reconsider the notion of reading pathways in its traditional form for digital texts, introducing the concept of 'reading as design': "The reader's interest determines how she or he will engage with the page and establishes the order in which its elements are 'read.' It is the reader's interest which provides the *design* of this page in that respect" (Kress, 2010: 175).

These texts, which are decidedly complex in nature, create new challenges for both designer and player, not to mention the teaching profession; they provide the opportunity to see new behaviors and techniques at work, including 'reading as design,' and make us think again about what 'creative writing' can mean.

INTERACTIVE GAME AUTHORING

Software for Game Creation

Adventure Author is a computer game authoring tool for children aged 10–14, developed at Heriot-Watt University with the goals of promoting literacy and creativity (Robertson & Howells, 2008). It is based on the commercially available Neverwinter Nights 2 (NWN2) game authoring software, which provides a toolset allowing children to design an interactive game world and people it with creatures and plot items.

The software also offers children the opportunity to create dialogue via the Conversation Writer, and children can add story text to objects such as journals and signposts to help the narrative unfold and bring characters to life.

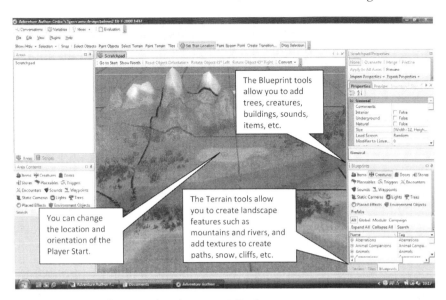

The Blueprint tools allow you to add trees, creatures, buildings, sounds, items, etc.

The Terrain tools allow you to create landscape features such as mountains and rivers, and add textures to create paths, snow, cliffs, etc.

You can change the location and orientation of the Player Start.

Figure 9.1   Area design within the NWN2 Toolset.

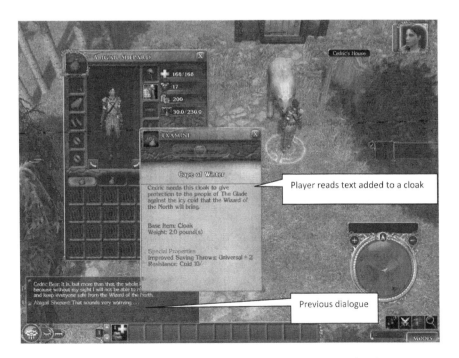

Player reads text added to a cloak

Previous dialogue

Figure 9.2   A cloak with added text gives further information to the player.

These games are complex, interactive, immersive texts combining typographic text, image, sound, and 3D spatial opportunities, and children have to go beyond the demands of conventional writing in order to create them.

Game Authoring in the Classroom

In order to explore the strategies young learners might use to tackle the complex task of game authoring, we undertook a naturalistic field study with the help of an enthusiastic teacher. The field study was conducted with a class of 25 pupils (aged 11–12) in a state-funded primary school in East Lothian, Scotland. The class teacher wished to try the Adventure Author software to support a cross-curricular project in fantasy literature themed around the novel *The Hobbit* by J. R. R. Tolkien. She chose to spend most of the class time for a six-week period on this project, although there were also regular timetabled slots for mathematics and P.E. By examining the strategies used by successful designers, we aimed to identify useful approaches that could be of assistance to other learners or teachers in the future.

Dialogue: Choices, Actions, and Conditions

Dialogue is the main means of taking the game forward in any chronological or sequential way—and given there is no descriptive text or narration the dialogue has to work harder than in a conventional written story. Dialogue also has a crucial part to play in terms of characters: children introduce their characters and their roles via dialogue and bring them to life through the words that they say and the actions ascribed to them. The Conversation Writer in Adventure Author makes it easy to branch a conversation (Figure 9.3) in order to give the player choices and to add actions or conditions to a line of dialogue, to set up rewards, attacks, and quests. Creating a choice for the player is relatively easy, but the designer must understand the tree-like structure that results from the choices. Sometimes the branching option helps to bring out the personality or feelings of a character. We illustrate these design choices through focusing on specific designers' decisions.

Stewart experimented with three dialogue choices for the player. Option one: the player does not agree to a character's request; option two: the player agrees to help; and option three: the player considers the request, but needs to be persuaded to continue. The player can explore all three, with attendant consequences.

Setting up actions in a conversation was popular. Tania confidently used a mixture of choices and actions with some witty dialogue to create light-hearted banter between the player and a pixie. The pixie warns, "Ah, you may choose to look through a rose tinted monocle or be wary and safe. Do you REALLY trust me?" The player can either agree (receiving 50 gold

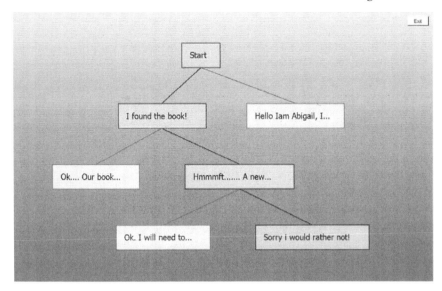

Figure 9.3   The structure of branching dialogue in the Conversation Writer.

pieces), or disagree and kill the pixie. If the player does trust the pixie, it ultimately becomes a bad-tempered ally, resulting in the frustrated player's outburst, "If you don't shut up, I'm going to clip your wings and take away your magic!"

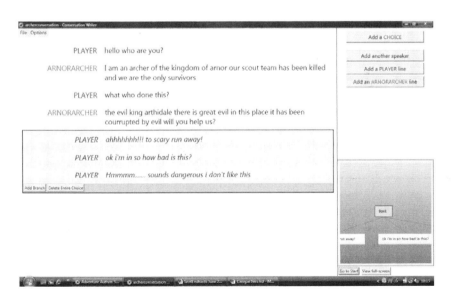

Figure 9.4   A dialogue with three choices; note diagrammatic representation bottom right.

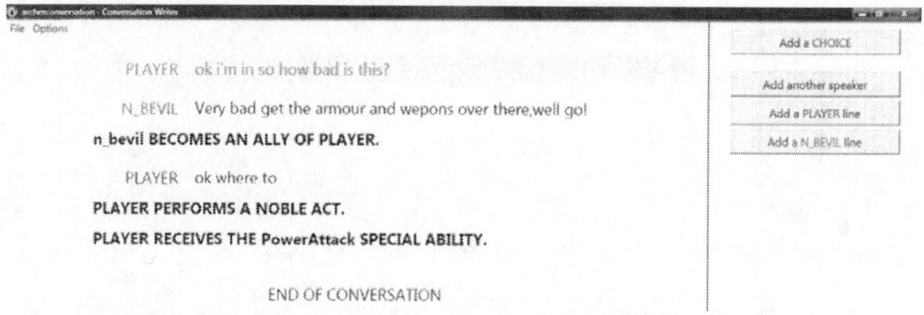

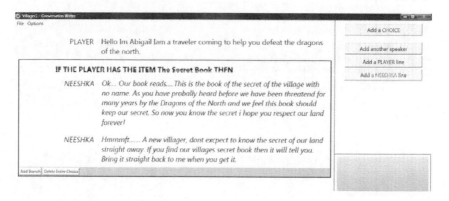

Figure 9.5   Actions (in bold) added to dialogue in the Conversation Writer.

Figure 9.6   Morag sets conditions.

The children enjoyed giving the player rewards, giving the player an ally, or specifying that a character should attack a player. They seemed to relish the opportunity to program the behavior of the game.

It is also possible in the Conversation Writer to set up conditions under which particular dialogue will appear to the player. The designer is essentially specifying a series of IF-THEN rules, such as "IF the player is carrying item x THEN say dialogue line y." Morag used a condition to set up a quest in which the player must find a secret book before she can help defeat the dragons that threaten the villagers.

Writing interactive dialogue is challenging at a number of levels. The learner must first master the technical and logical aspects of setting up choices, actions, and consequences. They must also think about the vocabulary for the conversation to make it genre-appropriate, as well as techniques for portraying personality or moods. Lastly, they must consider how this dialogue fits in with the plot, and particularly how the dialogue branches can lead to different plot outcomes. This is both cognitively and imaginatively demanding; most learners of this age require support with this task.

Story Locations

In the absence of conventional narrative or descriptive text, the designer uses the multimedia tools: visually, to create an exciting environment, and spatially, to draw the player in a particular direction. Many children take pains to make the setting fit their storyline, and create what we have called *story locations*, i.e., small scenes within the wider game setting (a cave with a glowing light at the door; a blacksmith's forge complete with the sound of hammering): significant places where significant events occur. These events, perhaps a conversation, or the acquisition of an item, a trap, or a transition to another part of the game, move the story forward. They happen in a significant location. Story locations and their associated events might be seen as the equivalent of chapters or episodes.

Stewart has given a lot of thought to such locations in his game, creating interesting settings in each quarter of the area grid.

The black dragon, critical to the quest, is placed in a hollow on a hillside, surrounded by special effects, drawing the player's attention and creating a dramatic arena for some important dialogue. Diagonally opposite, the glow spider, who will help the player, nestles in a curve of a stream with a waterfall as a backdrop—but beware the traps either side. An amulet, the object of the quest, is hidden bottom right, beside a rocky cave, guarded

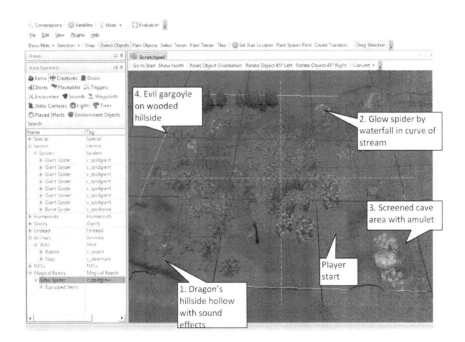

Figure 9.7   Stewart's game has four distinct story locations with effective landscaping.

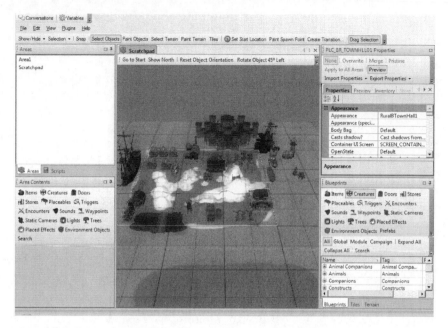

Figure 9.8   Screenshot of Angus' game showing a less coherent area design.

by goblins and trolls; this entire location is partially screened by hills and a building, but lighting hints at its presence. Diagonally opposite this, top left, across a stream and beside a forest, is the hillside location for the evil gargoyle that has to be defeated. Stewart seems to have a clear idea of what will happen in his game, where and when; in each of these locations the player receives new information or something significant occurs, and he has taken care to add supporting detail and interest.

Angus is less successful in harnessing the multimedia tools to create story locations. His area is packed with buildings and monsters and soldiers; it lacks coherence and suggests more random experimentation. For example, the bridge, which may seem inviting, leads nowhere, and the ships around the edge of the area are not in water. It may be that his storyline was less clear in his mind, or that he had less knowledge about how to 'chunk' his story into different locations across space and time.

The creation of effective (and genre-appropriate) story locations within the game world to support an unfolding story would seem to require a degree of sophistication. The designer needs a clear idea of the overall plan, a linking of visual, spatial, and temporal thinking, and an understanding of how the player might operate. It may be that additional help is required to map the game world in advance, with discussions about the way the story will move across this map from event to event.

Narrative Vehicles

Children can choose particular items (such as books, furniture, or other props) to play a significant role. They might become the focal point for a pathway through the game—e.g., to be collected as part of a quest, and narrative text can be added. For example, the designer might make a magic book containing information to be revealed only at a certain point in the game under certain conditions. When an item has been given this sort of role, we have called it a *narrative vehicle*, i.e., it helps to carry the story forward in some significant way.

Morag successfully uses narrative vehicles to contribute to her storyline. Her character Neeshka charges the player with a quest to find the potion of Lion's Heart, explaining that she feels weak and shy without it. When the player successfully delivers it to Neeshka, she is rewarded with both gold coins and storyline advancement, as Neeshka is now brave enough to help fight the dragons.

Kirsty also experiments with using narrative vehicles, but perhaps less successfully. She has written text for a series of genre-appropriate, carefully named objects: the Eidilon Temple Book, an invisibility potion, the village amethyst, the Starter Staff, and the Eidilon Crystal. The text in each gives tantalizing hints of the plot line—e.g., "A long time ago the people of Eidilon village were enemies, now this one gem is what brings peace over the land." Although the amethyst to which this text belongs is placed on a route that the player is likely to take through the game, it is not built into the storyline thereafter.

It seems that Kirsty is good at imagining potential plotlines for the fantasy genre but has not quite worked out how to build them into a spatial story environment. The player might reasonably expect to interact with the narrative vehicles in order to influence the plot, but Kirsty has not used the procedural aspects of the game authoring tool to program in these possibilities.

Children will need support to handle narrative vehicles effectively, balancing interesting textual content with careful thought as to how the player will find and interact with these important objects—e.g., by setting conditions.

Reading Pathways: Multimedia

Reading pathways, the routes through the game, can be indicated using the multimedia features of the software. The most successful children created pathway possibilities that were convincing, attractive, and supportive of their player.

Robert has given a lot of thought to supporting his player, creating a visually appealing and convincing world, but one where the possibility of losing the trail is minimized. Robert's intended pathway flows through a narrow strip of

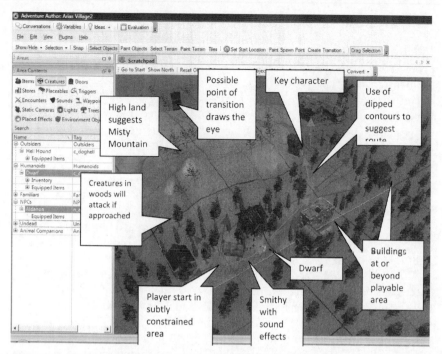

Figure 9.9   Red arrows show likely pathways created by Robert's use of multimedia tools; blue arrows show possible routes where player will quickly come to a dead end.

low ground at the foot of the area, and any interesting distractions (e.g., buildings in the distance) soon prove to be inaccessible, minimizing player frustration and helping to keep them en route to the main objective—crossing the Misty Mountains (suggested by the high ground behind). He carefully draws his player towards the smithy with the sounds of the blacksmith's forge, helping to ensure they meet the narratively important dwarf, and then draws them on to the rising ground behind the smithy by placing a decorated building and a key character where they will be noticed. As the player climbs further, his or her eye will be drawn to a distinctive gate, indicating a possible transition to Robert's next level.

Although Kirsty has clear visual pathways in her design, they are not effectively incorporated into her game and the player may actually have more success if he or she ignores them. She has a clear idea of how the story unfolds in her own mind, and the paths are more visually dominant than in Robert's design, but she is less successful in guiding the player. Kirsty uses cobbled paths, signs, and 'meet and greet' characters to try to direct the player, who has to find the red dragon to understand the purpose of the game. There are narrative vehicles containing excellent story information lying on the cobbled paths, but no clues as to how to find or use them. In addition, she fails to set conditions on significant lines of dialogue that

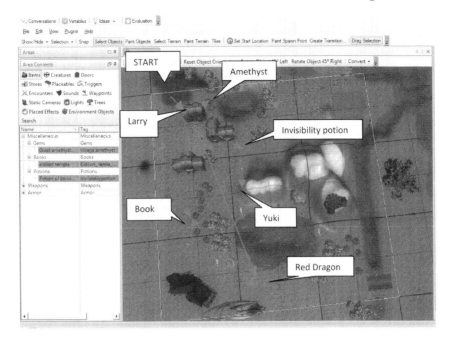

Figure 9.10 Kirsty's game. Solid red lines show the pathway her narrative seems to require; broken red lines show some of the other routes the player would be just as likely to take.

would allow her greater control over sequencing the spatial pathways. This means her player is at risk of missing the key facts of the game, and is certainly unlikely to come across them in the correct order.

Reading Pathways: Textual

The children used alphabetic text to indicate pathways through their game, giving instructions and guidance to the player via dialogue, narrative vehicles, and floating text overlays. The most successful games effectively combine both textual and digital support to guide the player through the 3D, interactive, immersive world.

Stewart's game (whose layout offers no overt visual paths at all—see Figure 9.11) uses textual cues to indicate pathways to his carefully crafted story locations. Unlike Kirsty, he has harnessed the condition function of the Conversation Writer, allowing him to control the progress of his player, and his clear story locations give a focal point to aim for. The result is a spiral route through the world of his game with conditions governing dialogue with the black dragon (location 5) such that the player must return via locations 3 and 4 with an amulet in order to gain additional information to complete the quest (6).

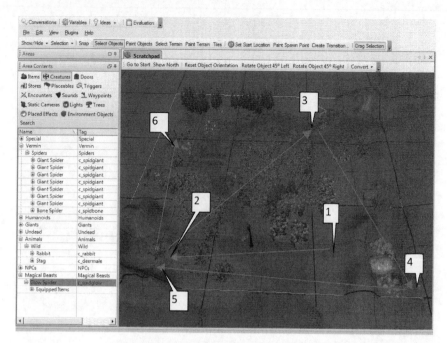

Figure 9.11   Stewart's area design, with likely reading pathways indicated by arrows.

Here is a typical example of Stewart's directional dialogue, between the player and the glow spider as he explains he must help the black dragon:

Spider: You will need his amulet, but the goblins took it and hid it somewhere in a cave in this land.
Player: I will find it.

If Stewart had not given such careful thought to his game world, this dialogue would be too open-ended, but he has seeded enough visual clues to ensure an alert player will head off in the right direction—the cave is tantalizingly visible beyond the southern hills.

By contrast, Angus's only example of dialogue is vague, offering little by way of pathways or purpose in what we have already seen is a very cluttered game world.

Hester creates floating text to appear in the game, via the Display Message action in Conversation Writer, which tells the player, "Go and search around and see what everyone is up to." This suggests a random or open-ended series of pathways, whereas Sandy chooses to display the more specific message, "Go to the woods." Kirsty's potion of invisibility gives the player an even more specific direction by saying, "Give this potion to Yuki of the winter wolf clan for a reward!"

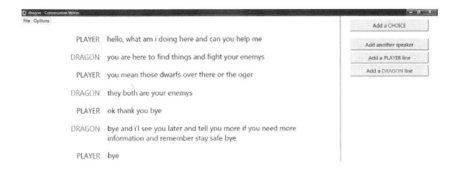

Figure 9.12   Angus' instructions are vague.

As a game designer, it is not enough to use text in order to set up pathways for the player; that text also has to make successful partnerships with the 3D spatial, immersive, and interactive aspects of the toolset to create effective multimedia pathways; the challenge for the children is how to combine all these features so that each plays an effective part in guiding the player through their world.

DISCUSSION

While considering these games, some points of interest emerged. Firstly, it became clear that storytelling skills from traditional writing tasks did not always transfer into the game authoring medium. Games with a lot of dialogue and narrative vehicle text are often not successful, particularly because players can get impatient with reading onscreen text during gameplay. Designers are sometimes disappointed to see a player scroll through their carefully crafted text without reading it. From the player's perspective, too much text slows down the action of the game and can reduce his or her sense of participation. Teachers can support learners by helping to identify sections of the game that are too text-heavy and by assisting dialogue editing. The writer's maxim "show, don't tell" is particularly relevant here.

Secondly, there are some new techniques to be mastered that go beyond traditional textual storytelling techniques—developing story locations, using narrative vehicles, managing pathways in a highly complex narrative environment, and making effective use of dialogue in this context. These are complementary elements that form a significant part of the storytelling and take it beyond conventional narrative. As designers, children have to make decisions, textually, visually, spatially, about how overt they want their reading pathways to be, how they want to use narrative vehicles, where and how to create and link their story locations, and how they will harness speech. These design decisions are a fascinating mix of modal meanings that need to be carefully combined; in order to facilitate this, teachers will need to become much more familiar with the possibilities offered by this form of storytelling.

Thirdly, learners who did not have much experience of playing computer games sometimes underestimated the importance of the 3D spatial aspect of the medium, or perhaps were unaware of how to use it to tell a story. A possible reason for this is that they did not visualize the game as the player would see it from beginning to end. The toolset defaults to a top-down view of the landscape that emphasizes the area as a whole rather than what the player will see minute by minute. When playing the game, the player sees the world from the point of view of the character rather than as an overview. To understand the player's experience it is necessary for the designer to regularly switch points of view by testing the game. In testing the game, the designer is explicitly trying out reading pathways in order to experience his or her work from the player's perspective. Anticipating the reader's needs is important in conventional writing tasks, but it can be difficult to encourage young authors to explicitly switch between the role of author and reader in order to improve a text; Adventure Author encourages switching between the roles of designer and player, and the process of checking and editing is much more immediate. To help learners with less experience of games, teachers could encourage learners to play example games before they work on their own games, and to regularly and systematically test their games throughout the process, ensuring that as author/designer they take the opportunity to change perspective and explore the needs of their reader/player.

CONCLUSIONS

Creating a 3D, interactive, immersive game provides new opportunities for authors. Dialogue has to work in new ways and be married with logical thinking and spatial awareness to manage a quest structure; the narrative vehicle and the story location are new concepts whose potential needs to be explored and understood; and the many ways of creating and combining reading pathways, the key to following the story, have to be mastered. Computer game authoring also allows children's own cultures and experiences to have a place in the classroom and provides an opportunity for both teachers and children to be creative in their approaches.

The challenges for the learner are many when designing stories in this medium. They must consider: How do I build a story spatially? How can I anticipate what my reader, the player, might do? Under what circumstances should I try to tell the story through words and when should I use visual design? The challenges for the educator involve supporting their learners in the creation of these new forms of text and the literacy behaviors that go with them. If educators are to acquire knowledge of successful new media authoring strategies, and assist their pupils in effectively expressing themselves, perhaps they need to become multimodal designers in their own right. They certainly need to prepare the structured teaching interventions, exemplars, assessment schemes, and software scaffolding to provide the well-judged frames of reference recommended in Jewitt's literature review (Jewitt, 2008).

Much of this is new and changing territory, which may take teachers beyond their comfort zones and challenge their understandings of what is meant by 'text' and 'literacy'; and indeed there are elements of risk attached as educators find their way forward. But the evident engagement, motivation, and wealth of learning opportunities afforded by computer game authoring(Robertson & Howells, 2008) increases the imperative on the education world to meet these challenges. Kress (2003: 175) warned: "*The young are teaching themselves because the old cannot or will not*" (Kress, 2003: 175). This chapter begins to bridge the gap between the understandings of the young, who hold the answers for the future, and the understandings of the old, who have the answers from the past.

ACKNOWLEDGMENTS

The images for this chapter were captured by the chapter authors, from interactions with Neverwinter Nights. The authorship of this game designing software is complex. The original holding company of the first game creators in 2002 was Infogrames Entertainment, SA, originally a French holding company which was the owner of Atari. Infogrames Entertainment no longer exists. A substantial part of software activity under the Neverwinter Nights activity is open source using the Linux platform. Attempts and written requests to track down the copyright holders have been made without success.

REFERENCES

Curriculum Review Group (2008). Technologies Cover paper Glasgow: Learning Teaching Scotland. Retrieved May 23, 2012 from http://publications.1fife.org.uk/uploadfiles/publications/c64_TechnologiesCoverPaper.pdf
Curriculum Review Group (2007). Literacy and English Cover paper. Glasgow: Learning Teaching Scotland Retrieved May 23, 2012 from http://www.hvlc.org.uk/hlp/docs/asg_transition/Literacy_English_Cover_Paper.pdf
DfE (2011). *The Curriculum: Aims Values and Purposes*. Retrieved January 13, 2012 from http://www.education.gov.uk/schools/teachingandlearning/curriculum/b00199676/aims-values-and-purposes.
Education Scotland (2010a). *Curriculum for Excellence: Literacy Across Learning. Principles and Practice*. Retrieved January 13, 2012 from http://www.ltscotland.org.uk/learningteachingandassessment/learningacrossthecurriculum/responsibilityofall/literacy/principlesandpractice/index.asp.
Education Scotland (2010b). *Curriculum for Excellence: Technology. Principles and Practice*. Retrieved January 13, 2012 from http://www.ltscotland.org.uk/

learningteachingandassessment/curriculumareas/technologies/principlesand-practice/index.asp.

Gee, J. P. (2003). *What Video Games Have to Teach Us about Learning and Literacy.* New York: Palgrave Macmillan.

Good, J. & Robertson, J. (2006). CARSS: A framework for learner-centred design with children. *International Journal of Artificial Intelligence in Education* 16(4): 381–413.

Grainger, T., Goouch, K., & A. Lambirth (2005). *Creativity and Writing: Developing Voice and Verve in the Classroom.* Abingdon: Routledge.

Jewitt, C. (2008). The visual in learning and creativity: A review of the literature. A report for Creative Partnerships. London: Institute of Education, University of London.

Juul, J. (2001). Games telling stories? *Games Studies* 1(1). Retrieved January 13, 2012. http://www.gamestudies.org/0101/juul-gts/.

Kress, G. (2003). *Literacy in the New Media Age.* London: Routledge.

Kress, G. (2000). Multimodality. In B. Cope & M. Kalantzis (eds.), *Multiliteracies: Literacy Learning and the Design of Social Futures.* London: Routledge.

Kress, G. & van Leeuwen, T. (2006). *Reading Images: The Grammar of Visual Design.* London: Routledge.

Kress, G. (2010) *Multimodality: A social semiotic approach to contemporary communication.* London: Routledge.

Lankshear, C., and Knobel, M. (2006) *New Literacies: Everyday Practices and Classroom Learning* (2nd ed.). Maidenhead, UK: Open University Press.

Marsh, J. & Singleton, C. (2009). Literacy and technology: Questions of relationship [Editorial]. *Journal of Research in Reading* 32(1): 1–5.

Merchant, G. (2009). Literacy in virtual worlds. *Journal of Research in Reading* 32(1): 38–56.

Murray, J. (1997). *Hamlet on the Holodeck: The Future of Narrative in Cyberspace.* New York: Free Press.

Pahl, K. & Rowsell, J. (2005). *Literacy and Education: Understanding the New Literacy Studies in the Classroom.* London: Paul Chapman.

Robertson, J. & Good, J. (2003). Using a collaborative virtual role-play environment to foster characterisation in stories. *Journal of Interactive Learning Research* 14(1): 5–29.

Robertson, J. & Howells, C. (2008). Computer game design: Opportunities for successful learning. *Computers and Education* 50(2): 559–578.

Sharples, M. (1999). *How We Write: Writing as Creative Design.* London: Routledge.

10 "I Oversee What the Children Are Doing"

Challenging Literacy Pedagogy in Virtual Worlds

Guy Merchant

INTRODUCTION

The impact of rapid changes in human communication brought about by digital technology and widespread Internet use is often compared to the 'revolution' instigated by Gutenberg's printing press. Whether this is a fair comparison will be discernible only from some future vantage point, but the fact of the matter is that in a single generation we have a witnessed a series of rapid changes—changes that have been facilitated by technological innovation. Communication devices available in the affluent West and elsewhere are increasingly sophisticated and ever more portable. From laptops, iPads, and smartphones we can access a wealth of information with a few keystrokes. But we can also maintain contact with others through instant messaging, texting, and email, and we can publish information, images, and ideas from almost anywhere. Compare that to a childhood in the 1950s, when two tins joined by a string defined the reach of imagined connectivity. Today very young children play with makeshift mobile phones when they are not playing with the real thing; keyboards and screens constitute the 'materials to hand'; and video games and virtual worlds are popular entertainment spaces (Merchant, 2007).

Literacy with all its concern for human communication and interaction is fundamentally challenged by these changes—and literacy education even more so. Admittedly sociolinguists have argued for a good many years that language is always changing, ever in flux. Typically they demonstrate how language varies *synchronically*—in other words between social groups, regions, and the like—and *diachronically*, over time, between generations and so through history. Furthermore it is more or less an established fact that spoken language varies far more than the written form along both dimensions. As an era marked by a phenomenal level of innovation in written communication, the early twenty-first century could well be the exception to this rule; again only time will tell. But if language and literacy as social phenomena are constantly in flux, then education, broadly speaking a conservative enterprise, has traditionally been concerned with controlling that change, ironing out variation, maintaining the 'standard' of written communication, and, in many instances throughout history, policing and standardizing language itself. Literacy education then is always double-edged—both emancipatory and regulatory in its endeavor. In striving to provide for full participation, literacy education always runs the risk of producing conformity or worse—alienation. Against the background of a sea change in literacy practices it might appear that the battle to impose conformity is already lost and reports of student alienation are widespread (Chandler-Olcott & Lewis, 2010).

These are the sorts of issues that have troubled many literacy theorists, researchers, and educators—particularly over the last ten years. And as our understanding of what Kress (2003; 2010) calls the "changing landscape of communication" has developed, many have also come to question established definitions of literacy itself. So not only have there been criticisms of the diet served up by schools under the banner of literacy on account of its traditional orientation, its preoccupation with print, paper, and pencil, but also there is at the same time the suggestion that the term 'literacy' itself is now outworn, unable to capture the full sweep of contemporary digital communication. Some of these tensions emerge across the various chapters in this book.

At this point in time it is clear that the uses of literacy as well as the technologies that are employed to produce and distribute it have changed and continue to change (Lankshear & Knobel, 2006). Children and young people occupy different positions with respect to these changes. Sometimes they are at the forefront of the changes, but this is not always the case—there are also occasions in which they themselves are confused, pressured, or excluded by the 'new literacies' (Livingstone, 2009). Schools are in a complex position too, encouraged on the one hand to prepare children for the digital future while at the same time being coerced and cajoled to raise standards—standards that are more often than not measured by success in traditional print literacies.

In this chapter I make an original contribution to the study of digital communication in the classroom by highlighting the factors that facilitate and hinder the adoption of new literacy practices. A simple model of the change process is proposed and then illustrated by using data from a case study on the use of a virtual world designed to promote literacy learning in elementary schools (Merchant, 2009a; Merchant, 2010). Before addressing the change process, though, I offer a short overview of existing work on the new literacies of video games and virtual worlds.

PERSPECTIVES ON THE NEW LITERACIES OF VIDEO GAMES AND VIRTUAL WORLDS

As a label 'new literacies' faces the same problems that 'modern art' does. By describing a new movement at a particular point in time it is in danger of rapidly becoming an anachronism. Modern art is generally used to describe a movement that lasted about a hundred years, beginning in the 1860s.

Contemporary art would rather not be labeled as modern art. Although we cannot predict the shelf-life of new literacies, some of the descriptions of it from the last ten years—including, I hasten to add, my own—are beginning to seem rather old. As newer technologies emerge with an ever wider range of affordances for meaning-making, the business of theorizing communication has to accept this fluidity. With this caveat in mind, and since there is no better term currently available, I will use the term 'new literacies' here to refer to some of the new literacy practices that associate with digital technology. This is a slightly narrower definition than that used by Lankshear and Knobel (2006) but will serve my purposes in this chapter.

One of the more influential tropes in writing on new literacies has its origins in asset models of education. This is shorthand for an ideology that prizes what learners already know and do—their capital in the Bourdeuian sense—and encourages educators to leverage these resources in the more formal settings of school. The parallel with moves to recognize 'popular culture' in education is immediately apparent and as the latter has developed it has inevitably come to acknowledge and incorporate digital culture (Marsh, 2005). But one of the conceptual and practical problems faced by both these educational discourses is the variation in children's capital resources. Although there have been some colorful and persuasive accounts of children and young people as experts, or 'digital natives' (following Prensky's 2001 description), these clearly do not generalize to all students.

New literacy practices have certainly diversified over the last ten years, and as a result the range of academic studies that address new literacies has mushroomed. One particularly interesting area of study encompasses the use of video games and virtual worlds. It has attracted researchers partly I suspect because of its apparent 'newness,' but also because these environments appear to capture the attention and imagination of children and young people in a notably 'strong' way—even sometimes to levels that are described in terms of addiction. The work of Gee (2003; 2004) is a major influence in this growing field. Gee's recent work focuses on the world of videogaming, and although much of it is applicable to virtual worlds they are not expressly his concern. However, the sophistication of his body of work is such that it speaks to other new literacy practices if not to education as a whole. The fact that not all children and young people are avid gamers does not disturb Gee's basic argument, although the suggestion that gaming can be more rewarding than school is provocative to say the least.

As a preamble to this consideration of new literacies in a virtual world, I will not attempt to provide a detailed summary of Gee's ideas here, but instead limit myself to underlining two central claims that are made in his work and are perhaps most clearly set out in *What Video Games Have to Teach us about Learning and Literacy* (2003). These are: 1) video games can be powerful learning environments because they are based on a sophisticated understanding of how we learn; and 2) the learning principles involved in video game design can be applied to other learning environments such as schools. Of these two claims, it is probably the first that has attracted the most attention simply because it is a very positive state-ment about a popular practice that is often demonized in public debate. My concern here with exploring the use of virtual worlds in classrooms also resonates with this first claim—that is, that they can be powerful learning environments (see also Dede, Clarke, Ketelhut, Nelson, & Bowman, 2006). This is set against the broader picture sketched out earlier that invites an exploration of new literacies in the classroom—an exploration that capital-izes on the interests and experience of learners and that prepares them for whatever digital future awaits them.

Either because of the impact of new technologies on literacy, or possibly because of the zeal of the advocates of new literacies, it is now broadly accepted by education policy-makers and by an increasing number of prac-titioners that some sort of classroom response is necessary. Now the burn-ing questions for educators concern not only *what* kinds of digital work to develop but *how* to go about it. Squire identifies this in his study of video games in the classroom when he underlines that the critical challenge for educators is "how we can use games more effectively as educational tools" (Squire, 2005). Implementation isn't just about educational efficacy—after all the path of educational research and innovation is littered with accounts of things that worked—it's also about fitting new work and new ways of operating into existing classroom life. The challenge for teachers then is twofold: firstly they themselves need to understand the significance of the changing nature of literacies, and secondly they need to know how to inte-grate new literacies into their practice.

NEW LITERACIES IN THE CLASSROOM— A QUESTION OF CHANGING PRACTICES

Introducing new practices into classrooms is a complex business. Whether such practices involve resources or materials, approaches to teaching and learning, or curriculum content, the extensive literature on school change repeatedly reminds us that it is no easy matter (Fullan, 2001; Hargreaves, 2005). Simply exhorting practitioners to incorporate new literacies into the curriculum and berating them when they don't is clearly a rather naïve position to adopt. If we are to learn anything at all from the last ten years of innovation, it is rather that new literacies sit in a complex web of inter-secting discourses (Scollon & Scollon, 2004). These are discourses about school improvement and teacher effectiveness, about literacy standards, curriculum and pedagogy, as well as those about new technology and the digital future. In schools, particularly in underperforming schools, trying something new brings with it certain risks, and as we anticipate the sus-tained implementation of new literacies work, this needs to be taken into account along with all the other lessons that the education community has learned about curriculum development over the last 30 years or so.

In this chapter I use a simple model for conceptualizing some of the challenges of using new literacies in the classroom. To present this I have chosen a financial metaphor—not because I feel particularly comfortable with financial truths, but more in recognition of the fact that school life is dominated by what Cintron (1997) calls the 'discourse of measurement.' The discourse of measurement is evident in the ways in which learners are segregated by age, organized in groups, allotted to particular places at particular times, and taught a curriculum that is categorized and leveled and enacted through quite specific timetable arrangements. Moreover it is currently the case that student performance is repeatedly measured, and that there is a growing tendency to judge teacher success and school effectiveness on these measures. This discourse of measurement produces a particular culture in which resources of all kinds are under pressure—a situation that, regardless of whether we like it, is akin to a competitive market economy. Buy-in, cost, investment, and interest therefore seem to be appropriate metaphors to apply to such a condition.

Admittedly aspects of new literacies challenge this discourse of measurement. The dynamics of distributed endeavor, the importance of shared content, and the increased collaboration that are evident in emerging practices contrast starkly with the current preoccupation with educational standards measured by individual performance on a narrow range of schooled literacy practices. Yet it is within this context that new practices will need to

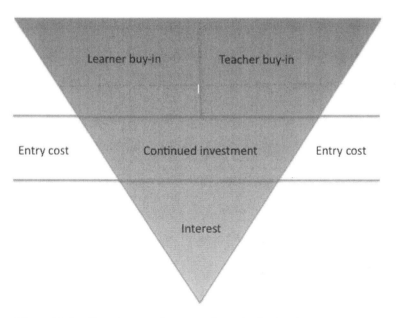

Figure 10.1 Changing practice—new literacies in the classroom.

take root. The model shown here (Figure 10.1) uses the financial metaphor to conceptualize the factors influencing the classroom implementation of new literacies. Its object of focus is the micro-system of the classroom and so it does not consider those important influences that shape both learners and teachers and the real world environment in which they meet—but it is based on the understanding that neither party is an entirely autonomous agent. Teachers are strongly influenced by school conditions as well as by the political and policy contexts in which they operate. And, like their teachers, students also have to function in these contexts and both parties bring their own everyday experiences of literacy practices (both the new and the not so new).

What follows is a brief commentary on each aspect of Figure 10.1:

Learner buy-in describes the degree to which students accept the new literacy practices that they are introduced to as something worth engaging in (in this case a virtual world);

Teacher buy-in describes the degree to which teachers accept the legitimacy of these new literacies and see the benefit;

Entry cost describes the preparatory stages, such as teacher planning and resource provision (hardware and software), computer access, and the prerequisite skills and support that learners need in order to engage with new literacy practices;

Continued investment describes that which is necessary to sustain involvement over time—factors such as motivation, ongoing preparation, support and encouragement, and so on;

Interest describes the benefits that relate to teacher and pupil engagement in the technological situation, whether these are judged in terms of motivation, perceived progress, or measurable outcomes.

The implementation model I have sketched out attempts to capture some of the forces that are at play in new literacies in the classroom. It should be clear from the foregoing commentary that there is considerable interaction between these forces. So, for example, learner buy-in and a relatively low entry cost can generate interest (in the motivational sense), which in turn may act upon teacher buy-in. On the other hand, a lack of continued investment might prove to be a barrier to sustained engagement, which could in turn influence interest and long-term buy-in from the teachers. With this model in mind I now consider a particular instance of implementing new literacies with an overview of the virtual worlds project. Then by juxtaposing students' and teachers' experience of the virtual world I investigate the changing practices that are involved.

CREATING A VIRTUAL WORLD FOR
THE CLASSROOM—A CASE STUDY

In the beginning it was simply an idea—an idea to capitalize on what was imagined to be the interest and enthusiasm of young children for engaging with digital worlds. A group of educators worked with private sector developers to build a 3D virtual world using funds available to boost achievement in underperforming schools in a school district in the North of England (see Merchant, 2009a for more detail). The world, called Barnsborough, was a simulacrum of real-world Barnsley and its surrounding environs and could be navigated from a standard keyboard by directing the movement of onscreen avatars. As Figure 10.2 shows, this virtual world contained familiar features together with a range of literacies, including: tool tips, available by mousing-over objects (clues such as "looks like someone's been here" and navigational information such as "you'll need a code to get in"), environmental texts (such as shop signs, graffiti, logos, posters, and advertisements), and hyperlinks (such as webpages, phone messages, and music clips). Avatars each with a unique point of view in the world could communicate with each other through a 'chat' function, which was displayed in instant-message format beneath the main display, with recent utterances also appearing in speech balloons above their heads. Figure 10.2 shows avatars interacting through this chat function.

In October 2006 teachers in ten pilot schools were invited to test out the world with their Year 5 and Year 6 students—children aged between 9 and

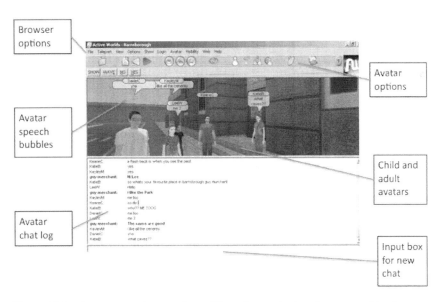

Figure 10.2   An annotated screenshot of Barnsborough showing some of its features.
Source: www.virtuallylearning.co.uk

11. In the project described here, teachers explained to pupils that Barnsborough had been hurriedly and mysteriously abandoned by its inhabitants. The broad objective for children was to solve this mystery by collecting evidence available in-world in a number of media and textual forms (e.g., telephone messages, newspapers, webpages, handwritten notes, videoclips, and so on). The texts located in the virtual world provided visitors with a number of possible accounts and solutions to the problem of why Barnsborough had been abandoned, which included a major biohazard, an alien abduction, and a political intrigue or big business disaster.

From 2006 to 2008, for the duration of the pilot project, I worked with the design team as a consultant and researcher following the development process from the initial planning stage into its classroom implementation. The case study material includes views of the project from a number of perspectives, including classroom observations, chatlogs, in-world avatar interviews with teachers (five sessions in total) and pupils (nine sessions in total), complemented by my fieldnotes on the planning process and the accompanying minutes and meeting documents. An evaluation questionnaire was distributed to project teachers at the end of the final summer term (July 2008). Classroom observations focused on the world in use and involved 'over-the-shoulder' observations of children and their avatars. These were conducted in two of the project schools on a term-by-term basis. Each observation was bounded by the timetabled session—being between 40 and 60 minutes in duration. Chatlogs of these sessions were archived by the researcher. During these observational visits, I negotiated follow-up in-world interviews with groups of pupils and by arrangement with their teachers. These normally took place in school break or lunch times, were located in Barnsborough, and were conducted through my avatar. Although the pupils were co-present in the classroom or computer suite at the time of the interview, I used my workplace computer and so they in turn communicated with me through their avatars. These interviews were semi-structured in form, allowing them to explore areas of interest. The pupil/avatar group size was four or five, and the group interview's average duration was about 20 minutes.

In addition to this material, documentary evidence and fieldnotes derived from approximately 18 hours of planning meetings were collected. This is hard to quantify with any precision, since the planning process was enriched by more informal email exchange and regular in-world meetings and visits. Between May and July 2008, I conducted one-to-one avatar interviews with five of the project teachers in the virtual world and distributed a short evaluation questionnaire to all ten (seven were returned). My overarching research strategy was to provide insight into the ways in which virtual worlds could be used to promote new literacies in the classroom by constructing what Stake (2003) refers to as an instrumental case study. Broadly speaking, then, the approach involved an exploration of what Markham (2004: 97) calls "the context of social construction," the negotiations of meanings, identities, and relationships that occurred discursively in and around the virtual world.

My observations in what follows are drawn from this pilot study and illustrate some of the rewards and challenges of integrating new literacies into mainstream classroom practice. In this, I look at the project first from the learners' perspective, and then from the teachers' perspective. I then interrogate this data using the curriculum implementation model introduced earlier.

Children Investigating Alien Abduction in a Virtual World

As stated earlier many of the children in the Barnsborough project schools were underperforming in terms of national benchmarks for literacy. Teachers frequently commented on their low levels of motivation, particularly when they were given classroom writing tasks. Whether this perceived motivation problem was assumed to be the cause or the effect of their writing difficulties was not immediately apparent, but the teachers' views seemed to be borne out by comments made by children in interviews. Many (but by no means all) children experienced classroom writing as a challenge. So, for example, one stated that *"writing used to be boring . . . it used to be very rubbish,"* whereas another offered some more detailed insights into why:

"Sometimes I dunno how to spell some hard words and I can't think of any ideas—erm—so then I get stuck what to put . . . I preferred writing when I were younger cos it weren't as hard."

In this case then, the challenge of writing related not only to its presentational features (the spelling) but also to the compositional element (the 'ideas'). What is harder to define is the nature of the routine writing tasks themselves, the kind of support that was available to meet these challenges (in themselves not restricted to struggling writers), and how exactly the demands of classroom writing change as children get older. Gaining detail concerning actual classroom writing practices before the Barnsborough project was beyond the scope of my research, but the schools were following the fairly prescriptive genre-based approach to writing advocated by the National Strategy (DfE, 2010) at the time and, hence, opportunities for exploring new literacies were limited (see Merchant, 2010).

Logging on to gain access to a virtual world then constituted a radical departure from the routines of classroom literacy. Barnsborough held the promise of providing a richer context and motivation to write than was normally provided. Futhermore, at least in their use of the chat function, the children were explicitly released from the obligation to produce conventional spelling. Here message content was privileged over form and at least some of the obstacles referred to earlier were obviated. But more than this, the project aimed to engage and motivate by providing a world to explore and a problem to solve. In order to access the children's experiences of this I want to illustrate some of these themes with reference to two short extracts from the project data. These are chatlogs taken from one of a series of in-world interviews with Year 6 children (for more detail on research design, see Merchant, 2010). In this extract the five children's initials have been changed for ethical reasons, but apart from that, the chatlog is an accurate record and includes the children's spellings and the 'conversational lag' that is characteristic of multiparty chat.

Guy:	So tell me what's going on in here in Barnsborough?
TK:	i think its aliens
Guy:	Aliens?
TK:	yep
Guy:	doing what?
BI:	someone or something has scared all the people away
HC:	people have gone missing and we think its aliens
HQ:	were not too sure
TK:	trying 2 take over
Guy:	That's terrible!!
TN:	i think it is aliens
BI:	i know
HC:	i know
TN:	i know
Guy:	Taking over the world?
TK:	I no were tryin 2 save avry 1
Guy:	You are?
TN:	we think
TK:	yep there takin over evaery thing
Guy:	But TK you're only young
TK:	but we all work as a team
HC:	and where trying to find out where they are

In this segment we gain a sense of the way children were engaged in the virtual world scenario that they had been presented with in Barnsborough. TK, often the first to respond to my avatar's questions, seemed to favor the alien abduction hypothesis (the thread runs: *i think its aliens—yep—trying 2 take over—I no were tryin 2 save avry 1- yep there takin over evaery thing*). TK, possibly quicker on the keyboard than others in the group—or maybe just faster to react—offers a short account of the scenario and also the children's own role in this. Perhaps it is also worth commenting on the presentational features that are used: there is no capitalization or punctuation in this thread; some abbreviation; the use of numerals to represent lexical items; and the use of the colloquial form of agreement—*yep*. These presentational devices borrow from the language of texting and show an awareness of the linguistic features of written language (Plester, Wood, & Bell, 2008).

If TK's contribution appears to offer the most coherent thread, the chat 'conversation' includes, and in some sense depends upon, the contribution of the others, either through agreement (the repeated chorus of *i know*) or by a more overt statement of the problem and hypothesis, such as HC's *people have gone missing and we think its aliens*. In all, this extract seems to me to show new literacies at work in the classroom—children engaged in problem-solving in a virtual world, meeting and communicating with onscreen avatars, and interacting through synchronous small-group chat. It also illustrates the collaborative nature of the online work as the children describe how they *work as a team* in order *to find out*.

In the second extract, the children in the same group explain the nature of some of the clues that they have come across in Barnsborough that appear to them to support their hypothesis of alien abduction.

TK:	weve found strange notes and green footprints
TN:	every oun is gon
Guy:	What notes?
HC:	its werid real werid
BI:	we have found out that a person is trying to contact his sister but cant
TK:	with codes on them
Guy:	maybe disappeared
HC:	green triangles on the floor
TK:	yep
TN:	yes
BI:	yes
HC:	yes

This shorter extract captures the sense of enthusiasm and involvement that many children experienced in their virtual world work. Here they talk with some excitement about the clues they have found in Barnsborough—clues that lend support to their alien abduction hypothesis. In some ways then it seems that the children had become immersed in the world in ways that are often observed in drama activities and gaming (Carroll, 2002; Merchant, 2009a). In other group interviews children expressed their enthusiasm for Barnsborough too, often describing it as *cool* or *mint* (Merchant, 2010). Some individuals commented on Barnsborough's game-like quality, explaining that it was *good because you can walk around and find clues—it's like a game, a virtual game*, or a sense of frustration with the lack of interactivity *if only there were some shopkeepers* (visitors to Barnsborough are able to enter a number of well-stocked shops but are unable buy any items).

Although children reported variable levels of engagement and enjoyment, the overwhelming verdict on Barnsborough was extremely positive. This does not mean to say that they were uncritical—as the foregoing comment suggests they had plenty of ideas of how the virtual world could be improved. But it is hard to find comments in the data that were negative, and this suggests a high level of 'buy-in' from the learners in this project.

Teachers of the World

The teachers' entry into Barnsborough was rather different to that of their students. Schools had been selected on the basis of local knowledge and were considered to be institutions that would be positively disposed to innovative practice, whereas the teachers themselves were identified by the age group of pupils they were teaching. Although these teachers were not exactly volunteers, and often had other pressing demands on their time, they were, on the whole, keen to be involved in the project. Teachers were introduced to Barnsborough in a day-long pre-launch training event, learning first about the concept and the design, and then being provided with an opportunity to explore and experience the virtual world in an unstructured 'playful' way. For all the teachers except one (who played online games) this was a novel and sometimes unsettling experience.

A year on, survey data from the participating teachers show how they were persuaded of the benefits of the virtual worlds project. Their responses highlight the fact that the impact on pupil motivation was by far the most influential factor for them. One teacher commented that:

> At first it was not something that I can say I got over excited about but as the project has grown so has my enthusiasm—it is a way of making learning fun.

Another summarized the project in terms of:

> Greater motivation of boys who had been low performers in writing, extreme interest in all children—girls and boys, excitement for teachers as well as children!

And yet it was also clear that the teachers' enthusiasm for Barnsborough was tempered by other factors—factors that were not directly concerned with the concept of new literacies or the use of the virtual world per se. The first of these is to do with school culture and the current widespread phenomenon of innovation fatigue; the second is about curriculum 'fit,' and the third is about access to hardware.

All the schools involved in the virtual worlds project had been identified by their low performance in statutory literacy testing at a time of intense concern about raising standards in schools. The high level of public and political interest in literacy performance, successive waves of curriculum reform, and regimes of accountability were most acutely experienced by those schools already working in challenging situations (Hargreaves, 2004). These factors combined to produce a pressured atmosphere in some of the project schools—little wonder, then, that a number of teachers complained about not being able to *find the time* to work on the Barnsborough project. The situation was exacerbated by local administrators who vigorously promoted and resourced interventions that were intended to 'solve the problem' of low performance. The virtual worlds project was somehow expected to find its place alongside a host of other programs, including at least two other literacy initiatives (the 'Big Write' and 'Shakespeare in Schools'). Survey responses from the teachers frequently referred to this issue, succinctly expressed by one teacher as *too many priorities in school—Barnsborough is yet another*. It is perhaps surprising then that Barnsborough survived at all in this hostile climate of innovation fatigue.

Project teachers were quite understandably focused on a view of literacy that was dominated by a genre approach—after all this was a central orientation in the official curriculum (see DfE 2010, for example)—and this view dominated the ways in which Barnsborough was used. A strong theme in teacher survey and interview data was the way Barnsborough was seen as a *stimulus* or *resource* for the officially sanctioned classroom routines of literacy learning and teaching. Despite the recognition by some teachers that *texting and chat are genres in their own right*, teaching approaches, the timetabled separation of literacy and technology, and the primacy of official versions of print literacy prevailed. And because they tended to see the virtual world as a way of enriching existing practice rather than transforming it, the idea of *virtual role play as a stimulus* made sense when it could be linked to literacy objectives such as report writing and note-taking, but not so well when literacy planning involved poetry or was related to preselected children's literature. In the survey data this was summarized in terms of a problem of *fitting into the curriculum*.

Despite the initial concerns of the planning group, virtual world work did not pose serious technical problems for the schools or the teachers. Some central support was made available to ensure that school computers had the Active Worlds browser software installed and that there were no problems with firewalls, but, apart from this, logging onto Barnsborough was unproblematic. Yet as Holloway and Valentine (2003) observe, computer use in school is about access as well as the resource itself. So in this project although there were no significant resource issues, often access to computers was a barrier. In all the schools the main resource was located in a computer suite that was also used by other classes for ICT lessons. This meant that access was limited and timetabled—often allowing space for only 1–2 hours per week. Consequently a high percentage of project teachers reported that infrequent computer access was a barrier to their work.

In summary the teachers faced a range of challenges in working with the virtual world. Interestingly these did not dampen their enthusiasm but they perhaps limited their level of use of the Barnsborough environment. Although teachers varied in their initial interest in the virtual worlds project, they were convinced by its benefits at quite early stages of its implementation. They were persuaded by the levels of pupil motivation that they saw and this was a very influential factor in terms of their 'buy-in' to the project. At the same time sustained involvement in the Barnsborough work was hampered by the immediate school context and the wider forces of curriculum and school improvement circulating through the education system. This made—and continues to make—continued engagement with the virtual world hard to sustain.

DISCUSSION

The model for understanding the dynamics of change proposed earlier in this chapter and illustrated in the diagram in Figure 10.1 provides a way of looking at the various forces at play in this new literacies project. Here I discuss the three layers of learner and teacher buy-in, entry cost and continued investment, and interest set out in that model, and how they apply to the project.

Firstly, the ways in which children reacted to the Barnsborough project suggest that *their* 'buy in' to the project was quite substantial. Their levels of enthusiasm for the virtual world and their sense of immersion in the narrative threads (notably that of alien abduction) were consistently high. Although no data was available about their engagement in similar virtual world or game environments in out-of-school contexts, it was evident that they adapted very quickly to the navigational and interactive features of Barnsborough and were positively disposed to the collaborative problem-solving they engaged in. In suggesting that writing and other aspects of the literacy curriculum *used to be* boring they convey this enthusiasm in a comparative way. They do, however, also emphasize that they are involved in *doing* something interesting. In contrast the teachers were more cautious—at least in the initial stages—and the virtual world environment seemed more alien to them. Furthermore they had little say in how the project was shaped and it might be predicted that this influenced their level of ownership and commitment. Curriculum developers repeatedly stress the importance of teachers' agreement on the need for change, and the appropriateness and priority given to new initiatives (Fullan, 1997: 34). Given the ways in which the virtual worlds project sat alongside a range of other initiatives, it is unlikely that time and attention were provided for considering these aspects of change at school-level. It could be concluded that teacher buy-in was rather restricted.

Secondly, the Barnsborough case study illustrates how the initial entry cost was offset by technical support, but also how repeat visits to the virtual world depended upon access to computer suites. Continued investment was not simply a matter of negotiating timetable constraints, but also a matter of accommodating the additional demand. This manifested in at least two ways: the first concerned finding a good curriculum fit and the second—a wider concern—was about justifying the additional investment in the face of competing school priorities. The implementation of the project was not guided by strong leadership or provided with ongoing support, and so teachers' beliefs and practices with respect to new literacies received relatively little attention. Despite this, the strongest motivator for teachers appeared to be the level of motivation that they observed in the students. As Fullan observed in his study of technology in Ontario schools:

> innovations are more likely to get implemented and stay implemented when they result in visibly improved student outcomes. (Fullan, 1997: 36)

In this sense student interest was one of the strongest features of the project. So thirdly and finally, this theme of interest captures part of the impact of new literacies work in the classroom. As has been repeatedly noted, pupil engagement in the story of Barnsborough was high and their motivation persuaded teachers of its significance, but, although by the end of the pilot project schools were able to demonstrate improved levels of attainment in literacy, because Barnsborough was itself part of a wave of interventions (see earlier) its specific contribution to this impact remained hard to evaluate. Furthermore since progress in literacy was based on standard measures of print literacy, a positive correlation would need to assume some sort of transfer between new literacies and more traditional ones. Admittedly it could be argued that students' use of new literacies in the context of problem-solving activities in Barnsborough at the very least provided multiple opportunities to 'put literacy to work' in what was to them a meaningful context, but wider contextual factors seemed to define what constituted longer-term interest or benefit. Again there are some interesting parallels in Fullan's work on implementation:

> The practicality of innovations also depends on the trade-off between the personal costs (time, effort etc.) and the actual benefits of getting and staying involved. (Fullan, 1997: 36)

In the light of unsuccessful attempts to re-launch Barnsborough in local schools (Merchant, 2010) it would appear that the evidence of pupil interest seems to have been an insufficient benefit to stimulate sustained involvement.

CONCLUSIONS

Given the widespread changes in communication in society at large it is important that children's experience of literacy in school reflects the digital dimension. The argument put forward in this chapter is that literacy learning in classrooms should be relevant, reflecting and extending children's everyday experience as well as preparing them for what is always an uncertain future. It has been suggested elsewhere that the new literacies are contributing to the emergence of a participatory culture (Merchant, 2009b), yet it is also clear that children and young people occupy very different positions in this culture. So, for example, Jenkins et al. (2006) argue that there is a pressing need to address the 'participation gap,' which could for some students lead to exclusion from these new practices. It would appear, then, that schools have a major role to play in ensuring that *all* children have a positive experience of digital communication and its possibilities. But, although the use of technology in the classroom has been incorporated into curriculum documents in the UK and elsewhere, examples of practice that fully address the new literacies in a principled and sustained way have yet to be reported (Burnett, 2009).

In this case study, the use of virtual world technology as a context for new literacies has been explored following Gee's (2003) idea that such environments can promote sophisticated kinds of learning. In providing an overview of children's and teachers' experience of this work I have focused on both the positive and the negative characteristics of the innovation process. Although there are pitfalls in generalizing from case study data (Flyvbjerg, 2006), the analysis of this virtual world work provided the raw material for a theoretical model—a model that may help to explain the factors at play when introducing new literacies into the classroom. In the Barnsborough work there were a number of key indicators of success, the most persuasive of which were the levels of enthusiasm and engagement reported by the children. The evidence here and that reported elsewhere (Merchant, 2009a; 2010) show children developing practices of online communication, and reading and writing a wide range of multimodal texts—key features of the participatory culture described by Jenkins et al. in their white paper (Jenkins et al., 2006).

The sustainability of projects such as this one must now be a concern for educators as we move from considerations of *what* to do to the concerns of *how* to go about it (Squire, 2005). The current research base in literacy and technology at the elementary school level is still patchy, and it is dominated by small-scale interventions. Out of 40 papers in a recent research review " . . . all but four studies cited reported interventions designed by researchers" (Burnett, 2009: 30). These studies tend to be short-term and grafted onto existing classroom practice. More substantial innovation is now called for in order to develop our understanding of new literacies in the classroom and to assess the tangible benefits for children and young people. We need to understand how new literacies can be fully integrated into the curriculum, and how the necessary skills, understandings, and dispositions develop. Such development can be achieved only through adequate investment and a strong partnership with practitioners, coupled with an understanding of how change in schools and classrooms really works.

REFERENCES

Burnett, C. (2009). Research into literacy and technology in primary classrooms: An exploration of understandings generated by recent studies. *Journal of Research in Reading* 32(1): 22–37.

Carroll, J. (2002). Digital drama: A snapshot of evolving forms. *Critical Studies in Education* 43(2): 130–141.

Chandler-Olcott, K. & Lewis, E. (2010). 'I think they're being wired differently': Secondary teachers' cultural models of adolescents and their online literacies. In D. E. Alvermann (ed.), *Adolescents' Online Literacies: Connecting Classrooms, Digital Media and Popular Culture*. New York: Peter Lang.

Cintron, R. (1997). *Angels' Town: Chero Ways, Gang Life and Rhetorics of the Everyday*. Boston: Beacon Press.

Dede, C., Clarke, J., Ketelhut, D., Nelson, B., & Bowman, C. (2006, April 10). Fostering motivation, learning and transfer in multi-user virtual environments. Paper presented at the 2006 AERA Conference, San Francisco, California.

DFE (2010). Primary framework for literacy and mathematics. Retrieved August 13, 2010 from http://nationalstrategies.standards.dcsf.gov.uk/primary/primaryframework/literacyframework.

Flyvbjerg, B. (2006). Five misunderstandings about case study research. *Qualitative Inquiry* 12(2): 219–245.

Fullan, M. G. (1997). *Successful School Improvement: The Implementation Perspective and Beyond*. Buckingham: Open University Press.

Gee, J. P. (2004). *Situated Language and Learning: A Critique of Traditional Schooling*. Abingdon: Routledge.

Gee, J. P. (2003). *What Video Games Have to Teach Us about Learning and Literacy*. Basingstoke: Palgrave MacMillan.

Hargreaves, A. (2005). Pushing the boundaries of educational change. In A. Hargreaves (ed.), *Extending Educational Change: International Handbook of Educational Change*. New York: Springer.

Hargreaves, A. (2004). Distinction and disgust: The emotional politics of school failure. *International Journal of School Leadership* 7(1): 27–41.

Holloway, S. L. & Valentine, G. (2003). *Cyberkids: Children in the Information Age*. London: RoutledgeFalmer.

Jenkins, H. (with Purushotma, R., Clinton, K., Weigel, M., & Robinson, A.) (2006). Confronting the challenges of participatory culture: Media education for the 21st century. Chicago: MacArthur Foundation. Retrieved August 21, 2010 from http://digitallearning.macfound.org/site/c.enJLKQNlFiG/b.2108773/apps/nl/content2.asp?content_id=<CD911571–0240–4714–A93B-1D0C07C7B6C1>&notoc=1

Kress, G. (2010). *Multimodality: A Social Semiotic Approach to Contemporary Communication*. Abingdon: Routledge.

Kress, G. (2003). *Literacy in an Age of New Media*. London: Routledge.

Lankshear, C. & Knobel, M. (2006). *New Literacies: Everyday Practices and Classroom Learning* (2nd ed.). Maidenhead: Open University Press.

Livingstone, S. (2009). *Children and the Internet: Great Expectations, Changing Realities*. Cambridge: Polity.

Markham, A. (2004). Internet communication as a tool for qualitative research. In D. Silverman (Ed.), *Qualitative research, theory, method and practice*. (2nd edn, pp. 95–214). London: Sage.

Markham, A. (1998). *Life Online: Researching Real Experience in Virtual Space*. London: Sage.

Marsh, J. (Ed.). (2005). *Popular Culture, New Media and Digital Literacy in Early Childhood*. London: RoutledgeFalmer.

Merchant, G. (2010). 3D virtual worlds as environments for literacy teaching. *Education Research* 52(2): 135–150.

Merchant, G. (2009a). Literacy in virtual worlds. *Journal of Research in Reading* 32(1): 38–56.

Merchant, G. (2009b). Web 2.0, new literacies and the idea of learning through participation. *English Teaching, Practice and Critique* 8(3): 107–122.

Merchant, G. (2007). Writing the future in the digital age. *Literacy* 41(3): 118–128.

Plester, B., Wood, C., & Bell, V. (2008). Txt msg n school literacy: Does texting and knowledge of text abbreviations adversely affect children's literacy attainment? *Literacy* 42(3): 137–144.

Prensky, M. (2001). Digital natives, digital immigrants. *On the Horizon* 9(4). Retrieved August 6, 2010 from http://www.marcprensky.com/writing/Prensky%20-%20Digital%20Natives,%20Digital%20Immigrants%20-%20Part1.pdf.

Scollon, R. & Scollon, S. W. (2004). *Nexus Analysis: Discourse and the Emerging Internet*. London: Routledge.

Squire, K. (2005). Changing the game: What happens when video games enter the classroom. *Innovate* 1(6). Retrieved August 6, 2010 from http://innovateonline.info/pdf/vol1_issue6/Changing_the_Game-__What_Happens_When_Video_Games_Enter_the_Classroom_.pdf.

Stake, R. E. (2003). Case studies. In N. K. Denzin & Y. S. Lincoln (eds.), *Strategies of Qualitative Inquiry* (2nd ed.). London: Sage. 134–164.

Part IV

Aspects of Participation

11 Scientific Literacy in a Social Networking Application

Christine Greenhow

INTRODUCTION

Improving adolescents' productive literacies, technological fluencies, and preparation for the twenty-first-century workplace are critical issues facing U.S. education (Bureau of Labor Statistics, 2007; Collins & Halverson, 2009; National Center for Education Statistics, 2005; National Research Council, 2000; Warschauer & Matuchniak, 2010) as research continues to document young people's dissatisfaction with and disengagement from school (Levin, Arafeh, Lenhart, & Rainie, 2002) and public life (Pew, 2008; Putnam, 1995). Increasingly, literacy researchers, learning scientists, and language and media scholars are examining students' informal, out-of-school media practices to improve theory, curricula, and the design of technology-mediated learning contexts (Black, 2008; Greenhow & Burton, 2011; Greenhow & Li, in press; Greenhow & Robelia, 2009a, 2009b; Greenhow, Robelia, & Hughes, 2009; Halverson, 2007; Peppler & Kafai, 2007; Robison, 2008; Steinkuehler, 2008).

Engagement with contemporary *socioscientific issues* (SSIs), or scientific issues shaped by political, social, and economic concerns (Sadler, Barab, & Scott, 2006), can facilitate scientific literacy. Engaging with SSIs requires learners to integrate scientific concepts with normative social practices. Deliberation of SSIs is also believed essential to addressing citizenship education because the issues are pressing and can help bridge school curriculum with students' out-of-school experiences and interests (Zeidler et al., 2002). Yet, inserting SSIs into time-strapped classrooms poses a significant challenge (Sadler et al., 2006), and few studies examine SSI negotiation within out-of-school, technology-mediated contexts popularized by youth culture, especially online social networks (Lenhart et al., 2010).

This chapter describes how young people (ages 16–25) engaged in SSI negotiation in a niche social networking application (HotDish), designed and implemented within Facebook.com. This investigation is part of a larger project examining young people's participation in social media (Greenhow, 2011a, 2011b; 2010). Specifically, I examine: 1) the nature of SSI argumentation in this network; and 2) whether participation in the networking application was associated with students' pro-environmental actions. HotDish was designed to evoke informal knowledge-sharing about environmental science issues and 'eco-friendly' behaviors in everyday life. This research contributes to our understanding of social media and learning and literacies therein.

SOCIAL NETWORK SITES

Like certain gaming environments, social network sites can be construed as self-generated, naturally occurring, indigenous online communities. HotDish is a social networking application within the social network site Facebook. A form of social media, social network sites are *networked communication platforms* in which participants: 1) have *uniquely identifiable profiles* that consist of user-supplied content, content provided by other users, and/or system-provided data; 2) can *publicly articulate connections* that can be viewed and traversed by others; and 3) can consume, produce, and/or interact with *streams of user-generated content* provided by their connections on the site (Ellison & boyd, in press). Unlike other virtual communities, SNSs rely on self-presentation and the display of one's social connections. SNS interactions can result in increased numbers and types of connections and can help users develop and maintain social ties (Ellison, Steinfield, & Lampe, 2007) based on shared values, goals, language, or identities (boyd & Ellison, 2007).

THEORETICAL PERSPECTIVES

This investigation of a niche SNS is guided by sociocultural activity and situated learning theories (Greeno, 1989; Vygotsky, 1978), learning ecology perspectives (Barron, 2006), and New Literacy theories (Coiro et al., 2008; Steinkuehler, Black, & Clinton, 2005). Sociocultural theories assume that learning derives from participation in joint activities, is inextricably tied to social practices, and is mediated by artifacts over time. These theories help researchers conceptualize and study learning, literacies, and community formation (Wenger, 1998) across contexts.

A sociocultural perspective is now evident in conceptualizations of scientific literacy, which have typically emphasized learners' coming to know science as practicing expert scientists do, but now reflect a broader emphasis on young people's engagement with science and technology communities and increased civic and personal understanding. Researchers argue that scientific literacy requires reading, meaning-making, writing, and communicating about contemporary science topics (Polman et al., 2010) and deliberating SSIs in science classrooms (Sadler et al., 2006; Zeidler et al., 2002). These skills and practices are often described as argumentation.

Highlighted by science educators and standards for its role in science learning (Yeh & She, 2010), argumentation is also seen as central to computer-supported collaborative learning (CSCL). Weinberger and Fischer (2006) proposed a four-dimensional approach to investigating argumentative knowledge construction in CSCL. The *participation* dimension considers the quantity and heterogeneity of participation, while the *epistemic* dimension analyzes "the content of learners' contributions" (p. 74). Extending Toulmin's (1958) framework, the *argument* dimension examines the construction of individual and sequential arguments, and the *social modes* dimension considers "to what extent learners refer to contributions of their learning partners" (Weinberger & Fischer, 2006: 77) through externalization, elicitation, and consensus-building.

Similarly, in their review of the environmental science literature, Heimlich and Ardoin (2008) stressed the importance of critical thinking and the ability to change behaviors based on knowledge and attitudes. They argue that providing learners with opportunities to *act* on knowledge of environmental science issues is essential because actions strengthen relevant knowledge and attitudes. Kollmuss & Agyeman (2002) advocate for opportunities to practice pro-environmental actions that seek to minimize the negative impact of one's actions on the natural and built world.

THE RESEARCH STUDY

To answer the questions described earlier, a semi-structured, mixed-method research design was employed (Green, Camilli, & Elmore, 2006). Data were collected and analyzed as part of a multiweek investigation of HotDish.

HotDish (apps.facebook.com/hotdish) is an open-source SNS within Facebook that facilitates information-sharing, commentary, and problem-solving 'challenges' among young people on environmental science and climate change (ESCC) topics. Launched in February 2009, HotDish registered 1,157 members over a four-month period. Youth (grades 10–16) were invited to join.

HotDish is both expert-driven and user-generated; an environmental partner continually updated HotDish with current ESCC information. Moreover, HotDish offered multiple channels for users to share knowledge about ESCC. Features included the ability to post original *stories*, or circulate online news articles. Members could read, vote on, *comment* on, *tweet*, or *chat* with others about entries.

An *Action Team* (AT) feature facilitated participation in problem-solving *challenge*s designed to address ESCC issues in users' communities through online or offline activities (Heimlich & Ardoin, 2008). Offline challenges included recycling electronics, volunteering for environmental organizations, writing letters to the editor, writing a lawmaker, starting a recycling program, and attending town meetings with ESCC issues on the agenda. Challenge completion was tracked through a point system and required uploading evidence of completion for subsequent evaluation.

Of 1,157 registered members, 346 users (ages 16–25) opted into this study and were observed regularly over several weeks for participation levels and other user statistics. Data were gathered from two sources: online survey and usage statistics/archived postings. In spring 2009, AT members (n=322) were invited to take an *online survey*, and 111 (38%) users completed it. Survey items assessed demographics; Internet/SNS use; environmental science/climate change knowledge; motivation and activities within HotDish; literacy practices; and civic engagement. *Usage statistics* per user and feature were also tracked. HotDish members contributed over 3,000 postings, predominantly comments, blog entries, and challenge documentation. Users were categorized into four groups based on total participation scores across all activity: inactive (registered but never participated), low, medium, and high.

This study sought to examine the nature of argumentation within Hot-Dish. A random sample of comments posted to stories (approximately 10% of the dataset) was double-coded for several dimensions of argumentation using both emic and etic codes. For the full paper, 20% of the data will be double-coded and inter-rater reliability will be calculated using Cohen's Kappa (1960). In addition, the frequency of participation (per user) and heterogeneity (per story) were calculated. Participation frequency was calculated as a proportion score (user's total comments posted to a story divided by the total number of comments on that story); heterogeneity was calculated as a proportion score (total commenters per story divided by the total number of comments on that story). Means for these two participation indices were calculated using all stories.

SELECTED RESULTS

Preliminary analysis of young people's purposes and the nature of argumentation and pro-environmental action within and beyond HotDish is ongoing. Usage statistics suggest that HotDish was successful in attracting a base of users (n=129) who actively participated in reading, posting, and commenting on stories.

Purpose

Social aspects of HotDish motivated young people to participate and contribute more than in other websites they frequented. The majority of survey respondents were more motivated to use HotDish to *interact with like-minded people* (72%) and to *express their opinions* (62%) than they reported for other websites.

Argumentation Practices

Across the study period, young people on HotDish read 2,103 articles, 89% of the total possible; they contributed 2,153 comments. Survey responses indicate that the majority of users connected with others by: *reading articles posted by other members* (77%); *reading comments on posted entries* (69%); and *completing problem-solving challenges with others* (53%).

Using Weinberger and Fischer's (2006) approach to analyzing the argumentative dimension of knowledge construction, initial analysis of story comment strings indicates that participants used commentary on posted articles primarily to construct arguments as well as develop a sequence of arguments/counterarguments on environmental SSIs. HotDish participants constructed single arguments ranging from simple claims to grounded claims using observations, personal experiences, and primary or secondary data sources. For example, Jane responded to an article describing a hotel's decision to stop giving newspapers to every occupant in order to reduce its carbon emissions. Her comment reveals the beginning of a constructed argument: "This is good. A lot of people in hotels don't even read them [newspapers]!" The first clause, "This is good," states a simple claim that the hotel is making the correct decision, while the second clause, "A lot of people in hotels don't even read them!," provides grounds.

Ava then countered that not providing newspapers is the wrong decision from an environmental perspective because guests will turn to reading news online, which ultimately costs more energy: "what about all the other components that go into making the plastics and . . . computer you use to access this online material? . . . not to mention the amount of energy you waste to access the article . . . the power to cool the hardware . . . paper is more easily recyclable . . . the carbon emissions are kept within the paper that can decompose and turn into fossil fuels . . ."

The debate continued with participants embedding links to other sources, such as statistics on Google's energy usage, to argue for or against Ava's claims. Further analysis will illuminate the epistemic, argumentative, and social modes constructed within the HotDish comment data and what these reveal about members' conceptions of environmental phenomena (i.e., cause, spread, solutions).

Analysis of the participation dimension of argumentation revealed that average proportionalized participation quantity in stories was .01 (SD = .09). Average participation heterogeneity in stories was .62 (SD=.23), meaning that the proportion of commenters to number of comments was moderately diverse (for most stories above three comments, at least two people commented). Analysis of variance (ANOVA comparing types of users revealed that high users had higher participation quantity scores compared to all users ($p < .001$).

Environmentally Responsible Behaviors

Survey findings and user statistics both indicated that HotDish users were engaged in local environmental activism and that these behaviors increased after participating in HotDish.

The post-use survey included items on environmentally responsible behaviors, including asking users to rate their behaviors before HotDish participation. A second set of questions asked users to rate their behaviors after HotDish participation. Results of a paired samples *t*-test indicated a significant difference between pooled pre-HotDish behavior scores and pooled post-HotDish behavior scores $t(109)=-4.98$, p<.001. Post-HotDish behavior scores were significantly greater (M=26.6, SD=5.2) than pre-Hot-Dish behavior scores (M=25.2, SD=5.1), with an effect size of $d=0.278$. Although this is a relatively small effect, it is explained in part by a ceiling effect; most HotDish users were already engaged in environmentally responsible behaviors when they joined. The fact that users still increased pro-environmental behaviors, as indicated in the survey results, despite a ceiling effect is an important observation that may be further illuminated in additional analyses described in future publications.

HotDish offered 56 different Action Challenges to help users enact pro-environmental behaviors, both in their local communities and online. HotDish users completed 1,173 problem-solving challenges during the eight-week period; of these, 332 completions (22%) were from the category of challenges known as *activism in the local community* described earlier. HotDish users enacted both formalized routes to citizen input and informal routes to citizen input and communication (Bennett, Freelon, & Wells, 2010), which will be described more fully in future publications.

CONCLUSIONS

Although critics assert that online social networking via mobile devices is contributing to declining social support, less diverse interactions, an inability to consider other points of view, mistrust, and a lack of community engagement in the U.S., on the contrary, researchers have found these practices to be associated with the cultivation of larger and more diverse social networks. Facebook users, for instance, have demonstrated more social support and more political action compared to other Americans of similar demographics, and the level of support has been shown to increase with the number of times a day an individual used Facebook (Hampton et al., 2011: 4).

In my research, preliminary results suggest that issue-oriented, online social networking applications implemented within the social media spaces youth already frequent hold promise for facilitating solutions to vexing problems facing U.S. education. Open-source applications can be designed cheaply to combine young people's interests in socializing with opportunities to practice socioscientific issue negotiation, media-sharing, and engagement in the community. Results also suggest that participation in similar SNS contexts may facilitate increased community engagement (e.g., pro-environmental behaviors) even among those already engaging in such behaviors. This finding is significant for those interested in improving theory, curriculum, and design of educational spaces because it confirms theories that providing learners' with opportunities for action strengthens relevant knowledge—to know is not enough—and demonstrates how sociotechnical features work to make this possible.

REFERENCES

Barron, B. (2006). Interest and self-sustained learning as catalysts of development: A learning ecologies perspective. *Human Development* 49: 193–224.

Bennett, L., Freelon, D., & Wells, C. (2010). Changing citizen identity and the rise of participatory media culture. In L. R. Sherrod, J. Torney-Purta, & C. A. Flanagan (eds.), *Handbook of Research on Civic Engagement in Youth*. Hoboken, NJ: John Wiley & Sons, Inc.

Black, R. W. (2008). Just don't call them cartoons: The new literacy spaces of anime, manga and fanfiction. In J. Coiro, M. Knobel, C. Lankshear, & D. Leu (eds.), *Handbook of Research on New Literacies*. New York: Lawrence Erlbaum Associates.

boyd, d. m. & Ellison, N. B. (2007). Social network sites: Definition, history, and scholarship. *Journal of Computer-Mediated Communication* 13(1): article 11. Retrieved October 9, 2008 from http://jcmc.indiana.edu/vol13/issue1/boyd.ellison.html.

Bureau of Labor Statistics (2007). The 30 fastest growing occupations covered in the 2008–2009 Occupational Outlook Handbook. Retrieved January 13, 2009 from http://www.bls.gov/news.release/ooh.t01.htm.

Cohen, J. (1960). A coefficient of agreement for nominal scales. *Educational and Psychological Measurement* 20: 37–46.

Coiro, J., Knobel, M., Lankshear, C., & Leu, D. (2008). Central issues in new literacies and new literacies research. In J. Coiro, M. Knobel, C. Lankshear, & D. Leu (eds.), *Handbook of Research on New Literacies*. New York: Lawrence Erlbaum Associates.

Collins, A. & Halverson, B. (2009). *Rethinking Education in the Age of Technology*. New York: Teachers College Press.

Ellison, N. & boyd, D. (in press). Sociality through social network sites. In W.H. Dutton (ed.), *The Oxford Handbook of Internet Studies*. Oxford: Oxford University Press.

Ellison, N., Steinfield, C., & Lampe, C. (2007). The benefits of Facebook "friends": Exploring the relationship between college students' use of online social networks and social capital. *Journal of Computer-Mediated Communication* 12(3): article 1. Retrieved July 30, 2007 from http://jcmc.indiana.edu/vol12/issue4/ellison.html.

Green, J. L., Camilli, G., & Elmore, P. (2006). *Handbook of Complementary Methods in Education Research*. New York: Routledge.

Greenhow, C. (2011a). Learning and social media: What are the interesting questions for research? *International Journal of Cyber Behavior, Psychology and Learning* 1(1): 36–50.

Greenhow, C. (2011b). Online social networks and learning. *On the Horizon* 15(1): 4–12.

Greenhow, C. (2010). The role of youth as cultural producers in a niche social network site. *New Directions in Youth Development: Theory, Research & Practice* 128: 55–64.

Greenhow, C. & Burton, L. (2011). Help from my "Friends": Social capital in the social network sites of low-income high school students. *Journal of Educational Computing Research* 45(2): 223–245.

Greenhow, C. & Li, J. (in press). Like, comment, share: Collaboration and civic engagement within social network sites. In C. Mouza & N. Lavigne (eds.), *Emerging Technologies for the Classroom: A Learning Sciences Perspective.* New York: Springer.

Greenhow, C. & Robelia, E. (2009a). Informal learning and identity formation in online social networks. *Learning, Media and Technology* 34(2): 119–140.

Greenhow, C. & Robelia, E. (2009b). Old communication, new literacies: Social network sites as social learning resources. *Journal of Computer-mediated Communication* 14(4): 1130–1161.

Greenhow, C., Robelia, E., & Hughes, J. (2009). Web 2.0 and classroom research: What path should we take now? *Educational Researcher* 38 (4): 246–259.

Greeno, J. (1989). The situativity of knowing, learning, and research. *American Psychologist* 53: 5–26.

Halverson, E. (2007). Reality television and participation in online communities of practice. In C. A. Chinn, G. Erkens, & S. Puntambekar (eds.), *CSCL 2007: Proceedings of the International Society of the Learning Sciences Computer supported Collaborative Learning Conference.* New Brunswick, NJ: International Society of the Learning Sciences.

Hampton, K., Sessions Goulet, L., Rainie, L., & Purcell, K. (2011). *Social Networking Sites and Our Lives.* June 16. Washington, DC: Pew Charitable Trusts. Retrieved May 20, 2012 from http://pewinternet.org.

Heimlich, J. E. & Ardoin, N. E. (2008). Understanding behavior to understand behavior change: A literature review. *Environmental Education Research* 14(3): 215–237.

Kollmuss, A. & Agyeman, J. (2002). Mind the gap: Why do people act environmentally and what are the barriers to pro-environmental behaviour? *Environmental Education Research* 8(3): 239–260.

Lenhart, A., Purcell, K., Smith, A., & Zickuhr, K. (2010). *Social Media and Young Adults.* February 10. Washington, DC: Pew Charitable Trusts. Retrieved July 14, 2010 from http://pewinternet.org.

Levin, D., Arafeh, S., Lenhart, A., & Rainie, L. (August). (2002). *The Digital Disconnect: The Widening Gap between Internet-Savvy Students and Their Schools.* August 14. Washington, DC: Pew Charitable Trusts. Retrieved May 20, 2012 from http://www.pewinternet.org.

National Center for Education Statistics (NCES) (2005). *The Condition of Education in Brief.* NCES 2005095. Washington, DC. Author.

National Research Council (2000). *Inquiry and the National Science Education Standards.* Washington, DC: National Academy.

National Science Board (2010). *Science and Engineering Indicators: 2010.* Arlington, VA: National Science Foundation.

Peppler, K. A. & Kafai, Y. B. (2007). From SuperGoo to Scratch: Exploring creative digital media production in informal learning. *Learning, Media and Technology* 32(2): 149–166.

Pew Research Center for the People & the Press (2008). Key news audiences now blend online and traditional sources. Washington, DC: Pew Charitable Trusts. Retrieved May 20, 2012 from http://www.people-press.org

Polman, J. L., Saul, W., Newman, A., Farrar, C., Singer, N., Turley, E., Pearce, L., Hope, J., & McCarty, G. (2010). A cognitive apprenticeship for science literacy based on journalism. In K. Gomez, L. Lyons, & J. Radinsky (eds.), *Learning in the Disciplines: Proceedings of the 9th International Conference of the*

Learning Sciences (ICLS 2010): *Vol. 2. Short Papers, Symposia, and Selected Abstracts.* Chicago, IL: International Society of the Learning Sciences.

Putnam, R. D. (1995). *Bowling Alone: The Collapse and Revival of the American Community.* New York: Simon & Schuster.

Rideout, V. J., Foehr, U. G., & Roberts, D. F. (2010). *Generation M²: Media in the lives of 8- to 18-Year-Olds* (Report No. 8010). Menlo Park, CA: Kaiser Family Foundation.

Robison, A. J. (2008). The design is the game: Writing games, teaching writing. *Computers and Composition* 25: 359–370.

Sadler, T., Barab, S., & Scott, B. (2006). What do students gain by engaging in socioscientific inquiry? *Research in Science Education* 37: 371–391.

Steinkuehler, C. (2008). Cognition and literacy in massively multiplayer online games. In J. Coiro, M. Knobel, C. Lankshear, & D. Leu (eds.), *Handbook of Research on New Literacies.* New York: Lawrence Erlbaum.

Steinkuehler, C. A., Black, R. W., & Clinton, K. A. (2005). Researching literacy as tool, place, and way of being. *Reading Research Quarterly* 40(1): 7–12.

Thurlow, C. (2006). From statistical panic to moral panic: The metadiscursive construction and popular exaggeration of new media language in the print media. *Journal of Computer-Mediated Communication* 11(3): article 1.

Toulmin, S. (1958). *The Uses of Argument.* New York: Cambridge University Press.

Vygotsky, L. S. (1978). *Mind in Society: The Development of Higher Psychological Processes.* Cambridge, MA: Harvard University Press.

Warschauer, M. & Matuchniak, T. (2010). New technology and digital worlds: Analyzing evidence of equity in access, use, and outcomes. *Review of Research in Education* 34(1):179–225.

Weinberger, A. & Fischer, F. (2006). A framework to analyze argumentative knowledge construction in computer-supported collaborative learning. *Computers & Education* 46: 71–95.

Wenger, E. (1998). *Communities of Practice: Learning, Meaning and Identity.* New York: Cambridge University Press.

Yeh, K. & She, H. (2010). On-line synchronous scientific argumentation learning: Nurturing students' argumentation ability and conceptual change in science context. *Computers & Education* 55(2): 586–602.

Zeidler, D. L., Walker, K. A., Ackett, W. A., & Simmons, M. L. (2002). Tangled up in views: Beliefs in the nature of science and responses to socioscientific dilemmas. *Science Education* 86: 343–367.

12 Seeking Planning Permission to Build a Gothic Cathedral on a Virtual Island

Julia Gillen, Rebecca Ferguson, Anna Peachey, and Peter Twining

INTRODUCTION

Schome Park was a virtual island, set in the middle of a sunlit sea beyond which none of its inhabitants could wander. Like all islands, it had a limited set of resources and so the islanders had worked out a system of local governance for allocating these. Most prized was permission to use prims, a kind of all-purpose material, to construct an exciting new building, perhaps the site for an event or new community facility—a club, a cooperative store, garden, race track, restaurant, or something equally appealing. One day, a newcomer who had recently landed from the U.S. onto this island, dominated by Brits, approached the planning permission committee. Carefully observant of legal and procedural niceties, he set out his request, in writing, as required. He wanted to build a Gothic cathedral. In many old-timers' views, this was a bad idea, something that threatened the community's history and ethos, perhaps to the core. A lively debate ensued.

We, the writers of this chapter, were staff members in this extraordinarily lively and unpredictable online project centered on a virtual world. The fourth author was the director of the project. This was the first European closed (i.e., 'protected') Teen Second Life Educational project, which ran for 13 months from 2007 to 2008. It was centered upon activities in a virtual world, accompanied by other online communication domains, including wiki and asynchronous fora. Since elements of the project were open 24/7 and several hundred people participated—for varying durations and intensity of engagement—the project had such an enormous variety of events and interactions that it would be impossible for anybody involved to witness or even have any knowledge about everything that occurred. Accordingly, as we've argued elsewhere, although certain kinds of overviews have been written (e.g., Twining, 2009; Twining & Footring, 2010), there is also a place in analysis of the project for deploying a 'team ethnography' approach (Creese, Bhatt, Bhojani, & Martin, 2008). This is an attempt to understand events and practices through accepting the existence of a "multiplicity of co-existing and sometimes directly competing points of view" (Bourdieu, 1999: 3) within the project, working together to construct a polyvocal account, remaining aware of the unfinalizable nature of any understandings. Since the project can be characterized as a lifelike flow of interactions and events online, more like life on a large island indeed than the bounded characteristics of a more standard educational intervention project, a multivocal ethnography appears to us an appropriate approach to studying the project, especially now that we take a retrospective examination (the project was also characterized by concurrent research methods that are not the focus of attention here). We have together selected examination of the 'Gothic cathedral debate'—our own construction—as a 'telling case' for this chapter. We will return to both methodology and our selection of this case later.

Before introducing the debate in more detail, it is vital, as within any ethnographic approach, to give a sociohistorical background to the setting. We have to explain the background to the project in the physical world and to introduce some of the social and cultural aspects of the environment we are examining.

SCHOME PARK: A BRIEF CULTURAL HISTORY

The Schome Initiative was set up under the auspices of a voluntary umbrella community of educationalists, young people, parents, teachers, and anyone who wanted to join online discussions about the future of education in the twenty-first century.[1] This online community has since 2005 been based at the Open University, UK (a distance learning university with a strong record of principles of high-quality learning and teaching, openness and innovation). The word 'Schome' derived from an early characterization of 'not school, not home' that, while not being a simple rejection of both those domains, suggested that the firm boundaries between them need to be shaken and was informed by the notion of 'the third place' (Oldenburg, 1989). The shared aim has been to investigate and attempt to enact new models of education, centered upon a cradle-to-grave ethos, providing participants with increased range, responsibility, and control of their learning and greater opportunities for collaboration. From the perspective of the director of the project (Peter) it was rooted in the experience of participating in an eStrategy Implementation Review team (Twining et al., 2006), which led to vision-building activities in schools (Rix & Twining, 2007; Sheehy & Bucknall, 2008; Craft, Chappell, & Twining, 2008) and an identification of key elements of what the UK's future education system should provide. A simplified version of that identification summary appears as Table 12.1.

The Schome Initiative was established with the aim of creating a new form of educational system designed to overcome the problems associated with current education systems in order to meet the needs of society and individuals in the twenty-first century. Technology is seen not only as a tool

Table 12.1   Summary of Key Elements of a Future Education System for the UK (based upon Twining, 2010)

Aims	Smarter learners better able to cope with changing contexts – focus on enhancing learning, motivation and lifelong learning.
Environment	Both the spatial and temporal aspects of the learner's environment will expand through greater emphasis placed on the home, working across physical and virtual settings and extending the school day.
Actors	An increase in the involvement and availability of actors (people and organisations involved in supporting learning) owing to ICT, especially in relation to interactions at a distance, accompanied by greater emphasis on the role of parents.Collaboration will be a key element to this diversification of actors and environments. Learners' choice, responsibility and control will become increasingly important .
Curriculum	The curriculum includes everything that learners learn and will be broadened in terms of the subjects available and learner choice. More vocationally-oriented options will be offered and there will be a greater emphasis on core skills.
Support	The range and nature of support, which includes teaching, will increase and diversify as the environments, actors and curriculum expand. There will be an increase in learner choice about when, where and how learners are supported.

to support and extend existing practices but also as having the potential to transform ways of representing the world and of supporting learning.

In 2006 the Schome community decided to explore the potential of virtual worlds, considering their capacity to act as spaces in which visions of future practices and pedagogies can be built and experienced, making it "possible to construct, investigate and interrogate hypothetical worlds" (Squire, 2006: 19). With funding from a number of organizations at various stages of the project and a great deal of further voluntary input (see Gillen et al., 2009; Sheehy, Ferguson, & Clough, 2010; Twining, 2009 for more details) the Schome Park Programme (SPP) was launched. The SPP decided to use *Teen Second Life*, the youth version of the virtual world *Second Life*, at the time with an incontestable claim to being the most technologically advanced open virtual world (Twining & Peachey, 2009)— that is, not a constrained and goal-oriented environment such as *World of Warcraft*. This made it necessary for the community participants ourselves to design and enact all activities on the island (later two islands), which, along with a wiki and forum, was the location for the project. Although at the beginning of the project a few resources were 'imported' as it were from elsewhere in *Second Life*, once the project was open it was up to participants to design activities, establish ground rules, and construct community practices. Having downloaded the client application, via their 2D computer screens, participants interacting remotely were physically located in homes, schools, workplaces, or after-school clubs—mostly in the UK but with some in the U.S. With a mixture of staff-led and student-led activities, which many people who tried out the project found exciting, a distinctive community emerged with an ethos that one of us, Peter Twining, the project director, has previously characterized in terms entirely dichotomous to a school regime; see Table 12.2.

In particularly crediting Table 12.2 to the director of the project, we are not seeking to disassociate us, the other authors, from it. On the contrary, the Schome ethos and aims are well encapsulated here for all of us. But still, in capturing a specific text and its articulation in just this form, we want to spring from it, drawing attention to how the culture of any community is constantly in flux. With Heath and Street we suggest it is fruitful to think of culture as a verb rather than a noun: an "ever-shifting active process of meaning-making" (Heath & Street, 2008: 7); thus newcomers to the community, for example, whatever their scale of knowledge about Schome before entering, will have at best an emergent sense of the project's aims and features as understood by the director and core participants. They, and we indeed, will shape and refine understandings of the Schome culture in ways at least partly dependent on initial interactions as well as developing interactions and a growing sense of shared community history.

Thus, as a brief but linked diversion we would like to remark at this point that the kind and quality of initial interaction were a constant challenge with which the project grappled throughout; if it was possible for a

Table 12.2 Features of Schome (reproduced from Twining, 2010: 141)

Features of School	Dimension	Features of Schome
Teacher = Expert Student = Learner (non-expert; empty vessel)	Roles	Everybody = Learner (all have something to offer)
Based on power (of the teacher)	Relationships	Based on equality
Externally imposed (e.g. by government, teacher)	Curriculum	Learner choice
Teacher imposed	Discipline	Community sanctioned
Piagetian (individual constructivist)	Theoretical stance	Situated social constructivist
Extrinsic (e.g. marks in gradebook)	Motivation	Intrinsic (enjoyment/satisfaction/interest)
Success of the individual	Focus	Health of the community
Competition (between individuals)	Perspective	Collaboration

project entrant to 'land' in-world at any time 24/7, how could we ensure that his or her first experience was a worthwhile one rather than of limited interest or even off-putting? This difficulty was a strong factor influencing the brevity of participation of many entrants, and is a common issue for virtual worlds in general (Au, 2008).

In the Schome Park Programme, both individuals and groups joined the project at various points during the three phases. The particular debate focused upon in this chapter occurred during the third phase, when school-based groups of students joined, some working with a teacher in an after-school club, others using Schome Park as part of lessons during school time. Their introductions to Schome Park were designed so that to some degree at least they understood they were joining an already well-established community of practice: "a group of people who share an interest in a domain of human endeavor and engage in a process of collective learning that creates bonds between them" (Wenger, 2001: 1).

BACKGROUND TO THE GOTHIC CATHEDRAL
PROPOSAL AND CONTEXT FOR ANALYSIS

The immediate context to the debate over the proposed Gothic cathedral is that a high-school group from the U.S. entered the SPP with their teacher. In this computer class, one opportunity among others that was given to them was to earn credit through carrying out a project in Schome Park. Projects generally involved building or creating artifacts on the island. This group, who called themselves the SpARTans, was given to understand, however, that any building proposal had to be put to the Schommunity before being undertaken. This was owing to limits on resources, including prims and space for building, and a shared community ethos that such projects should be outlined and agreed in essence before construction. (For more informa-tion and analysis as to the interactions between these groups, including discussion as to the conceptual relations between network and community as enacted in practice, see Ferguson, Gillen, Peachey, & Twining, 2011.)

In this chapter we seek to explore what happened in a debate about one planning application. As will be shown, we consider the debate to be a "telling case" (Mitchell, 1984) in that rather than being a 'typical case'—which in our compass here might be a delightful demonstration of how wonderfully well Schome matched up to its aspirations and characteriza-tions in practice—we find the events around the Gothic cathedral to be a less comfortable and yet fruitful instantiation of Schome Park life. We seek to analyze the debate as virtual literacies in practice, exploring the entwined relationships between communicative domain, participants, and meaning-making practices. We recognize that 'the debate' is our own con-struction, in that in order to narrow down the scope of analysis to some-thing practicable, we focus on the main location for communications about the Gothic cathedral proposal, one specific thread of the asynchronous forum. It would be better to make a brief consideration of other communicative domains where the debate occurred since the forum was so entwined with other interactions in practice, but beyond the scope of work in this chapter. Here our focus is on an extrapolated dataset of 90 postings, more than sufficiently challenging to analysis in its range and content. Before beginning to examine that data, however, it is necessary to explain its place within the various communicative domains of the project.

As was briefly mentioned earlier, the project was centered on an island, or, as the project expanded, an island archipelago, known as Schome Park. Participants in the project interacted and communicated through a pseudonymized identity, both on the simulated island 'in-world' and through other digital modes of communication. In-world, the mode of interaction is through an avatar, which interacts with the environment, including other avatars and objects, giving the illusion of three-dimensional space. All movement and communicative practices are controlled by the individual, who controls the avatar via a keyboard. The effects projected include movement by walking, running, or flying; communicating through written synchronous 'chat' and instant messaging; and building new objects and making them do things, through using the software that includes a programming language. At the same time communicative domains outside *Second Life* were extremely important, especially the project's wiki and forum. As the community of practice developed and learned which domains were most appropriate and effective according to various purposes, the wiki became increasingly specialized for recording events and for announcements of crystallized plans for future events. The forum was the site for a great diversity of purposes and indeed was the communicative domain most engaged in by project members—that is to say more time was spent engaging with it even than in-world. At first glance that seems perhaps a little odd, as the *Second Life* islands were the central focus for activity. However, the forum was even more popular for two reasons. The first is that it was relatively easy to access. Any participant could access his or her forum account from any computer; so if, for example, one was on the Internet, during a school break, for example, and using a shared computer without a *Second Life* account, it was easy to take a quick look at the forum. Secondly, it was well suited to discussions including asynchronous and even synchronous planning of events in-world. Although there were many other communication domains relating to the project—for example, blogs maintained by participants under their project pseudonyms but hosted outside the project—our ethnographic endeavor as a whole is constituted by the analysis of the project's virtual literacies, visible as textual records of chatlogs, wiki pages, and asynchronous fora, plus field notes and image captures. Hence, since in this project staff members interacted with students only online[2] we tend to describe our approach as a virtual literacy ethnography (Gillen, 2009).

Centering on the specific forum thread, which for simplicity we will from now on refer to as the 'debate,' we worked to identify the span of messages that were its focus, settling on 90 posts posted between April 11 and April 21, 2008. We carried out a small amount of editing to remove some material relating to other topics; since the thread was so focused in practice this was relatively easy to do. We did not edit out material when any of us felt it might have a bearing on the debate. Our approach to analysis is to illustrate the beginnings of the debate, to begin to discuss some of the issues immediately raised, and then to offer further analysis of a sample of postings.

THE FORUM DEBATE

Figure 12.1 shows the original posting in full, except that the name of the avatar (i.e., participant's pseudonym) and that of the thread on which the message appeared have been obliterated. This is the first posting in our data-set; it was actually the seventh posting in its thread, but from this point postings were centrally concerned with the debate. Although some of our writings about the project in the past have featured participants' (avatars') names (i.e., project pseudonyms), in accordance with consent given, other of our writings such as this paper have further introduced a new level of anonymity.

Applying Katzav and Reed's (2004) approach to the analysis of argumentation, there are three clearly identifiable arguments as follows:

Argument 1. I propose that I will build a cathedral. Therefore I need some things.
Argument 2. I suggest that there is a lack of time to do this. Therefore I propose it will be done gradually.
Argument 3. I suggest that I will open on May 26th. Therefore the significance of this opening should be marked by an event.

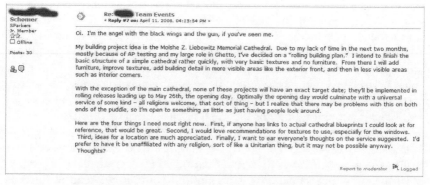

Figure 12.1   Original proposal to build a Gothic cathedral.

Each of these is fleshed out in more detail. For example, the things that are needed in Argument 1 consist of blueprints of actual cathedrals (i.e., materials from elsewhere that will inform the design activity), materials—here 'textures'—that can be used in the build activity, and thirdly suggestions for a location, or position to build it.

Taking a sociocultural framework to online discourse, that we relate strongly to a more general perspective on human communication, we can broaden our understanding of the posting further. Discourse is always mediated action (Scollon, 2001), which is to say that communications are always affected by the material conditions of the communication channel, and the cultural understandings of involved participants. As Haraway (1997: 218) proposes, discourses are "not just words: they are material-semiotic practices." We will have more to say about the material aspects of these postings later, but we can immediately point out that the posting is constituted by templated aspects and newly written elements. The structured template appears at the top, giving the posting precise temporal and spatial coordinates, while the left-hand column gives some details about the author (whom we shall call TA), including facts that to a practiced eye (i.e., core member of the community of practice) give clues as to the status of the author, as relative newcomer. Significant is the little box with 'offline' next to it. Although in reproductions such as here it will be shown as a blank square labeled 'offline,' during the life of the project, and specifically those April days in 2008 being revisited here, when a participant read a posting there might well have been an illuminated green square here and the label 'online.' This would mean that as one read, the author was actually online at the same time. If one were quick to post a response, it was likely that the original author would see that posting, and thus the forum was effectively operating as a synchronous channel. This is of course one of many aspects to communication that is partially occluded to any subsequent research, but our knowledge as participants enables us to know that this synchronicity, yet persistence, was often a feature in the intensity of certain exchanges. It is also a superb example of newly flexible ways of combining reading and writing practices (Lankshear & Knobel, 2006; Kress, 2010).

Every communication is not understood anew; all communications are crafted towards a sense of explicit and implicit audience, against a background of values and attitudes (Voloshinov, 1995). This first posting can be seen as including other elements than the arguments as identified earlier, indeed words that appear to indicate awareness that there may be elements in the proposal potentially troublesome to the community. In particular the idea of the 'universal service' is recognized as potentially problematic, yet the very act of recognizing a potential problem, picked up again at the end of the post, appears a tactful calibration to potential difficulties.

It was not enough to carry through the proposal. Within three minutes a response appeared; see Figure 12.2.

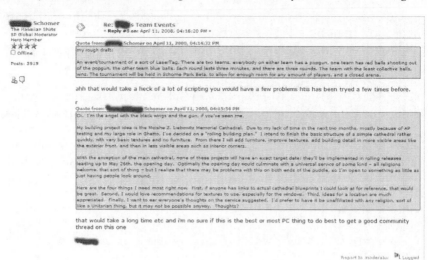

Figure 12.2   First response to Gothic cathedral proposal.

We must remark at this point that it was a difficult decision to make—
to decide whether it was sufficient to quote the direct response of this
responder, whom we shall call TB, to the initial proposal:

> "that would take a long time etc. and I'm no sure if this is the best or
> most PC thing to do best to get a good community thread on this one"

Displaying that response in the context TB designed, in Figure 12.2, gives
a somewhat different interpretive frame. We can read that TB has chosen
to respond to TA's previous initiating post together with another posted by
somebody else. (We will refer to TB as 'he' in accordance with our impres-
sion gained over the life of the project, but gender ascription is always
tentative. For example, in writing this we found that three of us thought
the SpARTans' teacher was female and one male. In practice we found it
impossible to avoid gender ascription.) He, TB then, in this posting groups
it together with another proposal that he is also negative towards. This
might make his objection less personalized, less hostile perhaps—although
of course this is only one possible reading. TB does choose to select the size
of quotation, in one case the whole post, in the first not, which makes it
clear what he is responding to. Finally, although negative, he does not present his negative response as a putative last word, but rather suggests further
discussion might be useful. As we have already mentioned, the result was a
total of 90 postings in 11 days. This intensity, and the broad range of topics covered, presents a considerable challenge to analyze relatively briefly.
Since the nature of a team ethnography implies some willingness to be open

about matters of process, we can say that piloted approaches have included an identification of all arguments and an attempt to map their relations; this rapidly revealed itself to be completely unmanageable, including when considered against the affordances of book pages or even screen presentation. Accordingly, we present a brief exploration of the breadth of debate according to participants and topic sampling.

Figure 12.3 displays the contributions per participant. Each participant is anonymized through being given a letter according to his or her place in the debate. The student who first brought up the idea that became the focus of the debate is therefore TA; the one who immediately responded to 'him' is TB. In this code 'T' stands for teenage participant and O for adult, since this difference was visible to everybody in the project throughout, through a distinct patterning of avatar 'surnames' that was necessary for child protection reasons.

Figure 12.3 demonstrates that the debate was widely engaged in and that furthermore everybody except three people found it worth posting to at least a second time. Some people were extremely engaged; these included the original proposer but also the fourteenth teenager to enter the debate. As we will show by more qualitative analysis, this is indicative of the continuing fertility of the debate; it did not feature mere rehashing of established positions set by a small number of combatants. The mean number of contributions per person is 5.29 (SD 4.51) and the median number 3. Adults appear to be fairly minimally involved in that OA posted twice and OB just once. However, our

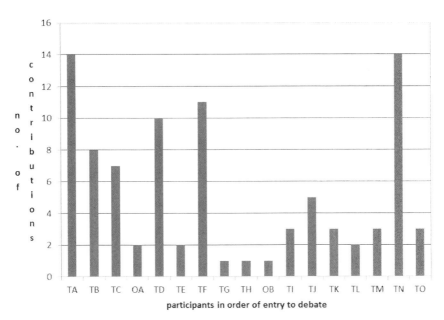

Figure 12.3　Contributions to the debate (Tx—teenager; Ox—adult).

sense was that the teenagers were aware that the thread was being read and monitored in some sense by adults, who played a part in topping and tailing the debate. Some postings made reference to the likelihood, or possibility of intervention, perhaps by the project director.

Now we turn to considering the content of posts. We decided to briefly describe, quote from, and relate to the debate as a whole, every tenth contribution (i.e., from number 10, to 20 . . . to 90), having checked that we all agreed that this sampling did result in a reasonably representative selection, according to dimensions of length, strength of relation to surrounding posts, and content. We recognize that necessarily the act of describing or summarizing the postings has the potential to skew the original intentions of the author or indeed how it might be read, both within the project and later.

Posting 10—TB4, 194 Words Long & Inclusion of One Quotation

This posting is coded as TB4 (i.e., it was the fourth posting by TB, who was of course the very first to respond to the TA's initiation).

TB again responds to TA, although this time by responding to a very short extract, in which TA criticizes Richard Dawkins, whose views have been introduced into the debate.

TB makes various points in alignment with TA, including agreeing that religion should be discussed, violence is wrong, and that Gothic architecture can be beautiful, citing York cathedral as an example. He interweaves these agreements with an assertion, backed up with a dictionary definition, that a cathedral building is necessarily associated with religious purposes and states that he does not want a religious building in Schome Park. He also adopts a strategy of mitigating the strength of his view by asserting he has no power to stop TA.

Posting 20—TA4, 507 Words Long & Inclusion of One Quotation

TA begins by quoting approvingly a contribution to the thread, outside the debate, which describes plans for a beach wedding by two participants, including "a chuppa, used by many Jews during the ceremony." TA moves to the body of his post by declaring he will make a general response to several points made in discussion, rather than taking each up separately. He rejects some notions of compromise that have been raised, making an argument that it would be pointless to build a cathedral without overt religious symbolism, as then it would not be a cathedral. He also objects to people being offended at the notion it necessarily involves religious practices, declaring: "I'm not planning this place as a place to regularly hold services. I was thinking of a sort of all-inclusive 'consecration' as an opening, but not to any specific religion. This building's religious presence would be a presence, but it would begin and end at the architecture." He displays attention to the wellbeing of the community, and approval of aspects of the cooperative tone of the debate, in calling it "reasoned, disciplined and intellectual, minus my provocative pass at Mr Dawkins" and proceeds to refine his earlier opinion, then stating: "This was a learning experience, one that never would have happened if discussion of the man was banned." He finishes his post by questioning other cultural presences in Schome Park—for example, as to whether the Japanese garden might be perceived as a Shinto presence.

Posting 30—TF4, 573 Words, Divided into Two Sections with a Subheading

The first half of the posting is a complex contribution to the debate, arguing that the root of opposition to the proposal is not that people would be offended by having a religious building as such: "I am sure we are all sensible enough not to be offended by a religious building. However, that doesn't mean there aren't other reasons against it, and Political Correctness is standing as a straw man here*. Instead, I think my reasons against it are best explained by Crick, tongue in cheek: 'Christianity may be OK between consenting adults in private but should not be taught to young children.'" Rather, he explains, religion is intensely personal and inappropriate to Schome Park as potentially invasive. The asterisk leads to the subheading for the second section, which is an extremely well-structured argument about the nature of political correctness, synthesizing various kinds of evidence and referring to American, Russian, and other histories.

Posting 40—TA8, 88 Words, in Two Parts, Interposed with Two Quotations

In part 1 of his posting, TA responds to a concern about the possibility of using too many prims in his project in a conciliatory fashion, asking for advice and adding (with reference to his computer class agenda): "I do have to make something, though; this IS our final project. " In part 2 he responds to a new enquiry about his reasoning for wanting to build a cathedral: "Originally, it was because 1) the layout is governed enough that I'd have a strong starting point and 2) because of the beauty of religious buildings in that style. Now it's a fight for free expression of ideas." This appears likely, in our view at least, to be a particularly powerful posting as attending to so many community norms and values, including contrasting the relative freedom, albeit always within certain constraints, of the Schome Park Programme and school, the realm with which it is most often (unfavorably) contrasted (Gillen, 2011).

Posting 50—TN3, 173 Words

Without directly quoting any other postings, TN here clearly locates her posting in the flow of a particular theme as to whether religion should be practiced in Schome Park. She expands on a previous posting through disclosing: "I myself am a Christian, I dont make a big thing of it, but in this case I do think I should say that I feel that these places are places in which to worship God, and therefore should not be copied just for recreational purposes." Finally, she expresses some degree of support with another contributor, who has declared she wishes to leave the project, as she feels strongly against the use of it for school-based assessed work.

Posting 60—TO3, 239 Words Including One Quotation and a Hyperlink

TO begins by quoting an extract from a posting by TN in which she distinguishes between religion, wars, and wars justified by religion, mentioning the Crusades. TO proposes a taxonomy for wars (civil, ideological, expansionist, and religious), and taking the Crusades as an example argues that organized religion has often been associated with war. "The idea of an afterlife and of salvation has always been, and will continue to be, a way to persuade otherwise moral people to commit atrocities. That is why I dislike organised religion, and why I think it should have no place in schome." He continues by making a distinction between religion used as justifying wars and distinctive religious leaders and their followers, naming "Abraham, Muhammed, Guru Nanak, or Siddartha Gautama" as proponents of contrary views (implicitly against war). In the second part of his posting he suggests other styles of buildings, including a hyperlink to an article on Leuven Town Hall in Wikipedia.

Posting 70—TN11, 41 Words, Spaced Out into Three Sections

The content of TN's posting has clear intertextual references to preceding posts, but those have to be read in order to fully understand her brief entries here. For example, her first, "I read them. . . . " responds to an earlier posting by TF, who in turn is synthesizing some earlier responses and postings including his own. Indeed, it must be interjected at this point that to describe TN's posting on this occasion would take far longer than the original posting and that, therefore, any notion of 'summarizing' is indeed impossible. The second element supports the idea of a vote relating to the proposal (this can be set up as a poll on any thread at any time), and the third extends somebody else's idea that symbolism can be used appropriately in Schome but relating to issues away from religion. Her suggestion is "Something about a personal hero. eg. Douglas Adams, and 42 pillars or something similar. Just an example."

Posting 80—TB8, 107 Words

TB begins by joining a long-running theme in response to TA's proposal—an objection that being set work and graded on it by a teacher is counter to the established Schome ethos. He mitigates any possible offense that might be taken (implicitly, presumably, by the teacher) and praises TA, culminating in the proposition: "For engaging in this debate alone and how well you are presenting your augment etc alone you should get a A*"" It's vital to recall that this praise sounds all the more genuine, and one might perhaps say intellectually mature, coming as it does from someone who has opposed the cathedral proposal from the outset. He finishes the post by again arguing secular builds would be better, in his opinion, as religious connotations affect his opinion of any building.

Posting 90—TJ5, 199 Words in Three Sections, Including One Quotation

TJ quotes a relatively emotional posting by TA in which he states, "I'm feeling pretty freaking persecuted as a religious person." She denies that persecution of anybody because of their religious beliefs can occur in Schome, also stating that any suggestion to the contrary is insulting. Secondly, she implicitly refers to her position as a "hero moderator" (visible on the left-hand side of her template) in threatening to close the thread down until the project director is available (to mediate).

However, in the third part of the posting she continues the theme that has appeared many times in the debate, of suggesting some kind of amendment to the original proposal, proposing this to be a "compromise."

A Brief Afterword

The debate did not end with Posting 90. It marked a kind of watershed, though, in that some of the interwoven themes petered out and others were resolved. TA decided to abandon the Gothic cathedral idea, and his teacher posted to explain why she had originally encouraged TA and how she had not foreseen the problems that arose, nor indeed felt she had come to a final understanding of them. Here and in other threads and project domains, as well as beyond, references to the debate and themes from it continued to be discussed, but beyond our scope here.

CONCLUSIONS

In conclusion then, we would echo the opinion of some of the participants that the debate was rich in multiple ways. Analysis shows how vital it is, when considering literacy practices, to take into account in very precise ways the affordances of the specific domain engaged in. The written, persistent nature of the forum made it possible to maintain several significant arguments in just one discussion. The ability to return to earlier issues, to keep multiple ideas in play, and to have the time to develop extremely complex turns in the conversation are all afforded by the medium. Participants were able to interweave arguments, dip in and out of them, arrange them in new patterns, and play on their resonances. The same debate could not have happened in any other medium; the qualities of the forum, as creatively taken up by the participants, had a profound effect on how the arguments played out. We offer support then for Haraway's (1997) characterization of discourses as "material-semiotic practices" as discussed earlier.

Yet the debate would be of very limited interest if it merely illustrated the potential affordances of one medium rather than another. Of more significance in the end is the extent to which it clarifies or at least raises significant questions about creating the foundations for the kind of collaborative discussions that are founded in a trusting community, supportive of individuals shaping learning identities in a creative environment (Peachey, 2010). Rethinking educational practice to include more authentic literacy engagements, asynchronous debates that are genuinely meaningful to participants, speak to their concerns, and relate to genuine opportunities for purposeful activity and indeed creativity, is surely a worthwhile exercise (Barton, 2007; Ferguson, 2011). How might then such ideas promote reshaping the aims of learning environments, even ultimately institutions of education?

A more skeptical question might legitimately be posed as to whether settling such disputes is relevant 'in the real world.' We are wholeheartedly convinced that, as more and more communication happens online, the capacity to interact online in ways far more sophisticated than the old caricatures of online interaction (flaming, flirting, etc.) imply is a vital component of effective professional and personal relations. Although it is beyond the scope of this article, the physical world is waking up to the economic, political, and hence legal ramifications of interactions in virtual worlds (Castronova, 2007). Tennesen (2009) argues that it is likely virtual world transactions, even if without commercial currency in the physical world, are likely to come under "bricks-and-mortar jurisprudence" as they do already in South Korea.

In the end, though, we would suggest it is not necessary to accept that because virtual worlds are becoming increasingly recognized as authentic theatres for human interaction that virtual literacies should be valued. Rather the capacity to build bridges either between communities, or even within communities where divisions of purpose and values suddenly open up into dangerous chasms, fruitfully involves consideration of the complexities involved in communicative practices.

> In communication, members of a community participate in the renewing, the remaking and the transformation of their social environment from the perspective of *meaning*. In the process 'the social'—as entities and forms, as processes and practices—is constantly articulated in (material) semiotic form: the social is re-*calibrated*, re-*registered* with semiotic/cultural resources. (Kress, 2010: 34, emphasis as original)

Ever-shifting active processes of meaning-making continually 'do' culture, as we find new modes for learning in the pursuit of multiple, entwined goals, in a necessarily social world.

NOTES

1. Informative webpages still accessible in 2012 about the Schome Initiative include http://www.schome.ac.uk/wiki/Schome_community_history (a collaboratively written history); http://www.schome.ac.uk/wiki/SPP_-_The_ spARTans (about the class from the U.S. mentioned here) and http://www. schome.ac.uk/wiki/Second_Life_demos#Schome_Park videos for machinima (in-world videos of some of the projects).
2. There were a few occasions where some staff members met some students, including when a few student participants visited the Open University, and when another group met a staff member when participating in the finals of a competition. Many staff members, including, for example, the first author, never met a student participant offline and the overwhelming majority of students never met any member of staff offline either.

REFERENCES

Au, J. Wagner (2008). *The Making of Second Life: Notes from the New World*. New York: HarperCollins.

Barton, D. (2007). *Literacy: An Introduction to the Ecology of Written Language* (2nd ed.). Oxford: Blackwell.

Bourdieu, P. (1999). The space of points of view. In P. Bourdieu et al., *The Weight of the World: Social Suffering in Contemporary Society*. Stanford, CA: Stanford University Press.

Castronova, E. (2007). *Exodus to the Virtual World*. Basingstoke: Palgrave Macmillan.

Craft, A., Chappell, K., & Twining, P. (2008). Learners reconceptualising education: Widening participation through creative engagement? *Innovations in Education & Teaching International* 45(3): 235–245.

Creese, A., Bhatt, A., Bhojani, N., & Martin, P. (2008). Fieldnotes in team ethnography: Researching complementary schools. *Qualitative Research* 8(2): 223–242.

Ferguson, R. (2011). Meaningful learning and creativity in virtual worlds. *Thinking Skills and Creativity* 6: 169–178.

Ferguson, R., Gillen, J., Peachey, A., & Twining, P. (2011, September 21–22). The strength of cohesive ties: Discursive construction of an online learning community. Paper presented at Researching Learning in Immersive Virtual Environments (ReLIVE 11), Open University, Milton Keynes, UK.

Gillen, J. (2011, April 8–12). Exploring a learning ecology: Teenagers' literacy practices in a teen Second Life project—Schome Park. Paper presented at Researching the Literacy Practices of Children and Young People in Virtual Worlds, American Educational Research Conference, New Orleans. Retrieved May 10, 2012 from http://www.lancs.ac.uk/staff/gillen/AERA2011_Gillen.pdf.

Gillen, J. (2009). Literacy practices in Schome Park: A virtual literacy ethnography. *Journal of Research in Reading* 32(1): 57–74.

Gillen, J., Twining, P., Ferguson, R., Butters, O., Clough, G., Gaved, M., Peachey, A., Seamans, D., & Sheehy, K. (2009). A learning community for teens on a virtual island—The Schome Park Teen Second Life Pilot Project. *eLearning Papers* 15. The New Learning Generation. Retrieved May 10, 2010 from http://www.elearningeuropa.info/en/article/A-learning-community-for-teens-on-a-virtual-island—-The-Schome-Park-Teen-Second-Life-Pilot-project

Haraway, D. (1997). *Modest_Witness@Second_Millennium.Femaleman©_Meets_Oncomouse™: Feminism and Technoscience.* New York: Routledge.

Heath, S. B. & Street, B. (2008). *On Ethnography: Approaches to Language and Literacy Research.* New York: Teachers College Press, Columbia University.

Katzav, J. & Reed, C. A. (2004). On argumentation schemes and the natural classification of arguments. *Argumentation* 18: 239–259.

Kress, G. (2010). *Multimodality: A Social Semiotic Approach to Contemporary Communication.* London: Routledge.

Lankshear, C. & Knobel, M. (2006). *New Literacies: Everyday Practices and Classroom Learning.* London: McGraw-Hill.

Matusov, E. (1996). Intersubjectivity without agreement. *Mind, Culture and Activity* 3(1): 25–45.

Mitchell, C. J. (1984). Case studies. In R. F. Ellen (ed.), *Ethnographic Research: A Guide to General Conduct.* London: Academic Press.

Oldenburg, R. (1989). *The Great Good Place: Cafes, Coffee Shops, Community Centers, Beauty Parlors, General Stores, Bars, Hangouts, and How They Get You through the Day.* New York: Paragon House.

Peachey, A. (2010). Living in immaterial worlds: Who are we when we learn and teach in virtual worlds? In K. Sheehy, R. Ferguson, & G. Clough (eds.), *Virtual Worlds: Controversies at the Frontier of Education.* Hauppage, NY: Nova.

Peachey, A., Gillen, J., & Ferguson, R. (2008, September 8–13). Fluid leadership in a multi-user virtual environment educational project with teenagers: Schome Park. Paper presented at Ecologies of Diversities: Meeting of the International Society for Cultural and Activity Research, San Diego. Retrieved May 10, 2012 from http://www.schome.ac.uk/downloads/Fluid_Leadership_Peachey_Gillen_Ferguson.pdf.

Rix, J. & Twining, P. (2007) Exploring education systems: Towards a typology for future learning? *Educational Research,* 49(4): 329–341.

Scollon, R. (2001). *Mediated Discourse: The Nexus of Practice.* London: Routledge.

Sheehy, K. & Bucknall, S. (2008). How is technology seen in young people's visions of future education systems? *Learning, Media and Technology* 33(2): 101–114.

Sheehy, K., Ferguson, R., & Clough, G. (Eds.). (2010). *Virtual Worlds: Controversies at the Frontier of Education.* Hauppage, NY: Nova.

Squire, K. (2006) From content to context: Videogames as designed experience. *Educational Researcher* 35(8): 19–29.

Tennesen, M. (2009). Avatar acts. *Scientific American* 301(1): 27–28.

Twining, P. (2010). When educational worlds collide. In K. Sheehy, R. Ferguson, & G. Clough (eds.), *Virtual Worlds: Controversies at the Frontier of Education.* Hauppage, NY: Nova.

Twining, P. (2009). Exploring the educational potential of virtual worlds—some reflections from the SPP. *British Journal of Educational Technology* 40(3): 496–514.

Twining, P., Broadie, R., Cook, D., Ford, K., Morris, D., Twiner, A., et al. (2006). Educational change and ICT: An exploration of priorities 2 and 3 of the DfES e-strategy in schools and colleges. Coventry: Becta. Retrieved November 16, 2011 from http://kn.open.ac.uk/public/document.cfm?docid=10101.

Twining, P. & Footring, S. (2010). The Schome Park Programme: Exploring educational alternatives. In A. Peachey, J. Gillen, D. Livingstone, & S. Smith-Robbins (eds.), *Researching Learning in Virtual Worlds.* London: Springer.

Twining, P. & Peachey, A. (2009). Open virtual worlds as pedagogical research tools: Learning from the Schome Park Programme. In A. Tatnall & A. Jones (eds.), *Education and Technology for a Better World*. New York: Springer.

Voloshinov, V. N. (1995). "Language, speech, and utterance" and "verbal interaction." In S. Dentith (ed.), *Bakhtinian Thought: A Reader*. London: Routledge.

Wenger, E. (2001). Supporting communities of practice: A survey of community-oriented technologies. Retrieved November 16, 2011 from http://www.ewenger.com/tech/.

13 Learning from *Adventure Rock*

Lizzie Jackson

INTRODUCTION

Having launched the BBC's social media services in 1998, as a long-standing member of the BBC's production staff, I completed a doctoral study in 2009 that looked at how BBC producers were engaging with the public in message boards, live chats, chat rooms, and via interactive television. The findings showed producers were often unsure how to organize participatory services such as message boards or live chat; there was a lack of reciprocity from the BBC's side. This pointed towards the need for more investigation into how a more creative relationship with audiences might develop.

In July 2007 the opportunity arose to undertake a year-long study of the beta (trial) version of *Adventure Rock* launched in April 2008 by the BBC Children's department. It is a public service virtual world for children, not run for commercial gain. Developed from *KetNetKick*, an earlier version of *Adventure Rock* created by Larian Studios for VRT, the Flemish public service broadcaster in Belgium, *Adventure Rock* is a 'third perspective' world; the child's view is above and behind his or her avatar. The world is more akin to a series of very complex 3D online landscapes with embedded games and creative studios.

The study was one of eight undertaken by researchers on new genres of public service content jointly funded by the Arts and Humanities Research Council and the BBC from 2007 to 2009. It aimed to find out whether producers might involve young people in the design of such new services. Professor David Gauntlett from the University of Westminster provided valuable advice and insights, particularly during the final data analysis, and I designed and delivered the research. The findings will be of interest to producers, researchers, educationalists, and media students.

By virtue of being an academic study, the analysis of *Adventure Rock* provided more sophisticated data than is normally available to producers. Typically the BBC would organize a user test (click-through) of a service before launch over a half-day with around 15–20 participants. In this study 90 children from across the UK, aged 9–11 and of mixed socio-economic backgrounds, were given access over two months from December 2007 to

January 2008. A mixture of elicited techniques termed by David Gauntlett Creative Methods (Gauntlett, 2007), including drawing, creating media diaries, and some model-making, encouraged the children to reflect and express ideas and opinions on *Adventure Rock*. The study also looked at producer intentions and offered an analysis of parental responses.

Several important studies on children's use of online environments (Livingstone, 2003; Buckingham, 2008) inform the approach. I also draw on child development theory (Ellis, 1973; Piaget, 2001; Pearce, 2007) to show how children and adults imagine and articulate possible 'other' worlds and futures through literature. Taking a sociocultural approach (see Black & Reich, this volume), I argue online play and exploration are important tools for the development of multimodal literacies. The use of environments that extend or mirror the real world offers important opportunities for learning and a site for the building of competencies, a bridge between the formal learning of school and the informal instruction for everyday life, at home.

The findings include '13 tips' for producers of virtual worlds for children and a deconstruction of orientations (player types) to *Adventure Rock*. These orientations may be useful for researchers looking at other virtual worlds and immersive gaming environments. The study was the first to look at how children can become involved in the production process and the first to look at an immersive, 3D, single-player environment free of directly commercial considerations.

To a degree *Adventure Rock* fulfills the criteria used by Castronova to define a 'synthetic world,' "any computer-generated physical space, represented graphically in three dimensions, that can be experienced by many people at once" (Castronova, 2005: 22). What is missing, however, is the interaction between players characteristic of online multi-user virtual environments (MUVEs).

There are exotic landscapes but no sense of others; this is solo play—there is no way children can communicate to each other 'in-world.' Messaging and the showcasing of player content are provided on an accompanying website. *Adventure Rock* is a serial exploration of an online 3D landscape for young explorers aged 6–12 years. The avatar created by these intrepid pioneers searches for clues about the 'world,' plays games, fights crocodiles, meets robots, and progresses though increasingly complex levels, gaining points and coins. The avatar (the child) is accompanied by 'Cody,' a flying robot.

The young participants of the study were invited to take part in two creative workshops that encouraged the imagining of virtual worlds, and analysis of *Adventure Rock* and four commercial worlds for children through drawing, mapping, and discussion. Children were recruited from middle schools in Glasgow, Cardiff, Belfast, Manchester, and London. Two separate sessions were run in each location for a younger group, 7–9-year-olds, and an older group, aged 10–11. I also attended production meetings at the BBC Children's offices in West London to observe the producers as they

Figure 13.1   Adventure Rock, an 'outside' virtual world for children. BBC Children's.

worked towards the launch. Lastly I gave a questionnaire to the parents of the children to find out what they thought of virtual worlds for children.

To preview the findings of particular interest from a literacy perspective, we discovered younger children have different requirements in virtual worlds from older children. We also found all children need to be sociable online, particularly more mature or confident children. Without sociability the opportunities for learning—for example, risk avoidance strategies and negotiation skills—are reduced. I therefore advise producers to produce a pedagogical strategy to deliberately support the development of multimodal literacies, and furthermore that these pedagogies take account of the progressive developmental and behavioral stages identified within the literature. For orientation, before describing the methods I used to obtain the subsequent findings, discussion of play theory and the value of creative imagining is presented alongside the consideration of child development within an online context.

CHILDREN AND PLAY AS A TOOL FOR MATURATION

The range of literature on the nature and function of play is vast; therefore I drew on a more limited range of psychological and psychoanalytical notions that will explain the theoretical frame that informed the project. Our growing understanding of immersive online landscapes such as *Adventure Rock* stemmed from the insights of Piaget on the maturation of children and further developed from a range of ideas in different fields from zoology to psychotherapy. Although these intellectual positions were developed for a world in which children acted directly only with a physical environment, the insights can be translated to immersive online gaming and virtual worlds.

In 1926 Piaget found play to be an essential element of the maturation of children, arguing that 7–11-year-olds accumulate conceptualizing skills through their physical experience and from there they begin to solve problems (Piaget, 2007). In the 1950s and 1960s psychologists began to look at the play activities of young animals; Ellis (1973) described how scientists noticed how young animals approached new objects, with echoes of Piaget's work on child development.

The procedure that commonly occurs is for the animal to first indulge in locomotor exploration. Investigating the situation by moving around the object allows the exploration of its properties by distance receptors, while preserving the options for escape (Ellis, 1973: 97–99).

This implies the gradual accumulation of risk avoidance skills. Social interaction amplifies opportunities for learning: "as more and more interactions are experienced, more and more connections between antecedent-subsequent events are made. More cause-effect relations are established" (ibid). In this way young animals find out the probable effect of different activities, therefore assisting them to adapt and deal with unpredictable situations.

Play has also been found to have cathartic properties, facilitating a form of suppressed communication: "In pretending, children often express indirectly or symbolically pressing worries or fears and repeat these themes again and again" (Garvey, 1977: 9). There is much literature in evidence on the use of play in therapeutic contexts for this reason. Newer studies centralize identity formation as being of even greater significance, reflecting the growing idea of child-as-citizen: "they have to be seen and respected as subjects in their own right who develop their own and unique cultural milieus" (Fromme, 2003: 5). These studies redefine childhood as a cultural site as well as a physiological progression.

I will now turn to the idea of imaginative play located within the literary traditions, as a constructivist activity supporting learning. Cook suggests, "Play, broadly defined, should exert an *influence* on learning," not replace it (Cook, 2000: 182). Goldstein also proposes "the early make-believe of children is the starting point for the development of narrative thought" (Goldstein, 1994: 26). 'Episodes' of imaginative play offer time for formative and preparatory physical or mental activities, but they are also useful as 'glue' between separate—but linked—play sessions that extend exploration and offer additional opportunities for consolidation.

In their general descriptions of play at home, children described how they brought *Adventure Rock* into the physical world play. "[We p]ut duvets over the kitchen table . . . a big monster came to get us" (girl, 8, Belfast), or "We put pillows on our trampoline" (girl, 9, Belfast). Those who described an ongoing imagined world (shared with others) felt it was important to "keep it in the same place and [have] the same things. Say if you had a place and next time it was completely different, you'd have to keep things the same" (boy, 8, London). Language, communicative acts, gift-giving and receiving, and an overall 'grand' narrative help to sustain 'naturally imagined' worlds.

For a story truly to hold the child's attention, it must entertain him and arouse his curiosity. But to enrich his life, it must stimulate his imagination; help him to develop his intellect and to clarify his emotions; be attuned to his anxieties and aspirations; give full recognition to his difficulties, while at the same time suggesting solutions to the problems that perturb him (Bettelheim, 1991: 5).

For Bettelheim storytelling is an important tool for the development of reflexivity, emotional intelligence, and empathy, and as an agent of motivation. Becoming a reflective learner is one of the most ubiquitous transferable skills in contemporary higher education, a skill for adult life.

John Carey lists 500 worlds imagined by adults in the *Faber Book of Utopias* (1999). The earliest is Plato's *Republic* (c.360 BC) followed by *Germania*, written by the Roman historian Tacitus in AD 98, "a work of political and moral exhortation" (Carey, 1999: 16). Moving forward in time, other highlights from the list are Plutarch's *Life of Lycurgus* (AD 120), Sir Thomas Moore's *Utopia* (1516), and Swift's *Gulliver's Travels* (1726) . . . and on and on. For adults and children imagining 'somewhere other' is an opportunity for critique, escapism, and creative play.

We have come a long way as a society from situating literacy solely within the narrow conception of reading and writing. David Buckingham describes how "those immersed in new digital tools and networks are engaged in an unprecedented exploration of language, games, social interaction, problem solving, and self-directed activity that leads to diverse forms of learning" (Buckingham, 2008: vii). The 'new' media offer good opportunities for collaborative learning—for example, in social media, virtual worlds, and immersive games. Interaction and connectivity in online games and virtual worlds assist the development of personal expression and negotiation, a foundation for group work (Drotner, 2008). The ability to build and sustain groups is a highly useful skill in the creative industries, where interdisciplinary working is common and the range of digital skills may be varied. Literacies around group work are increasingly considered in higher education contexts, particularly in practice-based curricula.

The Young People and New Media Project undertaken by the London School of Economics (LSE) with 15,000 6–16-year-olds (ending in 2002) found, "In gaining familiarity with new technological formats and interfaces, one key mode of engagement provides an entry point for children and young people, namely games-playing, favored for work or play, alone or in company, as part of learning or relaxing" (Livingstone, 2003: 229). In addition to validating digital play, Livingstone notes how

The multimodal nature of new media contents brings together multiple forms of engagement hitherto considered distinct forms of production (writing, drawing, designing) and reception (reading, listening, viewing, learning), as well as activities commonly distinguished from the reception of mass media (playing, talking, researching, performing). (Livingstone, 203: 221)

The potential value of informal learning environments online is clear, and the idea of play as a highly important tool for learning has been traced forward through developmental psychology, behaviorist theories in the maturation of animals, social skills, and the function of groups. Finally, the imagining of worlds has been shown to be a natural part of our linguistic, literary, and cultural expression.

I turn now to the case study of *Adventure Rock*, in which we wanted to find out how children could become involved in the design of new genres of programming. The BBC, as one of the leading public service broadcasters and the largest in the UK, has a commitment to: "Be at the forefront of harnessing opportunities offered by technological developments, to deliver both formal and informal learning" (DCMS, 2006: 15). In 2009 the UK business magazine *The Economist* recognized a continuing rise in the use of virtual worlds for children.

In America in 2008 eMarketer, a market researcher specializing in the use of digital media, estimated 8 million children and teens visited virtual worlds on a regular basis, a number the firm expects to increase to 15 million by 2013 (eMarketer, 2009). "As of January, there were 112 virtual worlds designed for under-18s with another 81 in development, according to Engage Digital Media, a market research firm" (*The Economist*, 2009).

Media outlets that create content for children were aware of this adoption. In 2007 the BBC Children's department commissioned *Adventure Rock* as one of a range of new services for CBBC, a nested website aimed at children within the highly popular BBC website (www.bbc.co.uk). These new services offer more immersive and personalized content and demonstrate a new strategic direction.

ADVENTURE ROCK, AN 'OUTSIDE' VIRTUAL WORLD

Concurrent with the BBC's commissioning of *Adventure Rock* in 2007 there had been a decline in the amount of commercial television content produced for children in the UK (Steemers, 2010). One of the functions of the BBC is to counteract market failure when in the public interest; therefore the BBC Children's department may have felt under pressure to address this. The same year the corporation redefined its six public purposes, the second of which is "promoting education and learning" (BBC Trust, 2007: 25).

Chitra Bharucha, acting chairman of the BBC Trust, the body that monitors how the BBC carries out its public purposes, "requested BBC management to prepare fresh proposals for how the BBC should deliver the Charter obligation to promote formal education and learning, meeting the online needs of school age children" (BBC News, 2007).

The BBC Children's department licensed *Adventure Rock* from Larian Studios for £250,000. Larian Studios are a Belgian media outlet that had made *KetnetKick*, an award-winning and popular earlier version of the virtual world for VRT, the Flemish language public service broadcaster in Belgium. The Belgian producers worked with the BBC Children's department for almost two years to change the 'look and feel,' producing new areas, changing characters, and creating additional objects. *Adventure Rock* is a single-player, simulated 'outdoor' game aimed at children aged 6–12. Unlike many virtual worlds for children that can be played online, the child (or an adult) must download files before playing the game, something the children in the study found difficult.

The 3D world, or series of immersive landscapes, offers progressive solo exploration and gaming. Children create an avatar to run, jump, crawl, and even swim around the world. There are seven studios for the creation of music, cartoons, animation, video, dancing, and 'inventing contraptions.' The players also find pages from a book and strange hieroglyphics that may, in time, begin to explain the mysteries of the *Adventure Rock* Island. Although this is for solo play, the adventurers also meet bots: robots and crocodiles (raptors) that guide them around the world and test their skill in combative games. The children can also collect coins found along paths, which translate into points that can be used in an 'Upgrade Centre' to buy

Figure 13.2 'Cody,' a cheeky flying robot. BBC Children's.

new clothes for their avatar or new equipment for Cody. This is a friendly and comic round metal robotic creature who hovers behind the child's avatar giving cheeky comments, tips, and hints. Over the two months of the fieldwork I saw something of a cult following develop around Cody; the children drew him repeatedly in their diaries, and later in the second workshop in response to the question "what was the most important object in '*Adventure Rock*'?"

After the fieldwork had ended new features were added before the launch (in April 2008). A snowboarding run, ski lift, and funfair slide were opened, and later a 'cinema' where the children could watch CBBC television programs 'in-world.' The children in the research study were highly excited by the idea of watching television within a virtual world, to the extent of *imagining* they could see video before any video was released into the world. The beta version of *Adventure Rock* included large TV screens on stands *ready* to offer news bulletins, trailers, or announcements.

Outside what Castronova (2005: 147) terms the 'membrane' of the world *Adventure Rock*, there was a website with a showcase area for children's work. A moderated message board was also offered for children to leave comments for each other. The children therefore either left the world if they want to chat to other explorers or opened a second browser window.

Figure 13.3   A child's avatar watches in-world 'television' with 'Cody.' BBC Children's.

In my opinion, the BBC's strategy to launch a virtual world for children was not at fault in itself as it is highly important for public service media to keep pace with commercial developments. At the same time I found significant evidence that *Adventure Rock* lacked important elements the children identified as being essential in an immersive world or game. Many of the children, particularly the younger 7–9-year-olds, enjoyed exploring, playing games, and creating content in the studios in *Adventure Rock*, but overall it did not retain their curiosity over time, as they were able to interact only with the bots (robots and crocodiles) and not with each other within the environment.

The BBC Children's department organized a workshop for me with CBBC producers to give the findings from the study. Adjustments were subsequently made to the registration and download of AR, and an instructional video was commissioned to help children with the initial setup. The *Adventure Rock* website was given higher priority and extended. In addition the CBBC website was zoned to aggregate content for 7–9-year-olds in one area and for 9–11-year-olds in another.

USING CREATIVE METHODS WITH CHILDREN

This is a producer and user study looking at the development and use of an immersive online environment through the use of a range of multimodal methods we term 'Creative Methods' (Gauntlett, 2007). The use of Creative Methods is appropriate as they encourage participants to communicate what they think through making, whether through drawing, modeling, video, or other means. The process of creating with the hands becomes part of the reflexive process. Articulating through making is highly suitable for studies involving children as the method does not suit only children who have higher reading and writing skills. It is a sociable way to explore ideas through making, deepening reflexivity and extending the range of communication, including through metaphors.

Twelve schools were approached from Glasgow, Cardiff, Manchester, Belfast, and London. One school had to drop out because it used Apple Macintosh computers and *Adventure Rock* would run only on PCs. Two workshops took place in December 2007 and January 2008 at BBC Regional offices. Ninety children aged 7–11 from mixed socio-economic groups took part, a sufficiently robust and varied sample to produce rich data. The children were split into two separate age groups (7–9- and 10–11-year-olds) for two separate sessions in order to test whether younger and older children had a different orientation towards *Adventure Rock*.

In addition I observed weekly production meetings at the BBC's Television Centre and gave out questionnaires to the parents of the children. The idea to undertake a producer and user study was important in order to examine whether the producer's intentions matched the children's subsequent use of *Adventure Rock*. However, the methods were more strongly focused on the audience rather than producers, recruiting the children as nominally 'CBBC consultants.' Each workshop was captured on video with a single camera on a tripod and gun microphone. This enabled the gathering of behavioral nuances and good quality sound. At the suggestion of David Gauntlett I cross-referenced any quantitative findings with qualitative data where possible.

Overall I aimed to find out:

A. What did the children think of *Adventure Rock*? How did it compare with other virtual worlds for children?
B. If children were creating their own virtual world, what would it be like?
C. Could children contribute usefully to the design process in any way?
D. Did the younger and older children approach *Adventure Rock* in different ways (7–9-year-olds and 10–11-year-olds)?

Figure 13.4   Children imagine and draw their ideal virtual world.

The first workshop took question B as a starting point. Children were encouraged to talk about the imaginary spaces they constructed for either group or solo play. They were then asked to draw their ideal imagined world on a large sheet of paper in groups. Tissue paper, stars, glitter, and 'stick on' speech bubbles were also provided.

Between the first and second workshops the children were given access to the beta version of *Adventure Rock* over the Christmas and New Year holidays. The BBC Children's department producers worked hard to ensure there was enough of the world to explore by January. We had intended to include a quickly captured analysis of the accompanying message board and gallery on the accompanying website, but this was not possible as it had not been fully completed, the production schedule having slipped due to technical issues. The children had faced considerable difficulties in accessing, downloading, and moving around the world. A good enough number of areas with sufficient variety, however, were offered to the children. This included an initial 'get started' tutorial, Star Square (the center of the world), the Upgrade Centre, where points could be exchanged for goods, the Music Studio, Cartoon Studio, Drawing Studio, and Rainbow Canyon (a space to explore).

I asked the children to record what they did in *Adventure Rock* in media diaries and suggested they also visit four other commercial virtual worlds (*Club Penguin, Nicktropolis, Habbo Hotel,* and *BarbieGirls*). As the fieldwork progressed new areas opened and there were fewer technical problems; however, one or two children in each group were never able to access *Adventure Rock*. Most of the children were able to log in and explore for enough days to produce adequate and representative data. A topic in the BBC Children's message board was opened to receive the children's technical comments.

The second workshop in January 2008 began with a discussion of what the children felt about *Adventure Rock*, and any of the other commercial virtual worlds. They drew and mapped out—on a paper plate—what they felt were the significant objects, places, and characters. I then asked the children what they would add, remove, or change if they had been the producers. At the end of the second workshop I collected the questionnaire from the parents and the children's diaries for analysis. Over 85% of parents completed the questionnaire, a high level of response.

Creative Methods are excellent for children; they all enjoyed being able to produce an idea for a virtual world and took the role of being a CBBC consultant very seriously. The media diaries were a more successful tool for the older children to use, while the younger children preferred to draw. It was useful to play and replay the videos, although the capture and storage of personally identifiable images of children meant a password-protected server had to be set up in advance, which took time. A selection of the findings now follows: those that inform our understanding of multimodal literacies have been foregrounded.

WHAT CHILDREN WANT FROM VIRTUAL WORLDS

'13 tips' are offered for producers of virtual worlds; the children were very clear about what they liked and disliked, and about what they would include and why. These same likes and dislikes were also true across all the commercial virtual worlds. Eight orientations to *Adventure Rock* were found; these augment Bartle's four types of player: Explorers, Socializers (sic), Achievers, and Controllers (Bartle, 2003: 130), as will be discussed later. From a literacy perspective the importance of being able to interact with others was clear, and there were significant differences in usage and competencies between the 7–9-year-old and 10–11-year-old players.

The younger players needed more orientation and help, but they were also happier to enjoy solo play; for this reason *Adventure Rock* fulfilled more of their needs. From the paper plate drawings and the maps of imagined virtual worlds drawn in group work, I found the younger children were significantly less ruled by the laws of nature, physics, or social norms. Their designs for worlds were surreal, fantastic, and energetic. They often included mappings of the universe or superheroes (the boys) or mystical or royal themes (the girls).

The 10–11-year-olds wanted to have more realistic places to 'live in' and they often produced schemes for worlds with complex social systems and hierarchies. This may reflect a greater influence of school rules and norms

Figure 13.5 'A Normal Cottage' (from the London 10–11-year-old group).

or a growing allegiance to pre-teen culture—the need to conform, albeit to new social imaginings.

All the children liked the *Adventure Rock* Creative Studios, but the older boys and girls also wanted some form of commerce (shops and trading) and to be able to compete against each other. Overall the 10–11-year-olds wanted more social activities, collaboration, and challenges. "It's fun creating the stuff but you can lose interest. It's not interesting enough and not something that I would do that much. There's not enough action" (boy, 11, Cardiff).

Several players documented their scores and progress. One boy from Cardiff (aged 7) carefully noted the number of pages he had collected (24), coins (407), and score (8946); status is a driver of participation. All the children documented having peaks of motivation such as finding a new area, swimming, or when they first played a new game. From a literacy perspective these periods of higher engagement may offer moments of opportunity for the introduction of more complex activities. Other learning opportunities were identified—for example, the older children often introduced younger children to *Adventure Rock*: "My brother, Thomas, who is four, really enjoyed watching this game with me. And got really excited when I was chasing Raptor" (girl, 8, Belfast).

Figure 13.6 "You and some of your friends get to go to a quest/journey together like secret agents."

As a single-player game the point of view for each player was above and behind the avatar. Being able to create a suitable online identity was therefore highly important: "I think I should know what my name is or at least make my name up" (girl, 8, Cardiff). Creating the avatar was also a significant moment. "It's good making the avatar," said one boy (aged 8), from Cardiff. This was echoed across all the groups (e.g., "I got to design a character" (girl, 7, London)). The choices of skin and hair color and the range of clothes offered were also crucial. One boy said the hair style choices made the male avatars "look like freaks" (boy, 11, Glasgow). One girl commented, "The girls outfits could be a bit better, they're a bit yuk," (girl, 11, London). The Muslim girls wanted to be offered a range of head scarves. Producers need to accommodate cultural differences as well as current fashion trends.

The need to have a purposeful activity was stressed by the children. Activities that challenged the participants and progressively increased in complexity were expected as a norm of immersive game play. Both the younger and older children felt it was important to have good transport— for example, a motorbike or space shuttle. All transport would need to be superefficient—for example, being able to go to London from Scotland in 40 seconds.

Overall the children demonstrated eight orientations to *Adventure Rock*, which emerged from my analyses, in coding entries in the children's diaries. For example, there were 22 children who said they collected things ('collectors'), 22 who felt they were experts at the game ('power-users'), and 32 who said they were exploring AR ('explorers'). All these eight orientations, described in Table 13.1, were triangulated with the video data and drawings. Some of the children exhibited dual orientation.

The children who exhibit these orientations are also likely to have varying degrees of sociability. For example, life-system builders are highly likely

---

Table 13.1   8 orientations to *Adventure Rock*

1. Explorer-investigators – had an imaginative engagement with exploring details of the virtual world;
2. Self-stampers –wanted to make their mark on the world through self-expression;
3. Social climbers –interested in ranking, and wanted to be visibly doing better than other players;
4. Fighters –wanted to be able to fight things in the world;
5. Collector-consumers –wanted to accumulate anything of perceived value within the game; and who wished for an economic system, and also, interestingly, wanted to be able to give (and receive) gifts;
6. Power-users –sought to become experts on the game, and how it worked; and to share their expertise with others;
7. Life-system builders –wanted to create new environments, and to populate them;
8. Nurturers –wanted to look after their avatar, and possibly pets.

---

to need other players to organize into social systems; social climbers need to be able to meet others in order to both demonstrate and measure their status. Explorer-investigators and collector-consumers might be relatively happy undertaking solitary activities within the world or immersive environment for much of the time; however, at some point even they are likely to seek out others to show their collections or tell their stories to.

A second set of findings, shown in Table 13.2, offers 13 principles for producers of virtual worlds for children. The list reflects the children's spatial, social, economic, citizenship, motivational, and emotional requirements expressed in the workshops and diaries.

The final point needs some further explanation. Several groups of children designed a virtual world that included a place where their parents could live. This space was separated from the children's part of the virtual world by a glass or force-field wall. Parents would be able to live separately and look at the children's world, but not interfere.

Virtual worlds constructed to contain these 13 elements are likely to provide a playful, engaging, and interactive alternative to more passive media. Becoming a creator and having more control over the elements of a world reflect other genres of media in which the distinction between producer and audience-participant is becoming blurred.

Adventure Rock was found to be less sophisticated than many commercial services, largely because of the lack of any connectivity or collaboration between children in-world. The players or 'Adventurers' would have liked to have competed against each other, but this was not possible. *Adventure Rock* was nevertheless valued by the children. They thought *Adventure Rock* was unique because it offers a space 'outside' that they can explore. In some ways this may be this may be due to the reduction in the 'real-world' outdoor areas in which today's children are typically allowed to play freely

Table 13.2   13 tips for producers of virtual worlds for children, as derived from a study of *Adventure Rock*

1. Sociable – meeting and chatting.
2. Creative – making avatar, making things.
3. Have control – owning and changing the space.
4. A big, outdoors world to explore.
5. Visible status – "how am I doing"?
6. Clear location – "where am I"? + easy transport.
7. Mission and motivation – what's the purpose.
8. Some humour.
9. Help when they need it.
10. Video clips made by the CBBC producers, their own work, and other children's.
11. Somewhere to live – a home, hotel or town.
12. Shops – buying stuff.
13. A space away from adult rules.

owing to security concerns, although this was not an issue I was enabled to pursue in this research.

The children were very excited by the quality of the 3D graphics. At the time of the study only one other virtual world had comparable quality of 3D experience (*My Tiny Planets*). They also liked the fact that *Adventure Rock* is free, with no need for payments or subscription. Some children felt frustrated that *Adventure Rock* was not available for Apple Macintosh computers or via Internet-enabled games consoles. The technology could be problematic, particularly for the younger children who often had to have initial help to register, download, and use the world. The children and their parents felt the world was a suitable service for a public service broadcaster to launch. They believed the strategy to include more immersive, playful, and personalizable services was correct as the BBC needs to keep pace with external commercial developments.

CONCLUSIONS

At the outset of the project I wanted to find out whether children could become involved in designing their own media, in this case virtual worlds. In the case study *Adventure Rock* the children articulated 13 elements that they would include in any complex environment online. Beals and Bers (2009: 1) identified six that producers should take into consideration when designing virtual worlds for children "(1) purpose, (2) communication, (3) participation, (4) play, (5) artefacts, and (6) rules". *Adventure Rock* lacked the sociability found in the commercial virtual worlds for children, and this had a detrimental effect on how long children would *remain* engaged, particularly older adventurers. Both the children and parents, however, applauded the BBC for moving towards more complex, immersive, and engaging media services; this was an appropriate and highly popular strategy for a public service media outlet.

From a literacy perspective, virtual worlds such as *Adventure Rock* offer opportunities for multimodal literacy. There are opportunities to develop a range of different competencies including risk-avoidance techniques, social skills (such as negotiation), technical skills, and a space for the overall stimulation of the imagination. Perhaps it could be simplistic to say this was merely informal learning as the progressive nature of the environment (acquiring coins and points, finding new places, and so on) indicates virtual worlds can offer a highly structured form of learning through complex media. As they explored *Adventure Rock* the children experienced peaks of motivation, which could potentially be moments when more complex tasks could be introduced; this could be a fruitful direction for further research.

The children were highly interested in exploring their projected identity—for example, through building their avatar. They also demonstrated a high awareness of fashion and cultural nuances, something producers should bear in mind. Although the children played alone, they exhibited orientations to *Adventure Rock* that could be clustered together. This analysis produced eight player types, the resultant typology augmenting Bartle's fourfold categorization. Media students, researchers, producers, and educationalists looking at virtual worlds or immersive gaming environments may find these analyses useful.

In 2009 the BBC Trust carried out a large review of the children's services provided by the BBC, concluding, "Providing content that children enjoy and learn from is one of the core public service functions of the BBC" (BBC Trust, 2009: n.p.). Significantly the review found that over time there had been a "decline in usage of the CBBC website" (BBC Trust, 2009: n.p.)), which the BBC Trust recommended the BBC executive should address going forward. This may indicate a transference to other platforms or providers. According to the data-gathering agency Comscore (2010), "The rise of social networking, availability of video content and growing mobile media consumption is changing the marketer's toolkit and creating new and unique opportunities to engage with the European consumer." In order to fully exploit the potential of participatory media for public service purposes and for learning and teaching it will be necessary to situate children—and all learners and teachers—at the heart of any design process.

REFERENCES

Bartle, R. (2003). *Designing Virtual Worlds*. Indianapolis: New Riders.

Beals, L. & Bers, M. (2009). A developmental lens for designing virtual worlds for children and youth. *International Journal of Learning and Media* 1(1): . Retrieved May 8, 2011 from http://www.mitpressjournals.org/doi/pdf/10.1162/ijlm.2009.0001.

BBC News (2007) BBC Trust suspends BBC Jam. 14 March. Retrieved 23 May, 2012 from http://www.bbc.co.uk/bbctrust/news/press_releases/2007/march/14_03_2007.shtml

BBC Trust (2007). *Annual Report and Accounts 2007/08: The BBC Trust's Review and Assessment*. Retrieved 23 May 2012 from
http://downloads.bbc.co.uk/annualreport/pdf/2007–08/bbc_ara_2008_trust.pdf

BBC Trust (2009). Trust publishes review of children's services. February 10. Retrieved January 16, 2011 from http://www.bbc.co.uk/bbctrust/news/press_releases/2009/february/childrens_service_review.shtml.

Bettelheim, B. (1991). *The Uses of Enchantment: The Meaning and Importance of Fairy Tales* (3rd ed.). London: Penguin.

Buckingham, D. (Ed.). (2008). *Youth, Identity, and Digital Media*. Cambridge, MA: MIT Press.

Carey, J. (1999). *The Faber Book of Utopias*. London: Faber.

Castronova, E. (2005). *Synthetic Worlds: The Business and Culture of Online Games*. Chicago: University of Chicago Press.

Comscore (2010). The 2010 Europe digital year in review. Retrieved May 15, 2011 from http://www.comscore.com/Press_Events/Presentations_Whitepapers/2011/2010_Europe_Digital_Year_in_Review.

Cook, G. (2000). *Language Play, Language Learning.* Oxford: Oxford University Press.

DCMS (Department of Culture, Media and Sport) (2006). *A Public Service for All: The BBC in the Digital Age.* London: DCMS.

Drotner, K. (2008). Leisure is hard work: Digital practices and future competencies. In D. Buckingham (ed.), *Youth, Identity, and Digital Media.* Cambridge, MA: MIT Press.

Economist (2009). Online playgrounds: There's life in virtual reality after all. *The Economist.* July 23. Retrieved January 16, 2011 from http://www.economist.com/node/14098380.

Ellis, M. J. (1973). *Why People Play.* Englewood Cliffs, NJ: Prentice-Hall.

eMarketer (2009). Real Kids in Virtual Worlds. May 21. Retrieved May 23, 2012 from http://www.emarketer.com/Articles/Print.aspx?1007095

Fromme, J. (2003). Computer games as a part of children's culture. *Games Studies* 3(1): 5–6.

Garvey, C. (1977). *Play.* London: Open Books.

Gauntlett, D. (2007). *Creative Explorations: New Approaches to Identities and Audiences.* Routledge: London.

Goldstein, J. (1994). *Toys, Play and Child Development.* Cambridge: Cambridge University Press.

Livingstone, S. (2003). *Young People and New Media: Childhood and the Changing Media Environment* (2nd ed.). London: Sage.

Pearce, C. (2007). Communities of play: The social construction of identity in persistent online game worlds. In P. Harrigan & N. Wardrip-Fruin (eds.), *Second Person: Role-Playing and Story in Games and Playable Media.* Cambridge, MA: MIT Press.

Piaget, J. (2001). *The Language and Thought of the Child.* London: Routledge.

Piaget, J. (2007) *The child's conception of the world: A 20th-century classic of child psychology* (2nd ed.). Lanham: Rowman & Littlefield Publishers.

Slade, P. (1995). *Child Play: Its Importance for Human Development.* London: Jessica Kingsley Publishers.

Steemers, J. (2010). *Creating Pre-School Television: A Story of Commerce, Creativity, and Curriculum.* Basingstoke: Palgrave Macmillan.

14 Playing Together Separately
Mapping Out Literacy and Social Synchronicity

Crystle Martin, Caroline C. Williams, Amanda Ochsner, Shannon Harris, Elizabeth King, Gabriella Anton, Jonathon Elmergreen, and Constance Steinkuehler

INTRODUCTION

Jaea sits at a desk with a laptop on each side of him and a keyboard and large computer monitor directly in front of him; he has three different keyboards and three different screens. He also wears headphones for both listening and speaking. Eyes shifting rapidly, he sometimes focuses on a quickly changing scene on a single screen and sometimes glances across multiple screens that each offer different information. At the same time, he receives feedback from voices coming through on the speakers, leading him to shift his attention elsewhere on one of the screens, and speaking into the microphone he returns information to the voices. With so much equipment and so much rapid movement and communication, one might guess that he is doing very important and very complicated work. Perhaps he is saving lives.

In a way, he is. In the scene described earlier, Jaea is playing the massively multiplayer online role-playing game (MMORPG) *World of Warcraft* (WoW), and he is playing it well. *Very* well. His role in the group is to act as a healer, keeping the rest of his raid members alive while they take large amounts of damage from intimidating and powerful enemies. The other group members are playing from other rooms, similarly equipped with screens, keyboards, and headphones, but located throughout the country, perhaps even across the world. Their work is just as complicated and is equally demanding.

What Jaea is really doing is reading. He is reading text conversations with his fellow players on the screen in front of him; he is reading the graphics he sees on the screen; he is reading the actions of other players; he is reading the needs and abilities of his own character; and he is reading his physical environment as well. After all, the girlfriend and three very large, very fuzzy cats that he shares this space with require attention sometimes too. (The cats, in fact, demand it!) This reading occurs in his physical environment as in the game world, where he maneuvers his avatar.

His temporal existence is also full of multiplicity: he simultaneously has an understanding of *when* it is in the room he plays in, where his raid group is in terms of progressing through their raid dungeon, and the time at which his character exists in the game's fantasy universe. This chapter will explore the multiplicity of presence that is exhibited within gameplay in *World of Warcraft*, and demonstrate how leveraging multiple presences is essential to successful high-end virtual literacies like MMOs.

EXAMINING ATTENTION

From the phenomena described in the introduction, many may think of existing explanations to describe what we are seeing. Terms like split attention, multitasking, and constant partial attention are often used to describe situations in which a person undertakes multiple tasks at once. These terms often carry a negative connotation. In theories of split attention, the research focuses on "the limitations of working memory" and the idea that multiple tasks "overburden working memory" (Kalyuga, Chandler, & Sweller, 1999). The theory of split attention views attention as something that is allocated, and when divided up it weakens the person's ability to accomplish tasks (Awh & Pashler, 2000; Tabbers, Martens, & van Merriënboer, 2000; Mayer & Moreno, 1998).

Multitasking is another explanation for attention paid to several tasks at once, and although multitasking is seen by many as a valuable skill that makes their world function, it is seen by others as a less than positive structure. González and Mark (2004, 2005) represented multitasking as an issue to be remedied. They used as an illustration the everyday example of working in an office and having to deal with multiple conversations, telephones ringing, people walking into other cubicles (2004: 115). The issue of multitasking was mitigated through working spheres, which they defined as "a set of interrelated events, which share a common motive" (117). González and Mark's (2005) suggestions turned to system design, namely that system design needed to take into account multitasking and help to reinforce workers' working spheres. In the context of this paper, the multiple activities that are undertaken simultaneously could be considered split attention or multitasking; however, these descriptions in the existing research are narrow in focus, negatively valenced at the outset, and do not capture the subtleties of the game experience on its own terms.

To help describe the nuances of the game experience, we explore a variety of research to illustrate the complexities inherent to the activity. Understanding these subtleties is important because it allows a clearer picture of the actions and information management engaged in by players. The literature will be framed in three contexts of gaming—that of literacy, time, and place—and will finish with new explanations for attending to several tasks as once.

GAMING AS VIRTUAL LITERACY

Gaming as a literacy has been studied by many researchers. Gee (2003), in his seminal book *What Videogames Have to Teach Us about Learning and Literacy*, described 36 learning principles that are manifested in good games. He claimed that in order to participate in a game the player must understand the literacy of the game and that playing was participating in a semiotic domain in which the player must understand rules, symbols, social interactions, and discourse to be successful. In addition to games, research has been conducted on online communities, which are centered on literacy practices (e.g., FacFiction.net (Black, 2007a, 2007b, 2008)). Black described the literacy habits of adolescents in online fan fiction communities, detailing their level of community interaction, their editing abilities, the use of the space by second language learners to develop their English skills, and their development of 'metavocabulary of editors.' Black and Steinkuehler (2009) stated that participants in virtual worlds engage in reading and writing in a variety of formats, which they found to align with national educational standards (*Standards for the English Language Arts*, as cited in Black & Steinkuehler, 2009).

Steinkuehler (2006, 2007, 2008) also studies literacy in massively multiplayer online games (MMOs) as both a discourse (which is both language-in-use and language-in-action (see Gee, 1999) and as a constellation of literacies, which includes the game and all of the resources (e.g., wikis, blogs, forums, videos, etc.) that are used as information sources by the game community. The constellation of literacies is the 'space' in which the information needed for success in a game or other affinity space exists. Gee's (2004, 2005) semiotic social and affinity spaces describe the 'place' of MMOs. The affordances of these perspectives offer flexibility, focusing on space and how it functions to bring people with common interests together. Steinkuehler and King (2009) used play within the place of an MMO to bolster the literacy practices of disengaged adolescent boys using the space of the constellation of literacies that surround the game to help them to become re-engaged. Martin and Steinkuehler (2010) explore another form of literacy that functions within the information constellation of an MMO, that of information literacy. By observing practices in the naturalistic setting of the game, Martin and Steinkuehler (2010) examine what and how resources are utilized to maintain success in a game—that is, how players traverse the space of the constellation of literacies in order to successfully retrieve information and resources they need.

Time can be viewed in a multitude of ways. Gell looks at the keeping of time in two ways (1992). He divided time up into what he termed A-series time, or standardized time as measured by a clock, and B-series time, or time that is run by the punctuation of activity (similar to Erickson's (2004) characterization of *kronos* and *kairos*). We appropriate Gell's classification and apply it to the distinction between a person's time spent in and out of games. Gamers live a hybrid existence of A-series and B-series time (Martin, in progress) where A- and B-series time becomes intertwined and entangled in the gaming activities. This is true in many genres of games but it is especially true in relation to MMOs. In an MMO, a player follows B-series time by focusing on the game world where much activity is punctuated by a cycle of activities rather than by the time increments of a clock. However, the player may at the same time keep track of when a certain time in the physical world comes—for example, when they need to eat dinner or when they need to make a phone call. Here, A-series time is intruding on the B-series time of the game. Participation in group activities in MMOs, although possibly starting at an A-series time, is punctuated by phases of the activity in B-series time. Although states of engagement and flow can be found in other activities, games offer an always available environment to delve into and MMOs offer the added benefit of constant social interaction in the virtual space, although the players are generally separated in the physical space.

Situating the activity of in-game activities within literacy, time, and space gives a basis for understanding the activities that take place within the game. Through this lens of activities a different approach of cognition could be taken. Distributed cognition (Hutchins, 1995) is an approach that emphasizes the use of resources expanding cognition beyond the individual's mind. This theory focuses on the coordination of enaction among agents within the community, which can include individuals, artifacts, and the environment itself (Hollan, Hutchins, & Kirsh, 2000), and here, the environment includes the game environment. This notion of the distribution of cognitive processes among the community, in this case the players of the MMO *World of Warcraft*, can be seen in Martin and Steinkuehler's (2010) idea of collective information literacy, also termed *distributed information literacy*.

METHODS

To comprehend the visual and information literacy experiences and practices of an expert-level *World of Warcraft* player, the researchers involved in this investigation used an instrumental case study model in which the actor being studied was selected for purposes of better understanding the surrounding problem space of one expert player during normative gameplay (Stake, 1995). Our goal is to identify the ways in which literacies are practiced and constructed in a complex, navigationally demanding, fast-paced, and visually elaborate digital environment in which successful literacy practices and problem solving efforts are essential to success. The goal of this case study was to develop a hermeneutic understanding of the practices common to expert-level WoW play in a holistic, empirical, interpretive, and an empathetic manner (Stake, 1995).

Selecting an expert-level player was imperative to understanding the advanced literacy practices and concomitant problem representations evidenced by many participants of this highly effective upper echelon of gameplay. Problem representations, such as determining the most effective visual and information literacy practices in order to achieve advanced game world success, were inherently designed by the participant and were grounded in his domain-related knowledge and subsequent semantic organization. Furthermore, experts solve problems differently than do novices (Chi, Feltovich, & Glaser, 1981) and we expected this difference to manifest even—or, perhaps, especially—in very complex problems spaces like *WoW*.

For this study, a 25-year-old, Caucasian, male, expert-level *World of Warcraft* player was observed playing *WoW* (Stevens, Satwicz, & McCarthy, 2008) on a weekly basis from January of 2011 until April of 2011. The researchers are familiar with *WoW* gameplay and are gamers themselves, although they do not play at the expert level of the case study participant. The expert-level player, Jaea (a pseudonym), typically plays *WoW* for about two hours each weekday, in addition to logging in about 8–12 hours of playtime over the weekends. He is a successful raider, and his guild is consistently first-ranked *server-side* (on their server) in ten-person raids, which are collaborative and complex in-game actions to defeat a series of high-level enemies usually called bosses. The guild has even been first on their server to complete some ten-person raids, a prized achievement.

Data was collected through the use of detailed and structured handwritten field notes taken by one case researcher present during gameplay. In

Figure 14.1   Jaea's physical context.

addition to constructing presence flow charts (see Figures 14.2 and 14.3) capturing Jaea's foci of attention, the case researcher also took abundant notes used to reconstruct each of the ten fast-paced and complex gaming sessions. The case researcher mainly observed Jaea's actions, both physically (in person) and on-screen, during gameplay, and occasionally asked questions when it was not obvious what was happening—on average about once or twice during each gameplay session.

To assist with data collection, the case study participant, Jaea, frequently thought aloud as he played, meaning he talked through the problems or experiences he encountered during gameplay. In addition, he modified his typical gameplay habits to play without headphones. This allowed the case researcher to hear utterances from Mumble, a voice-over IP application that he uses to communicate with other players, as well as contextualize his responses to Mumble. Having the case researcher carefully observe and note Jaea's head movement captured shifts in player focus (see Figure 14.1 for Jaea's physical context). A movement of Jaea's head to the left indicated focus on a second laptop, in which he would read Twitter or Reddit forums, a user-generated and rated news links forum, while playing. The second laptop was positioned far enough to the left that Jaea couldn't read the screen merely by shifting his eyes' focus, but had to turn his head slightly, which let the case researcher follow his presence more closely. The case researcher initially asked about Jaea's practices when he shifted focus to his information feed laptop, but he quickly developed a habit of automatically describing what he was doing. Jaea's engagement with the actual in-game WoW chat was also recorded whenever he typed a response. The case researchers also learned what the user interface (UI) customizations Jaea used looked like, so that they could identify times at which he tweaked or changed his UI without interrupting gameplay. A screenshot was taken of Jaea's screen at the end of gameplay so that the level of visual information captured on-screen could be paired with the other data collected by the case researchers.

For each observation a *presence visualization* was created while the observation was taking place. This visualization included graphic representations of where presence—operationalized as eye gaze, verbosity, and physical actions (including the physical actions necessary to create digital movement)—was most focused, as well as descriptors for the activities taking place within each delineation of time. Our operationalization of presence relied upon visual and audio indicators: Jaea's movement in physical space could highlight his physical presence (such as going to the bathroom), or it may indicate a shift from in-game WoW to information constellation (such as shifting his gaze from his primary computer screen, loaded with WoW, to his secondary laptop to the left, loaded with Twitter or WoW forums). Additionally, audio input from raid team members on Mumble would be represented in the information constellation layer, while audio feedback from the game itself would appear in the in-game WoW layer.

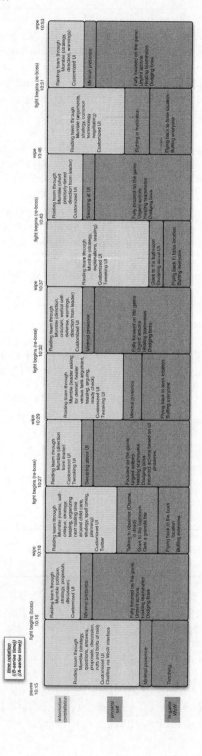

Figure 14.2   Presence flow chart 1.

time notation
((B-series time))
((A-series time))

	fight ends 8:07 p.m. / fight begins (elite only) 8:11 p.m.	fight ends 8:19 p.m.	fight begins (elite only) 8:26 p.m.	fight ends 8:33 p.m.	fight begins (boss) 8:40 p.m.	wipe 8:41 p.m.	fight begins (re-boss) 8:43 p.m.	wipe 8:48 p.m.
information constellation	Raiding team through Mumble (strategy, norms, self-critiques, curses) Customized UI Reading Reddit's WoW section online / Minimum presence	Raiding team through Mumble (strategy, norms, critiques, self-critiques, coordinating actions, curses, query and response) Customized UI / Minimum presence	Raiding team through Mumble (dividing loot, determining new boss, determining raid roles, explaining the upcoming boss to a new healer) J asks clarifying questions through Mumble Customized UI Reading Reddit's WoW section online	Raiding team through Mumble (query and response, activity direction) Customized UI / Minimum presence	Raiding team through Mumble (strategy, explaining the upcoming boss to a new healer) Reading Reddit's WoW section online Tweaking UI Customized UI	Raiding team through Mumble (strategy, wipe agreement) Customized UI / Minimum presence	Raiding team through Mumble (strategy, ready-checks) Reading the server forums Customized UI	Raiding team through Mumble (strategy, boss patterns, wipe agreement) Customized UI / Minimum presence until death Anger, relaxation	Raiding team through Mumble (strategy, query and response) Reading the server forums Customized UI
physical self	Yawning Talking to observer	Fully focused on the game Urgent actions Healing teammates Dodging boss	Goes to the bathroom	Fully focused on the game Actions perfectly timed with Mumble directions Urgent actions Healing teammates Dodging boss	J's presence here is based upon his casualness in the other two categories	Minimum presence	J is very focused on the game When he dies, the team wipes	J is very focused on the game When he dies, the team wipes	J's presence here is based upon his casualness in the other two categories
in-game WoW	Killing elites in dungeon Healing teammates Dodging elites		Flying through the air to the new boss location Following appropriate placement as discussed through Mumble		Just waiting with the raid group Some aimless movement		Flying back to this boss location Just waiting with the raid group Some aimless movement Buffing everyone		Just waiting with the raid group Some aimless movement Buffing everyone

Figure 14.3 Presence flow chart 2.

The player's ability to navigate within these different spaces and be successful in the game demonstrates a level of literacy, as the player must possess considerable information literacy as well as the traditional literacy of reading in order to interact with the information available around the game. Along with the literacy *space* players need to navigate for successful *WoW* play, our method is designed to capture both the *physical* and *virtual* spaces that Jaea regularly travels within. It is through the simultaneous traversal of such disparate places that makes expert—and even novice!—*WoW* play so difficult to understand and analyze. Our conceptualization of space is quite broad, capturing both digital and physical measurable space, as well as pursuit of information and the development of mental maps and plans.

Figure 14.2 represents 41 minutes of A-series time, while Figure 14.3 represents 38 minutes; the former is nine chunks of B-series time, while the latter is ten. From the data collected, Figures 14.2 and 14.3 were created for visualization and analysis. Each of the figures follows a similar format. Across the top are A-series time stamps that mark the demarcations between B-series chunks of time (Gell, 1992). Each section of time has a clear beginning and ending with 'fight begins' and 'wipe' appearing as the most common periods in these two presence visualizations. The former indicates that the raid group engaged in battle, while the latter indicates that all ten raid members died during battle and were unable to complete their goal. The emergent rule for breaking raiding up into B-series time is consequently 'fight begins' and 'wipe' (or 'win'), although in non-raid activities the time can be sectioned quite differently.

The framework for analysis developed for this study was originally inspired by Lemke's (2000) notion of timescales. Lemke focuses on activity in time and how timescales interact with one another. His view of the interactions of people within different timescales caused us to consider the presence or focus of an individual when engaging in a multifaceted activity like that of playing an MMO. The distribution of attention across multiple layers looks much more like Hutchin's (1995) distributed cognition than the description of split attention that plagues research on digital spaces (Kalyuga et al., 1999; Mayer & Moreno, 1998: 318; Tabbers et al., 2000; Awh & Pashler, 2000). Distributed cognition is an active process of engaging in multiple activities simultaneously and successfully. *Successful* here entails being able to learn from mistakes, being able to find needed information, and being able to cognitively manage multiple inputs from multiple presences at once.

From the four months of observations, two contrary examples are represented in Figure 14.2 and Figure 14.3. The first example (Figure 14.2) was a raid that Jaea's guild is very familiar with and that they were helping a new guild member through. Figure 14.3 is a raid that they had never attempted before, although the raiders had prepared beforehand by watching videos and reading guides. These two examples were chosen to illustrate a known activity and an unknown activity both in the context of a ten-person raid.

The digital contexts of Figure 14.2 and Figure 14.3 vary in important ways, even though both represent the presence flow of Jaea engaging in ten-person raids with his guild. Figure 14.2 was a familiar raid for Jaea and the guild, and one that they had successfully completed many times before. However, a new guild member had never encountered this particular content before and was being carefully guided by the nine other guild members. Figure 14.3, on the other hand, represents a new raid boss that none of the ten players, including Jaea, had attempted before. And while all the players had researched the raid information closely beforehand, strategies and coordination were developed by the guild *in situ*. Researching raids before attempting them is a common practice of raiding guilds. The reason for this is to familiarize the members with the layout of the environment, the types of enemies that they will be facing, and anything that is specific to a boss that they may come across. The information that is used for preparation is community-created and can take the form of resources like written walk-throughs or videos of actual gameplay. Information literacy skills are needed in order for the players to locate and understand the information provided in these resources as well as to evaluate the reliability of each resource.

In terms of time, the two presence visualizations are quite similar. The following is a description of the digital contexts for Figures 14.2 and 14.3. In order to maintain accessibility for readers who are not *WoW* players, the following accounts are considerably simplified. This simplified version is to make the description accessible for all readers regardless of whether they are familiar with *WoW*. As stated in the introduction, *WoW* is an online game played by millions of people across the world. Smaller groups within the game, called 'guilds,' play and plan together, often in order to complete 'raids' (that is, incredibly complicated and challenging battles with powerful boss monsters that require a group of people to defeat). During this playtime, the guild groups tend to communicate verbally and via text in order to coordinate their attacks, and teamwork, prior knowledge, and careful attention are necessary in order to succeed.

Figure 14.2 represents the first phase of the ten-person normal mode Al'Akir raid. Raids may be played in either the 'normal' mode or 'heroic' mode, for which the raid bosses are even more powerful and difficult to defeat. Al'Akir is a three-phase raid, and in the first phase, Al'Akir (the final boss of the Throne of Four Winds raid) stands in the center of a floating circular platform. Around Al'Akir spins a wall of damage-dealing whirlwinds that require players to either move close to the boss or to the very edge of the platform, requiring constant attention by the players. A general *WoW* strategy is to distract the boss into attacking a high-defense player (otherwise known as a tank) while other players deal damage to him (otherwise known as DPS-ers, named after the phrase *Damage per Second*). All at the same time, other players are healing the tank and DPS-ers to ensure they stay alive. As this strategy plays out, Al'Akir casts chain lightning, the damage of which is multiplied by the number of players near the afflicted players—so the players must maintain a carefully coordinated distance from each other. In addition, Al'Akir will occasionally cast a spell that pushes players a certain distance from him, requiring that players stay close enough to him so that they don't fall off the platform when pushed back. In order to prevent the pushback spell from being cast, the tank can run away from Al'Akir, but Al'Akir punishes the fleeing tank by doing extra damage to him or her, and consequently the healers need to be prepared to cast extra healing spells on the tank. There are more spells that Al'Akir casts during the battle (too many to describe here), each of which requires specific strategies that can sometimes conflict with one another.

Figure 14.3 represents the first phase of the ten-person heroic mode Valiona and Theralion raid, which—at the time of writing—Jaea's guild just successfully completed. During the observation that led to Figure 14.3, the guild was unsuccessfully attempting this raid for the first time. This raid has two bosses, both dragons, which periodically switch off between the roles of fighting on the ground and flying while attacking the raid from the air. During the first phase, Valiona is on the ground, casting proximity-based flame attacks while the tank tries to keep Valiona's attacks focused on him or her. The DPS-ers try to bring Valiona's health down (both dragons share a common health pool), and healers work to keep everyone alive. Meanwhile, Valiona has another attack that requires players to stack (in other words, get as close as possible to each other) in order to minimize damage, while Theralion has an attack that requires players to spread out as far away as possible, forcing the raid team to be constantly aware of their relative positioning and to be prepared to move as needed.

FINDINGS

Despite differences in the raid itself, as well as the group's familiarity with each raid, both show a strikingly similar pattern. During fights, the *in-game WoW* presence predominates, but the between-battle chunks show Jaea shifting presence heavily towards information flow. This strong pattern is, in retrospect, the very pattern that led to our B-series time demarcations. While fighting and not fighting may seem like simple activity changes that occur only within the virtual world that the in-game *WoW* self inhabits, the influence on presence flow in all three layers is sharp and clear. Furthermore, Jaea's smooth yet rapid movement from one distribution of presence to another is practiced and familiar and presents no evidence of cognitive confusion or adaptive difficulties, which might be seen if split attention and multitasking were an issue.

On the left of the figures are three labels, each of which represents a 'layer' of presence. At the top, the *information constellation* represents all the information accessed by Jaea that is not included by default in *WoW*. This information includes Mumble, the heavily customized user interface that Jaea relies upon, and any online resources or activities that he engages in, such as Twitter or email. In the middle, the *Physical self* represents Jaea's physical body, located within the physical world and subject to various distractions like bathroom breaks, cell phones calls, and aggressively playful cats. At the bottom, the *in-game* WoW represents the virtual body and the default WoW information, which includes virtual cues from fellow raid members and bosses, mana (magic points) and health information, equipment durability, and bag space.

The separation of the information constellation layer from the in-game WoW layer and the physical self layer is a complex one. While information comes from the physical world (such as in-body signals that say, "I'm hungry") and the in-game WoW layer (virtual indicators that say, "My avatar needs to eat"), this information is part and parcel of living in and being able to perceive and respond to those worlds. The information constellation layer includes only the information that is separate from the default physical messages (the hardness of the chair against your legs) and the default WoW messages (the attack upon your avatar by a monster). In other words, the information constellation includes the additional information that Jaea (and other players) choose to receive or not receive, to seek out or not seek out.

Within each chunk, text summarizes Jaea's activities by presence type. The order is not chronological because the actions overlap one another, and the text merely indicates what happened during that time frame. Each item represents an activity or exchange of some sort, ranging from going to the bathroom (physical self), listening to raid chatter via Mumble (information flow), to specific movements present only during boss engagements (in-game WoW). Repetitions of activities or exchanges are condensed and represented with only one label. For example, *Healing teammates* (in-game WoW) is an action Jaea engaged in repeatedly in each of the chunks; however, that entry is included only once, and there is no indication of frequency except indirectly by the height of the in-game WoW layer.

Time progresses from left to right, and the three layers co-occur within each B-series time column. The height of each layer within blocks indicates the proportion of presence: in Figure 14.2, for example, Jaea's presence in the first block is most strongly in information constellation, followed by in-game WoW presence, with the least amount of presence in physical self. In the following block, a distinct shift occurs, as information constellation and physical self become shorter, and in-game WoW nearly doubles. The dramatic shifts of presence accompanying events in WoW dictated the B-series time distinctions and help to foreground and background different elements of the data. Specific actions taken by Jaea are noted within the blocks by text but are otherwise backgrounded. Instead, we can clearly see the flow of activity and presence by backgrounding the details and foregrounding the descriptors of actions, which is key to our analysis. The graphs emphasize the proportion of overall presence allocated to each layer and the changes of those proportions based on activity.

There are two particular codes that are worth explaining briefly here. The descriptor *Minimal presence* is used to indicate that Jaea is barely present in that layer during a time chunk. It is used only in the physical self category to represent that some presence is unavoidable. Another descriptor, *Customized UI* (see Figure 14.4), is ever-present in the information constellation category, and represents Jaea's modified user interface. His reorganization of *WoW* information flow is so drastic that his every engagement with the virtual world is mediated by his unique design. Jaea's constant tweaking of his customized UI contributes to his level of expertise because his ability to process information included in the customized UI at a glance allows him to have faster reaction times and more precision when playing. A constant striving to improve the customized UI shows a perpetual striving to improve his gameplay. Just as in situations of other forms of fandom (Black & Steinkuehler, 2009) the player's ability to 'read' the text of the situation is important to success. Coiro and Dobler (2007) found that reading online required different skills than reading in traditional print format. The reader needed to understand more than the words on the screen—also the context clues and structure of the digital materials. The situation is similar for Jaea in-game; as Coiro and Dobler found for websites, Jaea must be able to interpret symbols, and understand the context clues and structure of the game interface. Modifying the interface could be seen as similar to writing fan fiction—tweaking the story and changing parts to make the readability more customized to his needs. While writing fan fiction and maximizing healing performance may seem quite different, both are examples of the same phenomena: participants acting upon their digital environments in order to rewrite their own stories. Jaea's UI modification could be conceived as intentionally modifying the spatial arrangement (Hollan et al., 2000) in order to simplify choice, perception, and internal computation.

One difference between the two presence visualizations is particularly clear. The physical self presence is similarly minimal during fights, but Figure 14.2 shows a shift towards a stronger physical self presence between battles, while the Figure 14.3 physical self presence stays quite minimal both in and out of fights. The differences in raid familiarity provide a possible rationale: Figure 14.2, as a familiar raid, required less attention from Jaea during non-battle times, as he was already comfortable with the actions required of him during battle, and didn't need to devote resources towards planning for the restart of battle. Figure 14.3, representing a never-before-attempted raid, required a consistently high presence in information constellation, thus limiting the physical self presence even during non-battle time chunks.

Note that although there is still a high information flow in Figure 14.2 during non-battle times, it contains some considerably different items that indicate a shift away from the in-game information. Instead of just raiding team discussions and user interface tweaking, Jaea is reading various forums and looking through Twitter, activities that are sometimes unrelated

Figure 14.4   Jaea's customized UI before Al'Akır.

to the game or his current activity within the game. This divergence in activity pairs with the increased presence in physical self, as Jaea stops devoting his presence to the game-related activities, and shifts into a more relaxed state.

VISUALIZATION OF EXPERTISE

Our expert's success at play, relying on more than just his ability to play his character well, requires fluid and rapid shifts of presence. As can be seen in the presence visualizations, Jaea's ability to distribute attention to different layers means that he can balance the influx of information and information needs that arise, as well simultaneously engage within the physical space and within the game. Jaea's expertise moves beyond his ability to control his character and relies on his ability to interact with his surrounding virtual and physical spaces, as well as informational resources.

Jaea's layers of presence vary in proportion with the activity he is currently engaged in during gameplay. The more temporally rapid the activity in the game, the larger the proportion of the game layer presence, whereas between activities the information layer or the physical self layer increases in proportion in the presence visualization. The information constellation layer always fills a larger proportion than the physical self layer. In Figure 14.3, the physical self layer is a smaller proportion because of the intensity of information flow both during fighting and non-fighting periods due to the fact that the raid is unfamiliar, which requires high levels of verbal coordination and information seeking even between fights. Despite the fact that all raid members studied the raid before they attempted it, the attempts were not going well and required just-in-time (Gee, 2003) information seeking in order to help them re-strategize. The information flow of a player is contingent upon the player's information literacy skills, and in this case the raid group's information literacy skills. Collective information literacy (Martin & Steinkuehler, 2010) is implemented within the raid group in order to pull from the group's collective knowledge of the game-at-large, raid strategy, player roles, specific raid layouts, boss phases, etc. Using this collective, connected cloud of information, the raid guild is able to be more effective and better informed together than they would be individually.

This method allows for the capture of more than just Jaea's movements in the space of the game, the information constellation, and his physical location. It captures social interactions, use of resources, and focus in correspondence with the activities in the B-series timescale. This connection of activities to time with reference to presence offers a deeper look into the intricate functioning of expertise in the game, and demonstrates the importance of distributed presence. From this conceptualization of distributed presence, we can extend the concept of distributed cognition as discussed by Hutchins (1995) and Hollan et al. (2000). Presence illustrates distributed cognition in several ways. First, it has a unit of analysis, in this case the larger unit of a coherent WoW activity and the smaller units of partitioned activity as demarcated by B-series time. Second, there are multiple actors in the cognitive process—in this example, members of a social group, as well as a variety of resources. Finally, the actions and process are distributed across time and previous actions affect the nature of later actions. Crucially, our examination of presence is based on the fact that "people form a tightly coupled system with their environments" (Hollan et al., 2000: 192), even as we extend the definition of *environment* to include the digital context of WoW and the complex constellation of information.

At the same time the actions we see here are reminiscent of collective information literacy (Martin & Steinkuehler, 2010), which could be viewed as distributed information literacy, in view of Hutchins' definition of distributed cognition. Collective information literacy occurs when multiple people in a group or affinity space work together to solve a problem. This happens in both examples given earlier but most notably in the example with the group facing an unfamiliar raid. In Figure 14.3, the strategy and problem solving sessions carried out at the end of each wipe are a perfect example of collective information literacy: the raid team always used that time to determine what needed to be changed from the prior strategy, and what information players were missing in order to accomplish the raid. The use of distributed cognition and collective information literacy is not surprising given the social nature of games. However, the evidence of these two models functioning in a punctuated way within the B-series time allows for a useful way to track the intellectual work as well as the action that goes into success in an affinity space or other collaborative spaces that requires joint activity. We offer Jaea as an exemplar of how expertise functions in a space like this, surrounded by other experts and experts-in-training working towards a common challenging goal.

THE SHIFTING NATURE OF EXPERTISE

Throughout his play, Jaea consistently engages in multiple simultaneous actions and thought processes. The number of actions he juggles at once combined with the speed with which he shifts between these actions is likely to seem overwhelming to a novice or non-player. This shifting distribution of presence should not be confused for partial or even split attention, but rather for the necessarily flexible nature of expertise. Jaea's focus is not splintered; rather, he is unquestioningly focused on playing his character well. The expert's shifting distributions of presence can be clearly distinguished from the metaphor of split attention: Jaea's increase in focus in one layer occurs because of activities in the other layers. Instead of 'losing' cognitive power (as in split attention), the expert's shift occurs because of a holistic understanding of the context and attentional demands. In fact, play at such an expert level cannot take place without such shifts in presence. Players who focus their attention on only one component of the game at a time cannot possibly play at the same level as Jaea. Only players who can engage in action with distributed attention and distributed information literacy across a group of players can successfully participate in high-level raiding activities. This ability demonstrates the literacy of the player to navigate the space of the game, the physical world, and the information constellation. These literacy practices, because of their ability to help the player succeed in the game, also affect the social identity of the player within the community. This method helps to visually identify the literacy practices that take place in the virtual space, the physical space, and the information constellation, all of which are contained in the constellation of literacies that a player or person uses and experiences. Through this visualization process we can observe the literacy practices as they take place and see what practices are layered together.

Expertise in *World of Warcraft* and other games requires masterful coordination of information resources across multiple timescales and spaces, and is the same no matter the physical age of the player. Jaea has to be able to sustain his attention across multiple spaces in his immediate vicinity, in the virtual game world, and with fellow players who are participating from other locations throughout the world. Considering that this delicate balance of shifting distributions of presence is necessary for expert-level play, we suggest that one has to consider the timescales and spaces involved all as equally valid.

CONCLUSIONS

This study of a single expert *World of Warcraft* player revealed important insights about activity as it occurs across multiple timescales and in multiple spaces, both real and virtual. For future studies that hope to continue with similar kinds of analyses, we recommend observing players with varied amounts of expertise. The methodology of presence that the researchers of this study utilize could be used to study the gameplay of any level of player. Novice players are not likely to engage these acts of distributed and collective cognition with the same ease with which Jaea is able to transition across times and spaces using both his physical self and in-game *WoW* self. Additional research could allow researchers to map out a trajectory of expertise development in terms of time, space, and literacy. We anticipate that such a trajectory will provide illumination into the development of facile shifts in particular layers of presence.

We also suggest that studying an entire raid group might reveal more about how attention is divided across multiple activities and events during high-level play of *World of Warcraft*. A sudden shift from in-game *WoW* self to physical self because of some event occurring in their physical space could have substantive effects on the attention of the rest of the players in the raid group even if they are distributed across multiple locations hundreds, if not thousands, of miles apart. As raiding players tend to operate at a fairly expert level, however, they may have means and strategies for coping with such interruptions and shifts such that it does not dramatically disrupt their play. Knowing more about how the players' manage their distributed attention to maximize their collective efforts could be useful for an array of contexts, both for study of games and beyond. Understanding how groups manage their resources across multiple spaces and times has a variety of implications in a globally connected world where teams of problem solvers are often located throughout the world as they work on shared problems.

REFERENCES

Awh, E. & Pashler, H. (2000). Evidence for split attentional foci. *Journal of Experimental Psychology Human Perception and Performance* 26(2): 834–846.
Black, R. W. (2008). *Adolescents and Online Fan Fiction*. New York: Peter Lang.
Black, R. W. (2007a). Digital design: English language learners and reader reviews in online fiction. In C. Lankshear & M. Knobel (eds.), *New Literacies Sampler*. New York: Peter Lang.
Black, R. W. (2007b). Fanfiction writing and the construction of space. *e-Learning* 4(4): 384–397.
Black, R. W. & Steinkuehler, C. (2009). Literacy in virtual worlds. In L. Christenbury, R. Bomer, & P. Smagorinsky (eds.), *Handbook of Adolescent Literacy Research*. New York: Guilford.
Bourdieu, P. (1977). *Outline of a Theory of Practice* (R. Nice, Trans.). Cambridge, MA: Cambridge University Press.
Chi, M. T. H., Feltovich, P. J., & Glaser, R. (1981). Categorization and representation of physics problems by experts and novices. *Cognitive Science* 5: 121–152.

Coiro, J., & Dobler, E. (2007). Exploring the online reading comprehension strategies used by sixth-grade skilled readers to search for and locate information on the Internet. *Reading Research Quarterly* 42(2): 214–257.

Erickson, F. (2004). *Talk and Social Theory: Ecologies of Speaking and Listening in Everyday Life*. Cambridge: Polity Press.

Gee, J. P. (2005). Semiotic social spaces and affinity spaces: From *The Age of Mythology* to today's schools. In D. Barton & K. Tusting (eds.), *Beyond Communities of Practice: Language, Power, and Social Context*. New York: Cambridge University Press.

Gee, J. P. (2004). *Situated Language and Learning*. New York: Routledge.

Gee, J. (2003). *What Videogames Have to Teach Us about Learning and Literacy*. New York: Palgrave Macmillan.

Gee, J. P. (1999). *An Introduction to Discourse Analysis: Theory and Method*. New York: Routledge.

Gell, A. (1992). A-series:B-series::Gemeinschaft:Gesellschaft::Them:Us. *The Anthropology of Time: Culture Construction of Temporal Maps and Images*. Oxford: Berg.

González, V. M. & Mark, G. (2005). Managing currents of work: Multi-tasking among multiple collaborations. In H. Gellersen et al. (eds.), *ECSCW 2000S: Proceedings of the Ninth European Conference on Computer-Supported Cooperative Work*. Paris: Springer.

González, V. M. & Mark, G. (2004). "Constant, constant, multi-tasking craziness": Managing multiple working spheres. *CHI 2004* 6(1): 113–120.

Hollan, J., Hutchins, E., & Kirsh, D. (2000). Distributed cognition: Toward a new foundation for human-computer interaction research. *ACM Transactions on Computer-Human Interaction* 7(2): 174–196.

Hutchins, E. (1995). *Cognition in the Wild*. Cambridge, MA: MIT Press.

Kalyuga, S., Chandler, P., & Sweller, J. (1999). Making split-attention and redundancy in multimedia instruction. *Applied Cognitive Psychology* 13: 351–371.

Lemke, J. (2000). Across the scales of time: Artifacts, activities, and meanings in ecosocial systems. *Mind, Culture, and Activity* 7(4): 273–290.

Martin, C. (in progress). *A-series and B-series Time Maps in World of Warcraft*.

Martin, C. & Steinkuehler, C. (2010). Collective information literacy in massively multiplayer online games. *e-Learning and Digital Media* 7(4): 355–365.

Mayer, R. E. & Moreno, R. (1998). A split-attention effect in multimedia learning: Evidence for dual processing systems in working memory. *Journal of Education Psychology* 90(2): 312–320.

Stake, R. (1995). *The Art of Case Study Research*. Thousand Oaks, CA: Sage.

Steinkuehler, C. (2008). Cognition and literacy in massively multiplayer online games. In J. Coiro et al. (eds.), *Handbook of Research on New Literacies*. New York: Routledge. Steinkuehler, C. (2007). Massively multiplayer online games as a constellation of literacy practices. *e-Learning and Digital Media* 4(3): 297–318.

Steinkuehler, C. (2006). Massively multiplayer online video gaming as participation in a discourse. *Mind, Culture, and Activity* 13(1): 38–52.

Steinkuehler, C. & King, B. (2009). Digital literacies for the disengaged: Creating after school contexts to support boys' game-based literacy skills. *On the Horizon* 17(1): 47–59.

Stevens, R., Satwicz, T., & McCarthy, L. (2008). In-game, in-room, in-world: Reconnecting video game play to the rest of kids' lives. In K. Salen (ed.), *The Ecology or Games: Connecting Youth, Games, and Learning*. Cambridge, MA: MIT Press.

Tabbers, H., Martens, R., & van Merriënboer, J. (2000, February). Multimedia instructions and cognitive load theory: Split-attention and modality effects. Paper presented at the AECT 2000, Long Beach, CA.

Virtual Literacies and Beyond
Some Concluding Comments

Guy Merchant, Julia Gillen,
Jackie Marsh, and Julia Davies

The chapters in this collection paint a vivid picture of the diversity of practices that constitute what we have rather loosely termed virtual literacies. A uniting feature of this body of work is its concern for how the communicative affordances of digital technologies are woven into the lived experience of children and young people. They feature in their daily lives across a variety of domains—in domestic settings, in educational institutions, in both public and private spaces. The contributors to this book have documented the emergence of new meaning-making practices, and new kinds of social interaction, both 'in the wild' (Beavis, this volume)—in the self-sponsored, voluntary, and self-sustaining communities that coalesce around online games, virtual worlds, and social networking sites—and in the innovatory work of educators, who are exploring the possibilities of harnessing the learning potential of these new technologies. Further, one of the book's strongest themes is to offer constructive ways in which connections can be made between home and school—the domain boundaries that Kendall and McDougall (in this volume), drawing on the work of Bernstein, characterize as potentially 'heavily insulated' and then crossable in transgressive acts. As Marsh (this volume) argues, online and offline spaces are mutually constitutive in children's lives, and as we suggest later, some of the most exciting developments involve ways of describing the fluid movement between these domains.

It is a truism to say that things constantly change, but while we have been compiling this book, and in the discussions that preceded it, we were conscious that the environments and technologies we were studying would not remain the same up to and after the point of publication. Some of the virtual worlds that were popular when the studies outlined in this book were undertaken have now been closed (for example, *BarbieGirls*, *Teen SL*) and a recognition of this ephemerality is a necessary condition for conducting work in this field. There are numerous reasons for the disappearance of some of the sites, and these include issues of design and structure as well as use. Furthermore, changes in political and economic environments worldwide may have constrained appetites in policy-makers' quarters to invest in innovations unless these can demonstrably 'make a difference.' Therefore our concern has been to unite a series of carefully situated studies, attentive to features of time and place, with a desire to contribute to discussions that would be useful beyond the very specific and to bring out ideas that will be helpful for anybody interested in the field, from whatever role or vantage point.

In this concluding chapter we tease out key themes that run through the chapters, and highlight some of the dilemmas and questions that will inform future research and practice. However, in doing this, we are aware that there are other significant themes that will occur to readers, or indeed those that will emerge with the passage of time. In order to provide a synthesis and to indicate possible ways forward, we have organized our reflections into five themes. We begin with an overview of the new ways of meaning-making that have been described in the chapters, making the point that these are multiple, and intersect with more familiar practices at a number of levels. This is followed by a focus on the playful, imaginative, and creative aspects of virtual literacy practices. Here we explore issues such as the creative, imaginative acts of world-making and identity play. Aspects of sociability are underlined in the section that follows, as we look at the centrality of the playfully social in this work. We follow this with an exploration of the theme of informal and formal pedagogics, suggesting that the norms and values that lie behind these virtual literacies are important to consider. Finally, we address some of the methodological issues and challenges that have been raised in the previous chapters.

NEW WAYS OF MAKING MEANING

In their landmark text *New Literacies: Everyday Practices and Social Learning*, Lankshear and Knobel (2010) describe these literacies as both new communicative practices and new habits of mind, and many of the chapters in this book have shown both these aspects at work. They have also described fluid movements across different spaces. This sort of media multitasking often involves actions and interactions that interweave with activity in the physical environment, creating a rich tapestry of meanings. Collectively, these observations begin to suggest that some of the binary distinctions explored in Chapter 1, and particularly the notion of online/ offline, may constrain our thinking and limit further progress in this area. The boundary between online and offline activity has been described as a porous membrane (Castronova, 2005). We argue that there is even more fluidity than the membrane metaphor implies—perhaps a state of affairs that is, in essence, little different from the way in which we navigate our way through the rich textual spaces of a contemporary urban environment, as a largely continuous experience.

The characteristics of new textual processes and practices have been illustrated in different ways throughout this book, and taken together illustrate some of the new media tropes that can be found elsewhere in the literature. For example, Lankshear and Knobel (2006) have written about the practice of remixing or reworking existing materials, and Bruns (2008) has explored the blurring of the distinction between consumption and production, coining the term 'produsage.' Work on social network-ing sites has highlighted the ways in which alternative connections are being made with both known and unknown others (Marwick and boyd, 2011), whereas Hull and Stornaiuolo (2010) have explored how these sites provide opportunities for multiple presentations of the self. In the work of Kress (2010) the nature of multimodality and the emergence of modular-ized approaches to design are described, and the collaborative and dis-tributed nature of knowledge-building in new media has been analyzed by Gee (2003).

Although it is helpful to reflect on how these new ways of making mean-ing are reflected in the various activities and practices described in this volume, it is also important to avoid the temptation to force unifying con-ceptions onto material and activity that are actually quite diverse in nature. As Postill suggests:

> . . . the Internet and indeed the world—is becoming ever more plu-ral and [. . .] no universal "logic of practice" (not even the logic of *techne*) is gaining ascendancy at the expense of all other logics. (Pos-till, 2010: 649)

This plurality is amply illustrated here, where we have seen participants involved in a variety of actions and interactions in which content has been generated, shared, uploaded, and downloaded in different ways. Often the participants do have a sense of common purpose, although this may be as limited as an interest in accessing a particular environment at the same time—as in the 'chaos' of entry to *Club Penguin* (Marsh, this volume). The affordances of such an environment then constrain the opportunities for interaction, but we can see in these an emerging nexus of practice (Scollon, 2001). Thus, when considering these environments it is important to rec-ognize the qualities of each that give rise to such plurality of experience, as we have seen discussed in the different chapters. For example, the interac-tive dimension of virtual worlds such as *Barbie Girls* or *Chimpoo* contrasts with the solo-player *Adventure World*. And even though the *Active Worlds* format used to create Barnsborough (Chapter 10) allowed for plenty of interaction, opportunities for modifying the world, uploading content, or building (as in *Schome Park*) were not available. There are also contrasting aesthetics across these virtual spaces. The stylized designs of *Club Pen-guin* differ sharply from the representational qualities of *Second Life*. The affordances of the sites for literacy are also very different and vary from the rather constrained literacy environment offered by *Webkinz* (Black & Reich, this volume) to the rather more generative space offered by *Teen Second Life* (Delgarno & Lee, 2010; see Gillen et. al., this volume). This confounds attempts to see virtual worlds, let alone virtual or online spaces in general, as one thing.

Even the definitions commonly used to identify different kinds of virtual worlds and different versions of virtual world gameplay—terms such as '3D' and 'immersive'—come to seem rather vague. None of the environments categorized here as 3D worlds actually exist in three dimensions, nor do they create the same sense of space that 3D cinema or television does, yet at the same time, there is clearly a greater sense of 'depth' in some worlds as opposed to others. Similarly, although a number of contributors apply the concept of immersion, any game or activity is truly immersive only to the extent that individual users become immersed in it, and furthermore, as we have seen, levels of immersion vary considerably between gamers and even within individual gamers' experiences. Similarly the boundary between virtual world and online gaming is distinctly fuzzy. We noted in Chapter 1 how players often invent games to play in virtual worlds that are not driven by an overall purpose or narrative. The reverse is true, too. Often players of MMOGs visit game locations simply to 'hang out.' Furthermore, in the design of virtual spaces, the extent to which a narrative is embedded or foregrounded can vary considerably. In Barnsborough and *Adventure Rock* there was a backstory, intended to provide an impetus for exploration, whereas *Schome Park* depended more on the inventions of participants.

This all goes to illustrate some of the difficulties that attach to the work of building robust categories in an area that develops so rapidly and unpredictably. It also supports the view that life online is as diverse as life offline, if indeed the two can be held separate in the first place. It might be fitting to conclude that, in documenting virtual literacies, we see that while the essence of meaning-making remains relatively stable, from a psychological point of view, the rapid multiplication and diversification of textual spaces demand more sophisticated descriptions of the processes involved than have been deployed to date.

PLAYFUL, IMAGINATIVE, CREATIVE

The role of the imagination, and the capacity for creative engagement offered by new media, has been described in detail elsewhere (Willett, Robinson, & Marsh, 2008). Here, though, we have seen again how learning and learner identities can be shaped through playful, and often self-motivated, activity. This is perhaps best illustrated through the descriptions of informal and less-bounded practices, such as those that constellate around virtual worlds and gaming 'in the wild' (Beavis, this volume). However, it does seem that innovative educators are able to draw on these attributes in classrooms, although they may experience some conflicts with entrenched routines and structures (Merchant, 2010). The extent to which new habits of mind imply new school pedagogies may well warrant further investigation (see Squire, 2005). In general, though, it seems to be the case that more tightly defined conceptions of learning, coupled with more extensive controls—often as a response to discourses of risk—continue to characterize formal educational initiatives.

Here, we have seen repeated examples of how online play is important in developing the sorts of understandings of multimodal texts that are central to virtual literacies. Whether this play involves an element of planning and design, or whether it is simply undertaken as a participant, the game-like quality remains. Underscoring this is an often implicit view of the relationship between play and learning. One line of development that is particularly striking here is the significance of imagined places and the narratives that develop in and around them. This reaches its apotheosis in the roles that are taken up, and the work that gets done, in virtual worlds and MMOGs. Nonetheless, it is also identifiable in the ostensibly more 'real' activities of social networking sites.[1] A number of authors in this book allude to the cultural significance of imagining fictional worlds. It seems likely to us that this is a universal human need or function of mind, as Bruner (2005) argues, but it is sufficient perhaps to suggest that the cultural understandings of both formal and informal learning represented in these chapters draw attention to the part played by the imagination. As was argued by Gillen & Merchant (this volume), the idea that 'world-making' (Bruner, 2005: 691) is some sort of bizarre aberration created by Internet 'nerds' in environments like *Second Life* or *World of Warcraft* just does not hold water. Such activity has much longer, well-respected antecedents, stretching back to the limits of human history and beyond, as Jackson (this volume) reminds us.

Vygotsky (1987) argued that opportunities for creative and imaginative exploration are important, not only for our psychological wellbeing, but also in providing opportunities to reflect upon or critique other aspects of our lives; so therefore they are essential to learning. Pinker (2011) has recently argued that literature provides important opportunities for the kinds of empathy with others that are necessary for social integration and harmony. We might extend this thesis further to suggest that interactive world-making could offer the same possibilities. This is, of course, highly speculative, but certainly provides an important counterpoint to the well-rehearsed discourses of moral panic (Bennet & Maton, 2011).

Identity play and building and furnishing homes and other structures are a related set of activities that contribute to world-making. In some environments, dressing a character and acquiring possessions or attributes can become part of developing a sort of narrative history. How do we talk about the avatars that represent us, but are not us—those representations that may not exactly have a life of their own, that exist independently of us, and yet may quickly develop characteristics and recognizable routines and collect around them a history of use that is something like a narrative of identity? These questions have their parallel in the world of social networking in which performances of the self are often playful and selective, and yet may still contribute to what Giddens refers to as the ongoing narrative of the self (Giddens, 1991).

Jackson (this volume) reminds us that the activities associated with this world-making are diverse and that certain players or learners may well exhibit particular preferences—for example, for nurturing (avatars or pets), for developing one's status within the game, or for socializing—and that these orientations are not exclusive. There is, then, an emerging sense of the rich possibilities for a variety of kinds of imaginative play and creative engagement in the nexus of practices that have been described in earlier chapters. This involves not only aspects of self-expression—a class of activity often upheld as culturally significant in liberal democracies—but also plenty of social interaction and negotiation, collaborative problem solving, and other forms of joint activity. What has been described as the 'playfully social' (Graham, 2008) is an important feature of this work and begs the question of what models of development and play are appropriate to the study of virtual literacy practices.

SOCIABILITY

From the early days of computer-mediated communication to the present time, the rapidly mutating forms of technosociability have been described and analyzed by researchers (see, for example, Herring, Stein, & Virtanen, 2012). The widespread take-up of mobile devices has, if anything, accelerated this trend. More recently, the rising popularity of sites like Facebook and Twitter has fuelled the notion that social networking is somehow synonymous with the connections made on social networking sites (Merchant, 2011). It is perhaps more accurate, though, to think of levels of mediation, in which different communicative spaces provide layered and intersecting networks of connection. In looking at the virtual literacies described in this book, it seems that these kinds of social interactions play an important role in motivating and sustaining participants' interest. Unsurprisingly these environments are often referred to as *social media*—"technologies that enable communication, collaboration, participation and sharing" (Hughes, 2009: 5)—and it is these characteristics that seem to provide opportunities for both formal and informal learning. As Waller (this volume) demonstrates in his analysis of young children's use of Twitter, a social media site that was originally intended for out-of-school communication, children are motivated by the kind of social engagement that these spaces offer and this can lead to productive kinds of learning.

Sociability seems to increase learning opportunities, and enables collaborative problem solving and strategizing. This can be stimulated by dynamic features of an ARG, an online game, or a virtual world, or alternatively by the careful design and choreography of a skilled teacher. We have seen how challenges such as the invitation to influence what an environment looks like, to organize a raid, or simply to collect or trade objects—challenges that often depend upon collaboration and interaction—may be more motivating for some participants, than opportunities to find out, or solve a mystery. The level of challenge may be something akin to what Gee describes as being pleasantly frustrating.

> Learning works best when new challenges are pleasantly frustrating in the sense of being felt by learners to be at the outer edge of, but within, their 'regime of competence'. That is, these challenges feel hard, but 'doable'. (Gee, 2005: 10)

In many examples in this book challenges become 'doable' through the collective action of networked individuals.

Parry (2011) uses the term hyperconnectivity to describe how social media can connect learners with those outside immediate classroom contexts in advantageous ways, and this sense of enhanced sociability is certainly a theme that is picked up by a number of contributors. The widespread use of social media among teenagers makes this a key area of concern (Lenhart, Ling, & Campbell, 2010; Livingstone, Haddon, Gorzig, & Olaffson, 2011; Ofcom, 2011). While much has been made of the risks involved, there is increasing recognition in the literature that under certain conditions, social networking sites can provide an important context for knowledge-building and more conventionally recognizable kinds of learning (Greenhow & Robelia, 2009; Merchant, 2011). The same sentiments are reflected here, and the net is cast wider to include a broader range of practices.

PEDAGOGIES

Virtual literacies, and the environments that support them, are not value-free. As with any designed space they are informed by a worldview in which particular identity positions are favored, and particular representations are made available (Holland, Lachicotte, Skinner, & Cain, 2001). Social relations and material practices are part of a discursive field that constitutes the background context of these virtual literacies. This is not to say that individuals, such as the children and young people in the studies reported here, do not have agency—in fact we have argued strongly that they do—but it is to recognize that this agency is acted out with, or against the grain of a matrix of norms and values. When we are considering commercial or institutional environments, we therefore think it is important to look at the pedagogical dimension, whether that is explicit or hidden. In this sense we follow Giroux and Pollock in suggesting that we should not lose sight of:

. . . how learning occurs by providing the ideas and narratives that shape how people see the world and themselves . . . (Giroux & Pollock, 2010: 5)

Although such a task may seem more pressing when we look at *Barbie Girls*, as Carrington's work indicates (this volume), or more straightforward when we consider some educational projects that incorporate social media, as in Greenhow's study (this volume), the underlying concern is the same. While individuals enact their identities in their interactions with each other, these identity performances are shaped by the contexts they operate within.

This raises the question of whether there is space for critical practice in social media. It may be the case that the sort of approach described by Burnett and Merchant (2011) constitutes a way forward here. Burnett and Merchant argue that existing paradigms of critical literacy and critical media literacy are restricted in their ability to engage with the fluid and densely interwoven spaces of social media. In its place they propose a practice-based model that focuses on the interplay between purposes, contexts, and resources. Their conception of new media practices is based on a view of how identities are formed and performed, and how these are in turn embedded in social networks.

Resources are of course a key issue for all those involved in schools and other formal educational institutions. Although formal, public education has a long tradition of being resourced by suppliers of educational goods, specialist publishers, and so on, the impact of technology both in terms of hardware and software provision (Jewitt, Moss, & Cardini, 2007) and in the global circulation of curricular and classroom materials (Nichols, 2006) has been transformative. The relationship between commercial and educational interests is perhaps more complex in the contemporary world than it has been in the past, and also varies considerably, not least according to features of the national setting. In the UK and Australia, for example, there is, still, a tradition of allowing schools, and to a degree even teachers, a certain amount of discretion in their decision-making—a form of agency that is sometimes denied in the U.S., where, in some states, commercial programs have been bought into as programs that prescribe in very close detail not just curriculum and assessment, but also nearly every detail in between. This raises the uncomfortable specter of the development of virtual worlds for schools that become very prescriptive and programmatic in their design in their attempt to deliver particular learning objectives. It will be important for educators in the years ahead to ensure that online educational spaces do not follow the reductive track of the commercial publishers, but instead allow for the kinds of creative practices that are outlined in some of the studies discussed in this book. A further challenge for those who wish to produce virtual learning spaces for schools is that the frequently high expectations generated by commercially available applications, which are often rich in graphics, make it hard to generate competitive bespoke creations for education.

The use of social media in classrooms certainly adds to this growing commercial interest in formal education. At the same time we note how, with the growing recognition of informal learning, the entertainment industry repeatedly aligns itself with an educational interest. Since its inception in 1922, the BBC, a UK public broadcasting service with a mission to promote informal learning, has had a broad educational function, and this mission is now clearly articulated. But at the same time it is still driven by a need to both attract audiences and protect audiences (see, for example, Chapter 13). Those with an interest in new media and new literacies are often critical of the way in which educational institutions reduce and regulate what is possible, and contributors to this book are no exception. On the other hand, those with an interest in formal education continue to suggest ways in which school curricula might incorporate or learn from the growth in informal learning in social media (Davies & Merchant, 2009). Despite the difficulties of implementation found in the regimes, routines, and timetable constraints of public education, as well as perceptions about what should and should not take place in school—perceptions that may be as strongly held by students as they are by their teachers—the importance of bridging the in-school/out-of-school divide is spelled out clearly in a number of chapters in this volume.

A further pedagogical consideration that is raised by a number of authors is that of the role of the teacher in the use of virtual environments in the literacy curriculum. Merchant (this volume) notes the innovation fatigue of educators in an environment in which new initiatives are constantly developed. This may create barriers in the adoption of virtual spaces for teaching purposes. Further, for some teachers, virtual worlds and online spaces may be unfamiliar, or they may be anxious about online safety issues, which may give rise to pedagogical practices that limit children's agency. Yet the work of Waller (this volume), Howells and Robertson (this volume), and Colvert (this volume) illustrate how teachers can, through creative approaches that foster pupils as autonomous learners, facilitate a range of innovative literacy practices in online spaces. These approaches require teachers to recognize the opportunities of virtual domains, understand their affordances (see Delgarno & Lee, 2010), and create curriculum spaces in which pupils can explore and experiment, supported by an adult who can advise, question, and challenge at appropriate points. The challenge for future developments in these areas is to develop approaches to assessment that enable pupils to demonstrate their skills, knowledge, and understanding in relation to literacy in online spaces and enable teachers to plan for future learning accordingly.

METHODOLOGIES

Virtual worlds, MMOGs, and other social media practices pose particularly challenging problems for researchers. Many of these problems are a product of the fluidity of textual practices that are involved. Not only does meaning-making in new media lack the fixity and boundedness of traditional print text, but features such as multiple authorship, regular updating, and dense interconnection within and between sites challenge traditional forms of analysis. Commentators have also observed how participants may navigate multimodal elements in different ways, and how a particular 'page' may well take on a different appearance when viewed on a different screen, through a different browser, or on a mobile device (Kress, 2010). Further to this, increased personalization means that each person's viewpoint is slightly different, as in Facebook, and updates may occur regularly and unpredictably throughout a single day. Moreover, media themselves are situated in multiple networks, thus confounding established notions of context and intertextuality. In sum, the very essence of textuality slips through our fingers unless we freeze it in time through a screenshot. This means that researchers need to be reflexive in their approaches to study in this arena. Here, some studies have alluded to the emergence of new kinds of ethnography. Gillen et al. (this volume) construct team ethnographies in order to honor the multiple perspectives of online worlds. Through this approach, they build a richer picture of environments that are usually seen only from an individual perspective.

This book has provided a number of examples to demonstrate the dangerous misunderstandings that can occur if we are too quick and easy with our interpretations. For example, Marsh (this volume) outlines how one user of *Club Penguin*, Sally, used set phrases rather than open chat with other users, and while on the surface one might assume that was because she was unconfident in writing, or a reluctant writer, in fact it was a deliberate strategy to ensure that she could communicate quickly with other avatars in order to prevent them from moving away while she was typing. Thus, in this study, close observation of online activity was combined with interviewing in order to investigate children's choices and decision-making processes in the use of this virtual world. Other studies also used a mixed method approach, as attempts were made to trace how subjects move between different sites, and back and forth into their immediate physical context. Martin et al. (this volume) utilized observations, interviewing, and think-alouds to trace the traversals of a 25-year-old expert gamer interacting in and around the MMOG *World of Warcraft*. The methods employed were sensitive enough to capture the complexities of his gameplay, his engagement with paratexts, and how these activities were situated in his everyday life. Thus, creative methods that include a variety of elicitation devices, such as those described by Gauntlett (2007), have proved useful to some as ways of exploring children and young people's views and engagements with virtual literacies. Researchers continue to grapple with problems, such as finding ways of dealing with the sheer volume of textual material that can be generated and the analytical challenges of dealing with rapidly changing and interlinked multimodal texts that intersect with more traditional activities and interactions.

FINAL THOUGHTS

Throughout this book, the editors and contributors have established a working understanding of virtual online spaces, and we conclude this chapter by revisiting our views of the practices that are associated with these virtual literacies. One of the key features that we have identified in a number of kinds of environments is the sense of affiliation or community that is engendered among participants. This sense of affiliation is sometimes built on existing social relations, such as with a dispersed group of colleagues or friends, or it may simply exist as a virtual community in which participants are unlikely ever to be in face-to-face communication. Whatever the balance, and the particular characteristics of the environment, literacy practices play an essential part in the social construction of these spaces. In some of the classroom studies reported in this collection, and indeed in other instances, too, these spaces exist in close relation to offline worlds that often include more familiar literacies. Nevertheless the studies all illustrate how new forms of literacies are emerging even when they are often intricately interwoven with existing practices (Davies & Merchant, 2009; Lankshear & Knobel, 2010).

The virtual spaces that we have been concerned with serve to mediate social interaction. They are united by the fact that literacies are being used to create online spaces—spaces that in turn encouraged new kinds of communicative interaction. In social media, new literacies are involved in maintaining and developing relationships, and these new literacies are characterized by:

- their collaborative or participatory nature
- the blurring of distinctions between reading and writing
- multimodality—the orchestration of various semiotic systems
- creativity and playfulness
- their flow across spaces and time
- the possibilities for the construction and use of a wide variety of generic forms in a single meaning-making event

The chapters in this book have, collectively, illuminated the way in which literacy practices in online spaces can demonstrate some—or all—of these characteristics. The authors have variously outlined the complexities involved in communication in virtual domains and highlighted the laminated, multilayered nature of online identities, practices, and spaces. In this way, we offer some insights into virtual literacies as social practices and highlight the areas that still need much work in the years ahead. This work is imperative, we would suggest, if we are to understand fully the nature of literacy in globalized, networked, and online worlds.

NOTES

1. Ostensibly more real in the sense that online identity performances, biographies, and friend lists may appear to have a closer correspondence with offline activity. However, the mapping may not be as tidy as that, in actual fact.

REFERENCES

Bennet, S. & Maton, K. (2011). Intellectual field or faith-based religion: Moving on from the idea of "digital natives." In M. Thomas (ed.), *Deconstructing Digital Natives: Young People, Technology and the New Literacies*. New York: Routledge.

Bruner, J. (2005). Life as narrative. *Social Research* 1(3): 691–710.

Bruns, A. (2008). *Blogs, Wikipedia, Second Life and Beyond: From Production to Produsage*. New York: Peter Lang.

Burnett, C. & Merchant, G. (2011). Is there a space for critical literacy in the context of new media? *English, Practice and Critique* 10(1): 41–57.

Castronova, E. (2005). *Synthetic Worlds: the Business and Culture of Online Games*. London: University of Chicago Press.

Davies, J. & Merchant, G. (2009). *Web 2.0 for Schools: Learning and Social Participation*. New York: Peter Lang.

Delgarno, B. & Lee, M. (2010). What are the learning affordances of 3-D virtual environments? *British Journal of Educational Technology* 41(1): 10–32.

Gauntlet, D. (2007). *Creative Explorations: New approaches to identities and audiences*. London: Routledge.

Gee, J. P. (2005). Learning by design: Good videogames as learning machines. *E-Learning* 2(1): 5–16.

Gee, J. P. (2003). *What Video Games Have to Teach Us about Learning and Literacy*. Basingstoke: Palgrave MacMillan.

Giddens, A. (1991). *Modernity and Self-Identity: Self and Society in the Late Modern Age*. Cambridge: Polity Press.

Giroux, H. A. & Pollock, G. (2010). *The Mouse That Roared: Disney and the End of Innocence* (2nd ed.). New York: Rowman & Littlefield.

Graham, L. (2008). Teachers are digikids too: The digital histories and digital lives of young teachers in English primary schools. *Literacy* 42(1): 10–18.

Greenhow, C. & Robelia, E. (2009). Informal learning and identity formation in online social networks. *Learning, Media and Technology* 34(2): 119–140.

Herring, S. C., Stein, D., & Virtanen, T. (eds.). (2012). *Pragmatics of Computer-Mediated Communication*. Berlin: Mouton.

Holland, D., Lachicotte, W., Skinner, D., & Cain, C. (2001). *Identity and Agency in Cultural Worlds*. Cambridge, MA: Harvard University Press.

Hughes, A. (2009). *Higher Education in a Web 2.0 World*. Bristol: JISC. Retrieved January 14, 2012 from http://www.jisc.ac.uk/media/documents/publications/heweb20rptv1.pdf.

Hull, G. A. & Stornaiuolo, A. (2010). Literate arts in a global world: Reframing social networking as a cosmopolitan practice. *Journal of Adolescent & Adult Literacy* 54(2): 85–97.

Jewitt, C., Moss, G., & Cardini, A (2007). Pace, interactivity and multimodality in teachers' design of texts for interactive whiteboards in the secondary school classroom. *Learning, Media and Technology* 32(3): 303–317.

Kress, G. (2010). *Multimodality: A Social Semiotic Approach to Contemporary Communication.* London: Routledge.

Lankshear, C. & Knobel, M. (2010). *New Literacies 3/e: Everyday Practices and Social Learning.* Maidenhead: Open University Press.

Lankshear, C. & Knobel, M. (Eds.). (2006). *New Literacies: Everyday Practices and Classroom Learning* (2nd ed.). Maidenhead: Open University Press.

Lenhart, A., Ling, R., & Campbell, S. (2010). *Teens and Mobile Phones.* Washington DC: Pew Internet & American Life Project. Retrieved December 21, 2011 from http://www.pewinternet.org/Reports/2010/Teens-and-Mobile-Phones.aspx.

Livingstone, S., Haddon, L., Gorzig, A., & Olaffson, K. (2011). *EU Kids Online* London: LSE. Retrieved December 21, 2011 from http://www2.lse.ac.uk/media@lse/research/EUKidsOnline/Home.aspx.

Marwick, A. E. & boyd, d. (2011). I tweet honestly, I tweet passionately: Twitter users, context collapse, and the imagined audience. *New Media & Society* 13(1): 114–133.

Merchant, G. (2011). Unravelling the social network: Theory and research. *Learning, Media and Technology.* 34(2): 119–40

Merchant, G. (2010). 3D virtual worlds as environments for literacy teaching. *Education Research* 52(2): 135–150.

Nichols, S. (2006). From boardroom to classroom: Tracing a globalised discourse on thinking through internet texts and teaching practice. In K. Pahl & J. Rowsell (eds.), *Travel Notes from New Literacy Studies: Instances of Practice.* Clevedon: Multilingual Matters 173–194.

Ofcom (2011). Communications market report: United Kingdom. August 4. Retrieved December 21, 2011 from http://stakeholders.ofcom.org.uk/market-data-research/market-data/communications-market-reports/cmr11/uk/.

Parry, D. (2011). Mobile perspectives: On teaching mobile literacy. *Educause Review* 46 (2): 14–16 . Retrieved January 14, 2012 from http://net.educause.edu/ir/library/pdf/ERM1120.pdf.

Pinker, S. (2011). *The Better Angels of Our Nature: Why Violence Has Declined.* New York: Viking.

Postill, J. (2010). Researching the Internet. *Journal of the Royal Anthropological Institute* 16(3): 646–650.

Scollon, R. (2001). *Mediated Discourse: The Nexus of Practice.* London: Routledge.

Squire, K. (2005). Changing the game: What happens when video games enter the classroom. *Innovate* 1(6). Retrieved January 14, 2012 from http://innovateonline.info/pdf/vol1_issue6/Changing_the_Game-__What_Happens_When_Video_Games_Enter_the_Classroom_.pdf.

Vygotsky, L. S. (1987). Imagination and its development in childhood (lecture 5). In R. Rieber & Carton, A. (eds.), *The Collected Works of L. S. Vygotsky: Vol. 1. Problems of General Psychology, Including the Volume 'Thinking and Speech'* (N. Minick, Trans.). New York: Plenum Press.

Willett, R., Robinson, M., & Marsh, J. (Eds.). (2008). *Play, Creativity and Digital Cultures.* London: Routledge.

Index

171–176; 182, 245, 252, 254.
See also Literacies; Scientific
literacies
New London Group, 67, 127
Newman, A., 182
Newspapers, *Club Penguin*, 79; origin
of virtual worlds, 16; attention
to social networking, 129; use
in *Mighty Fizz Chilla* game,
114–116, 114f
Nichols, S., 251
Nip, J., 37
Nonplayer characters (NPCs), 31
Nurturers, 221

O
O'Brien, W., 89
O'Mara, J., 64, 73n2
O'Rouke, M., 127
Observation, 13, 23, 27, 28, 57, 65, 71,
80, 82, 84, 95, 108, 168, 185,
186, 231, 234–236, 253
Occupy Wall Street, 126
Ocean Estate webpage, 108, 109f
Ofcom, 75, 90, 250
Offline, activities, 44–45; challenges,
183; space, 222; world, 134,
137
Olaffson, K., 250
Oldenburg, R., 191
Online, communities, 2, 16, 19, 21,
36, 39, 41, 50–51, 182, 186,
204, 228, 244; identity, 221;
safety, 33, 34; services, avail-
ability, 126–127; spaces, 50, 80;
surveys, 184. *See also* Gaming,
Virtual worlds
Open-source applications, 186
Open University, 191
Order-complexity-chaos spectrum, 76
Organized religion, 201–202
Out-of-game storytelling, 93
Out-of-school literacy practices,
79–80. *See also* Literary
practices
Outside space, 222
Overby, M., 75

P
Pahl, K., 127, 128, 142, 143
Palmer, S., 10, 86
Parallel social space, 9–10
Paratexts, 49, 68, 72
Parents, *See* Family

Parry, D., 250
Participation gap, 176
Participatory culture, 51, 85, 176, 185,
194
Pashler, H., 227, 234
Passwords, 109, 131–132, 218,
Peachey, A., 192, 194, 204
Pearce, C., 209
Pearce, L., 182
Pedagogy, 89, 127–128, 250–252
Peer-to-peer learning, 50
Pelletier, C., 67
Peppler. K. A., 181
Performance, 165
Performativity, 89
Persecution, 203
Personal information, 33. *See also*
Safety
Pets, 29, 30, 31, 35–37, 78, 221, 249
Pew Research Center, 181
Phillips, N. C., 77
Phones, 10, 34, 81, 122–123, 161, 167,
168, 227, 229, 237
Physical interfaces, 11
Physical self layer, 237, 238, 239. *See
also World of Warcraft*
Piaget, J., 209, 211
Pictures, downloading, 136, 136f
Pinker, S., 248
Plato, 78
Play, maturation 210–213; reclaim-
ing, 97–100; role in computer
games, 65; role and new media,
247–249
Player, definition and computer games,
145–146; interaction and model
of games as action layer, 66;
interpretation in *Mighty Fizz
Chilla* game, 115; mapping and
model of games as action and
games of text, 71; types and
learning from *Adventure Rock*,
221, 221t, 222
Playing together separately, examining attention, 227; findings,
236–239; gaming as virtual
literacy, 228–229; methods,
229–236; shifting nature of
expertise, 241; visualization of
expertise, 239–241
Plester, B., 170
Poetry, 49, 60, 173
Point system, 183
Policies, 86, 90, 166